From his insightful discussion of r
the church as a weed, from his thou
porary postmodern culture to his
biblical texts, Matthew Clarke of
gift: a vision of the church that casts off heavy baggage and scatters across the world spreading freedom and aliveness. More and more of us know that the days of the church as it has been are numbered; Matthew helps us imagine the church as it could be. If you're like me, you'll feel new hope, new motivation, and new creativity building through each chapter.

—**Brian D. McLaren**, author/speaker/activist

Around the world we sitting on the cusp of massive change. Thus, as always, this affects faith and expressions of faith. Theologies change, as Walter Brueggemann said to us in a conversation "Theology is thinking and responding to God and the world. God might be consistent but the world/context changes." So does the way we think and act about being church. Matthew Clarke has picked up what so many people are sensing about these changes and offers fresh ways to think and act - and once more offers the invitation to risk the exodus to a new promised future.

—**Fuzz Kitto**, Co-Director at Spirited Consulting and National Co-coordinator of Be Slavery Free

The very title *Scattering Church* suggests that Matthew Clarke's new book takes a very different view to the traditional view of the church. Matthew confronts those of us who really care about the role of the church with the challenge of completely turning the church as we know it upside down and inside out.

—**Dave Andrews**, Australian Christian anarchist author, speaker, social activist, and community worker

One of these days, when our dying church has been resurrected and looks very different than it does today, someone will say that Matthew Clarke saw it all coming—and even took it for an early test run. In language that is simple, vivid, personal, and theological astute, Clarke imagines churches that are scattered instead of gathered, fundamentally decentralized and subversive, divesting their power to the margins. The hour is coming, and now is, when stained glass and by-laws will be no match for table talk with loved ones who share a vision of the kingdom. Read this book, and then scatter as many copies as you can across this weary world.

—**Rev. Dr Robin R. Meyers**, Senior Minister, Mayflower UCC
Church, Oklahoma City, Distinguished Professor of Social
Justice, Oklahoma City University, author of *Saving God from
Religion: A Minister's Search for Faith in a Skeptical Age.*

This book is timely. Today the 'church' is an institution under threat and more and more Christians are leaving it or enduring it. We need to rethink 'church' strategically – and Matt's book gives us language to do just that. He offers a paradigm shift by moving metaphors from 'assembly' to 'scattering'. In so doing, he is following what smart organizations always do – go back to your purpose and rethink your vision. He wisely does not offer trite solutions for us. Rather he opens the doors of our mind to help us find new answers that will suit our local situations.

—**Dr Tony Golsby-Smith**, organizational strategist
and co-founder of Gospel Conversations

SCATTERING CHURCH

EFFECTIVE MISSION IN THE POST-INSTITUTIONAL WORLD

MATTHEW C. CLARKE

Turning Teardrops into Joy
Newcastle, Australia

Published by Turning Teardrops into Joy
www.turningteardropsintojoy.com/books

Scripture quotations taken from The Holy Bible,
New International Version® NIV®
Copyright © 1973 1978 1984 2011 by Biblica, Inc.™
Used by permission. All rights reserved worldwide.

Scattering Church / Matthew C. Clarke —1st ed. (A)
ISBN 978-0-6487248-0-3

Contents

Preface

WHAT MIGHT CHURCH LOOK LIKE if, rather than being a controlled, institutional garden, it was a radically decentralized weed?

My wife Annabella is an expert at creating spaces that welcome people into conversation. Through décor, food, colors, and her own enthusiasm, she invites people to share and be nourished. On one such occasion we had about 20 people at our house. We gathered around an outside table in the midst of an amazing permaculture garden in suburban Australia, with mango, lemon, and lime trees, native frogs and bees, herbs, sugar cane, vegetables, rainwater tanks, and solar panels. The evening's theme was the movie *Chocolat*—one of Annabella's favorites—so every dish of the banquet included chocolate, from the cauliflower, walnut and white chocolate soup to the braised chicken with citrus and chocolate sauce.[1]

In the movie, a French village is disrupted when the wild north wind blows free-spirited Vianne and her daughter into town right when Lent has commenced: a time for reflection and abstinence. Vianne opens a chocolate shop, much to the distaste of the village leader, the Comte de

Reynaud. With the conflict between the two established, the villagers now have to make their own decisions about how to respond to change, and to outsiders.

Significantly, Vianne and Reynaud are both looking for their own place in the world while trying to help those around them to flourish. While Reynaud thinks this can only happen via the traditional ways and discipline, Vianne encourages everyone to taste something new.

The conflict deepens when Johnny Depp arrives with a band of river gypsies. But for the rest, you'll have to watch the movie yourself.

Around our table we all reflected on the movie and our own experiences of life, hardship, and friendship. We thought about whether God can be found in the traditional church, where leaders like Reynaud control the congregants by rules and shame. We thought about what it means to be an outsider and what it means to belong.

What were the results of that dinner? We do not know, and we will probably never know how the seeds of that night grew in the lives of those who attended.

What we do know is that, however much we feel that life and faith are problematic, there are times like this with good food, wine, and stories to share around a table where we are able to catch a glimpse of something better; something more nourishing. We were nurturing a community that honors the insider as well as the outsider.

This is kingdom-building ministry. This is the shape of an effective church in the modern world. It is an approach that does not rely on a massive denominational bureaucracy, nor centrally controlled doctrine, nor paid priests, nor purpose-made buildings. It is fundamentally decentralized and subversive. It is a church that deliberately scatters its influence and divests power to the margins.

That is the kind of church I want to investigate in this book.

I do not claim that the scattering church is the only way to be the church. Instead, I build a case in this book for two things. First, that the idea of a scattering church is a Biblical model on equal standing with the dominant model of a gathering church. To get to that point, I establish a hermeneutic approach based on the importance of metaphors in the Bible. I trace the development of the dominant way of thinking about the shape of "church" and the way it emphasizes some of the Biblical metaphors while excluding others. I bring to the forefront the Biblical metaphor of scattering and show how it would inspire a different type of church.

Second, I argue that the scattering church is more suited to the post-institutional world of the 21st century. To get to that point I will explain what post-institutional means and how the traditional approach to church fails to work in that context. Then I describe what a scattering church looks like and how it is a better fit for the global culture in which we live.

STORIES

Annabella and I are much more interested in *being* the church than *attending* a church. I will explain that distinction more fully in Chapter 6, but an important aspect is that our whole lives as followers of Jesus are part of Jesus' ongoing mission to build a new sort of kingdom; one radically different from every other kingdom in history.

We are part of an Anabaptist group that meets each month in Sydney. We are part of an informal group of misfits inspired by the ikon collectives in Belfast and New York. We facilitate a sort of home church in Newcastle where we founded a group called "The Escape Goats," whose aim is to create a safe space for those who have become disillusioned or damaged by the traditional church to continue their faith journey. Inspired by the decentering approach of Peter Rollins, we curate transformance art events.

Annabella runs a sustainable social enterprise—"Turning Teardrops into Joy"—that raises money through several mobile coffee carts for developmental projects in Africa. My recent work has been with a Christian international development organization and previously with the church in South Africa during the national transition out of the Apartheid era. We have spent much of our lives in intentional Christian communities: groups that seek to live together in a faith-filled demonstration of the kingdom of heaven.

Throughout this book you will find stories from Annabella's and my experiences from those varied activities. I hope they illustrate the core ideas behind the "scattering church" model. In most of those stories, I have given the people false names to protect their privacy. (Writing a story is so much easier if you can use a name rather than endless he's and she's!) I don't think any of those stories give away personal details to make the people identifiable, but my apologies to anyone who may be embarrassed or disagree with my interpretation of the events.

AUDIENCE

We seem to be in the throes of a significant rethinking about theology and ecclesiology. The shape of Christian faith and its practical application in the world is in the process of revision. Established ideas and practices are being questioned and many new approaches are emerging.

Some historians have noted that this same rethinking happens in the church every 500 years or so, with the most recent being the Reformation, and 500 years before that with the Great Schism, and 500 years before that with the fall of Rome. That continues a regular cycle that goes back at least a further 1,500 years of Jewish history.[2]

As with previous cycles, today's church is rethinking and arguing internally about core commitments, including the important question of where ultimate authority rests. Living in this period of change, at the end of the current 500-year cycle powered by the Reformation, is uncomfortable and disorienting. This book is written as a contribution to the emergence of whatever God is giving birth to in the next cycle.

I throw these thoughts into the mix of Emergent Church, Simple Church, Alt Worship, and Fresh Expressions with two types of people in mind.

The first are followers of Jesus who already seek some expression of their faith outside the organized, institutional, traditional church. My message to you is that you need not feel guilty about being in that position. There is good reason to suppose this is where God is most actively building the new kingdom that Jesus spoke of. I hope you resonate with the vision of church I describe here and find some inspiration for approaches suited to your own context, along with new ways to describe it to others.

I also expect some people from inside the traditional church structures will read this book, looking at the "emerging church" movement with suspicion, confusion, frustration, or perhaps even envy! My message to you is not to fear such new expressions of church, but to recognize there are many, wildly varied and yet legitimate ways to follow Jesus.

THANKS AND APOLOGIES

Everything I have written is derived from things I have read and experienced. Clearly I owe a huge amount to other authors and the thousands of people who have been part of my own life journey.

Not the least of those are my immediate family and the people who have shared in experiments of Christian living over many years. My outlook has been greatly influenced by my first wife and the lessons we learnt together across two continents, two children, and numerous engagements with diverse faith communities.

Through many of the examples I include in this book you will sense the influence of my current wife Annabella. More than anyone else she re-tuned my eyes from seeing in black and white to seeing God's world in full color.

I draw on many other sources for this book and am very aware that the conclusions I come to will not always be shared by all those people. My apologies to anyone whose views I have misrepresented.

Key aspects of my conclusions are at odds with the dominant approach to church structures. Many readers will disagree—at least I hope they will disagree!—with my understanding of Christian missional practice and even with my understanding of the purpose of mission. I don't apologize for the disagreements because it is through this I hope we all can learn and grow. But I do apologize if I have inappropriately disparaged your position or spoken too dogmatically or certainly about my own.

I invite all readers to join the conversation with us at www.turningteardropsintojoy.com/books.

Part 1:

Foundations

[1]

METAPHORS

A CORE THEME OF THIS BOOK is the notion of a metaphor. I propose that the metaphors we use to think about the church play a significant role in how the church operates and whether it will be effective or not.

To explain this, I need to first explain what metaphors are and why they are so important.

MY ENGLISH TEACHER

When I was in school, my English teacher was quite clear— "A simile says one thing is *like* another thing, whereas a metaphor says one thing *is* another thing."

- "My love is like a red, red rose" (the first line of a poem by Robert Burns) is a simile.
- "All the world's a stage" (from William Shakespeare's play *As You Like It*) is a metaphor because it doesn't use "like."

Oh, and my English teacher said you can also use "as" in a simile too. "My love is as deep as the ocean" would count as being a simile.

That technical distinction, however, is too narrowly grammatical to be of much use except for passing English exams. My use of "metaphor" is more conceptual than grammatical. In what I write here, equating two different ideas is the core concept of metaphor regardless of how that equation is worded.

Listening to my English teacher, one could easily fall into the trap of thinking metaphors are just poetic lacework around the edge of communication. But on the contrary, metaphors are fundamental to the whole tapestry of understanding.

We come to understand a concept by seeing its connections to other concepts, which is the core reason for using a metaphor. A metaphor assumes you know one thing then uses that knowledge to help you understand another thing.

- Do you know how beautiful, and vibrant, and full of life a freshly budding red rose is? Well, they are the attributes that come to mind when I think about you. (But Robert Burns said it better!)
- Do you know how actors perform different roles on a stage to impress their audience? Well, that's the same with the whole world: we all play different roles throughout life, seeking to impress the people around us. (But Shakespeare said it better!)

With this understanding of "metaphor," whether something is a simile or not is relatively unimportant. We could also have lengthy debates about the differences between allegory, analogy, and parable, but I'm going to circumvent all of those debates by just asking you to subsume them all under the general term "metaphor." I'm not saying the distinctions between those varied forms are unimportant, just that they are all special cases of the core concept of metaphor. Similes, allegories, parables, and analogies are all effective because, at their core, they rely on a metaphorical way of thinking.

AN ARROW FROM KNOWN TO UNKNOWN

There are two core components to any metaphor, forming a sort of calculus—which simply means a way of doing things.

The first is a juxtaposition of two objects or ideas that on the surface seem quite different. Love and a rose. The world and a stage.

The second is an invitation (normally implied rather than explicit) to take attributes about one of those things and transfer them to the other thing. Life and beauty are attributes of a freshly budding rose that Robert Burns wants us to apply to his love. The acting of different roles is what Shakespeare draws attention to.

These two components define the way of doing things metaphorically—the metaphoric calculus.

Metaphors work by drawing on what you know about one object/idea and applying it to the other object/idea.

The metaphoric calculus normally has a clear direction, a trajectory, like an arrow shot from a known starting point to an unknown target. This is what makes metaphor such

an effective teaching tool: knowledge of the source concept
helps you to understand the target concept.

METAPHORS ARE PERVASIVE

Metaphors sneak into our language all the time and are
crucial for communication.

In their seminal work ("seminal"! now there's an evocative metaphor!) *Metaphors We Live By*, George Lakoff and
Mark Johnson show by example how dependent we are on
metaphors in our everyday use of language.

For instance, they point out that when we talk about arguments, we often use words drawn from warfare.

- Your claims are *indefensible*
- He *attacked* every weak point in my argument
- Her criticisms were *right on target*
- I *demolished* his argument
- I've never *won* an argument with her
- If you use that *strategy*, he'll *wipe you out*
- She *shot down* all my arguments.
- She forced me to *retreat*.

In a commentary on that metaphor, they write:

> *It is important to see that we don't just talk about argu-
> ments in terms of war. We can actually win or lose argu-
> ments. We see the person we are arguing with as an
> opponent. We attack his positions and we defend our own.
> We gain and lose ground. We plan and use strategies. If we
> find a position indefensible, we can abandon it and take a
> new line of attack. Many of the things we do in arguing are
> partially structured by the concept of war. Though there is*

no physical battle, there is a verbal battle, and the structure of an argument—attack, defense, counter-attack, etc.—reflects this. It is in this sense that the ARGUMENT IS WAR metaphor is one that we live by in this culture; its structures the actions we perform in arguing.³

METAPHORS IN THE BIBLE

Given that metaphors are so common in human communication, no one should be surprised to find them throughout the Bible.⁴ Some examples where this is quite explicit are:

- "Praise the greatness of our God! He is the Rock" (Deuteronomy 32:4)
- "The Midianites, Amalekites and other eastern peoples ... came up with their livestock and their tents like swarms of locusts" (Judges 6:3–5)
- "I have calmed and quieted myself, I am like a weaned child with its mother" (Psalm 131:2)
- The description of old age in Ecclesiastes 12:1–7
- "We are the clay, you are the potter" (Isaiah 64:8)
- "Your love is like the morning mist, like the early dew that disappears" (Hosea 6:4)
- "The day of the Lord will come like a thief in the night" (1 Thessalonians 5:2)

... but there are many more.⁵

JESUS' USE OF METAPHOR

All of Jesus' "I am" sayings recorded by John (e.g. "I am the good shepherd" in John 10:11) are metaphors, as are Jesus' instruction to the Twelve to "be wise as serpents and harmless as doves" (Matthew 10:16) and his declaration in the Sermon on the Mount, "you are the salt of the earth" (Matthew 5:13).

In a more complex way, parables, which are often described as "earthly stories with a spiritual meaning," are great examples of the metaphoric calculus.

Jesus' strategy in his extensive use of parables was to start with objects and ideas his listeners were already familiar with—"earthly stories"—and then invite the listeners to transfer what they knew from that familiar context to the unfamiliar context of the kingdom of heaven.

The metaphoric structure is explicit in statements such as the seven parables in Matthew 13 that all start with "The kingdom of heaven is like ..."

There are also many less obvious examples of metaphors in the Gospels.

For instance, Jesus said "The wind blows wherever it pleases. You hear its sound, but you cannot tell where it comes from or where it is going. So it is with everyone born of the Spirit" (John 3:8). In this discussion with the Jewish leader Nicodemus, Jesus uses the metaphoric calculus to challenge assumptions about what it means to "come from God" (v2). He invites Nicodemus to apply what he already knows about the wind to the new life in the kingdom of heaven made possible by the Spirit of God.

Nicodemus is confused by the metaphor, and this pattern is repeated in most of Jesus' parables. Nicodemus can tell that the arc of the arrow goes from wind to spirit, but I think he, and we, are left wondering which attribute of the wind is supposed to be transferred to the realm of spirit. Is it that those who are born of the Spirit can't tell whether they are coming or going? Sometimes it can seem that way!

There is a double layer of metaphor in this interchange between Jesus and Nicodemus. Jesus is taking earthly ideas about birth and inviting Nicodemus to transfer that knowledge into the spiritual context. But he is also engaging in clever metaphorical word-play around the concept of spirit. The Greek word for "spirit" is "pneuma," which means literally "wind" or "breath." The same is true in Hebrew: the word "ruach" means equally "spirit," "wind" or "breath." When either word is applied to God's Spirit they do so metaphorically. Built into the very Hebrew and Greek words is the metaphoric assertion that God's Spirit is like wind, and that the Spirit is God's breath.

I'll have more to say about that later. At this point, however, I'll just note the ambiguity in many Biblical metaphors and point out that Jesus rarely explains the meaning of his parables.

Ambiguity is an inherent outcome of any metaphor. A more technical way to say this is that every metaphor is multivalent: it can suggest multiple meanings. That may seem unfortunate, because it means we can often be uncertain of which meaning is intended. On the other hand, it is the foundation of all the value we gain from metaphor. Like every piece of art or poem, parable, sacrament, symbol, analogy or allegory, the richness of a metaphor triggers this multivalence. Metaphors evoke rather than define. And what they evoke will not only be different for each person but be different for the same person over time.

The way the Gospel writers present Jesus, we have to assume that ambiguity was a deliberate part of his teaching strategy.

MISSING THE MARK

Like an arrow, a metaphor can sometimes miss the mark. They can be misguided and they can be misunderstood.

One thing to keep in mind is that metaphors are not literally true. Love is not actually a red rose. Jesus is not actually a vine (John 15:1). Nor was he ever a shepherd (John 10:11,14) as far as we know.

On occasion, a metaphor can be used so often that it comes to be taken as the literal truth.[6]

Sometimes there are disagreements as to whether a linguistic expression is a metaphor or literally true. An important example is the disagreement between Catholic and Protestant traditions about the interpretation of Jesus' words "This is my body."

You also have to be careful about which attributes are carried over from the known thing to the unknown thing. Not all attributes survive the transfer. Burn's love is not red, nor does he expect that his love will wilt and die within a week. When Jesus compared the kingdom of heaven to a mustard seed (Matthew 13:31) he was not suggesting you can crush up the kingdom of heaven to make a spicy condiment to add to your ham sandwich!

Every metaphor has both intended and unintended connotations. There are specific attributes the author intends the metaphoric arrow to transfer, but it is not always easy to determine what they are.

For instance, when Jesus said, "unless you change and become like little children, you will never enter the kingdom of heaven" (Matthew 18:3), which child-like attributes does he intend for us to emulate? Is it their innocence? Their curiosity and question-asking? Their dependence on their parents? Possibly all of those things, though to know for sure we'd have to look at other things Jesus said in light of the social context in which he spoke.

Considering what Paul wrote in 1 Corinthians 14:20—"stop thinking like children"—we certainly cannot say that to enter the kingdom of heaven one must exhibit *every* characteristic of children.

Imagine, for instance, that the metaphor of becoming like children was believed with such completeness that we thought only short people can get into the kingdom! Although short height is an attribute of children, Jesus probably did not intend the metaphoric calculus to transfer that attribute across!

What easily and often happens is that once a metaphor starts being used, it gathers momentum and starts being applied in ways far beyond what was originally intended. People start transferring all sort of attributes across the metaphoric trajectory, causing them to completely miss the mark.

Whether other attributes of children should be transferred is less obvious. For instance, a common proverb in the Western English-speaking world is that "children should be seen but not heard." Likewise, I often heard during my own childhood that children should not question but do as they are told. Did Jesus intend principles like that to be carried across by the metaphor?

In some circles that would be considered an intended connotation. A preacher expounding Matthew 18:3 may well say that part of Jesus' meaning was to warn people that if they wanted to be part of God's kingdom then they should not question, but simply obey. The metaphor can then become a means of control: threatening to exclude people if they do not toe the line.

Other expositors of that verse would be horrified at such an interpretation and argue that Jesus intended no such thing.

METAPHORS ARE OFTEN IMPLIED RATHER THAN EXPLICIT

In most of those examples from Lakoff and Johnson, there is no *explicit* metaphor. The sentences are not structured in the forms "this is like that" or "this is that." The point they are making is that most of our language only works because of assumed metaphors. "Your claims are indefensible" only makes sense if you assume that claims in an argument are the type of thing that can be "attacked" and "defended." The unstated metaphor that "arguments are like war" allows us to take war-like concepts such as defending territory and, by the metaphoric calculus, apply them to arguments.

Through constant use, we end up forgetting that the application of "defense" to arguments is only a metaphor and we start believing and behaving as though arguments are much more war-like than they need to be.

The Bible also contains many implied metaphors.

In Romans 4, for instance, Paul writes that "Without weakening his faith [Abraham] faced the fact that his body was as good as dead" (v. 19) and that Abraham "was strengthened in his faith" (v. 20). I point out these verses because they assume faith is like a physical power: it can become stronger or weaker. That metaphor is not explicit but has to be assumed to make sense of the sentence—at least in English. The metaphor relating faith to a physical power is useful because it enables us to transfer, via the metaphoric calculus, ideas such as the value of practicing our faith in the same way we exercise our muscles. We should not, however, deduce that faith is the kind of thing that can be used to force our way onto others. We do not pit one person's "strong" faith against another's "weak" faith in a spiritual fight. Rather, the strength of our faith reflects our assurance of the power of God, as noted in verse 21.

A few verses later, Paul writes that we have gained access into grace (Romans 5:2). Underlying that phrase is a thought that grace is like a physical space that we can step into through faith. Now, we cannot literally step into grace because grace is not literally a physical space. But nevertheless, it is a useful and evocative metaphor.

In that same chapter, Paul writes that "God has poured out his love" (Romans 5:5) and that grace "overflows" (Romans 5:15). Those phrases suggest that love and grace are liquids: they can be poured and they can overflow.

Although that's not literally true, it is nevertheless a powerful implied metaphor.

This type of implied metaphor is very language dependent and seldom retains its meaning when translated. The last example above is a good case in point. The Greek word translated as "overflow" in the NIV is *eperisseusen* (ἐπερίσσευσεν) whose root meaning is to abound, to go over and above, to exceed. The idea of a liquid overflowing is a natural way to express that in English, but I do not think a Koine Greek speaker would naturally visualize the same image. The implied metaphor is quite appropriate for us, but it is not there in the Greek. Conversely, I have no doubt there are implied metaphors in the Greek that are not captured by the word choice in any English version of the text. Consequently, English readers very easily infer different connotations from the linguistic associations than readers in other languages.

THE DIRECTION OF THE ARROW

In any metaphor, the two juxtaposed ideas play the role of source and target. Sometimes, however, the direction of a metaphor is unclear, maybe even deliberately ambiguous. A great example is what Paul says in Ephesians 5 about two radically different things: the relationship between a husband and wife, and the relationship between Christ and the church. From verse 22 to 33 he builds a metaphor between the two things, but which is the source and which the target?

- "The husband is the head of the wife as Christ is the head of the church ..."

- "Husbands, love your wives, just as Christ loved the church ..."
- "Nobody ever hated his own body, but he feeds and cares for it, just as Christ does the church ..."

Is Paul helping us understand the relationship between a husband and wife by drawing on what we know about the relationship between Christ and the church? Or is he helping us to understand Christ's relationship to the church by drawing on what all his readers already know about the relationship between a husband and wife?

That's deliciously ambiguous!

Then Paul ends with a quote from Genesis 2:24 and says, "this is a profound mystery." He is not saying that the idea from Genesis—that a husband and wife become one—is a profound mystery. That is indeed a mystery, but not the profound point Paul is making. Rather, Paul is pointing out that the principle of a husband and wife becoming one can be applied, via the calculus of the metaphor, to Christ and the church. But doing so raises a deep and unanswerable question—how could Christ and the church become one flesh?

At first reading, the passage looks like it is informing us about human marriage, but when you stop and think about it, that understanding had been around for centuries—ever since Genesis 2:24! This means the new idea to which the metaphor's transference is applied is not the husband/wife side of the metaphor but the Christ/church side.

ANYTHING WE SAY ABOUT GOD IS METAPHORICAL

Is Jesus a door, as we read in John 10:7? Well no, of course not. Jesus is conceptually the entryway to a different life than what can be experienced without him. He is not literally a door, but he is metaphorically a door.

Is God a male? Well no, God hasn't got a body with any biological sex, nor genetic material with X or Y chromosomes. In the beginning God *created* male and female. God not only created a male person and a female person but created the very categories of male and female. The two sexes were jointly made in God's image, and God's character displays traits that our cultural stereotypes would label as both masculine and feminine.

Is God big? Well no, God is not an object that has any measurements. God is only big metaphorically in the sense that nothing can contain God. No box, physical or metaphysical, can define, constrain, or limit God.

In fact, no label can ever literally be applied to God. Anything we say about God is metaphorical. By that I do not mean that God is nothing but a metaphor. I believe there is a real, literal entity beyond the physical: something, or more correctly someone, whose form is beyond complete knowing, and yet is able to interact with the created world in ways we can experience.

But we can only speak about God in words, and no words can adequately describe God. Any word we apply to God assumes that the hearer knows the meaning of that word in relation to what they have already experienced in this world. To say, "God is love," for instance, is to invite the hearer to bring to mind what they already know of love (which is itself a partial and changing knowledge), and then apply that mental image to God. This is an inevitable result of the way language works when we assign known attributes to something unknown.

Those who think they can assign literal attributes to God miss the fundamental truth that God can never be objectified. By "objectify" I am pointing to the distinction between subject and object that is essential to our human language structures. If I were to say, "Matthew is writing a book," we label "Matthew" as the subject—the one performing the action—and "the book" as the object of Matthew's action.

All too often we think we can make ourselves the subject and God the object, as though we can stand aloof and independent in judgement or in control of God. We see this displayed in sentences like, "Matthew knows God" and "Annabella seeks God." Matthew and Annabella are the subjects of those sentences, instigating actions towards the object of God. From a philosophical point of view, the same is true of a claim like "God is good," because it implies a stance that positions God as a thing to which we can assign attributes. But in Christian thought, God is always the source, the instigator, the actor rather than the acted-upon.

That's why Paul corrects himself in Galatians 4:9— "Now that you know God – or rather are known by God ...." God is not an object about which we can make judgements or assertions. God is always the subject. The problem is that the limitations of language make it impossible to say *anything* about God without treating God as an object. The best we can do is to remind ourselves that anything we say about God will be faulty, incomplete, provisional, and metaphorical because the truth about God is fundamentally inexpressible.

Language is not rich enough to "capture" the full image of God. The metaphoric calculus is the best we can do when trying to express the nature of God using words. This limitation of language is an important part of the reason God came to live among us—that we might not have to rely on words describing God but instead *see* the glory of God in living flesh (John 1:14, 1 John 1:1–3). We know God not because of abstract words, but because of the tangible demonstration of Jesus, who is the visible image of the invisible God (Colossians 1:15).

METAPHORS FOR CHURCH

The Bible uses many metaphors for the church. Just as Jesus is called the way, Emmanuel, a lamb, and the son of man, so too the people around him were called many things: followers, disciples, Christians, etc. Collectively they were called the gathering, the body, the family, and many other names.

None of those descriptive terms can be taken as a pure definition. Rather, each word suggests some attribute which, by the calculus of metaphor, weaves together to form a multi-layered concept. Jesus is not just the door, not just the good shepherd, not just the savior. Instead, each of those appellations suggest attributes that need to be included in our understanding of who Jesus was. The church is not just the household of God, not just Christ's bride, not just the flock. But each of those images suggest attributes to be included in our understanding of what the church is.

Each choice of metaphor adds something to the meaning, but the meaning of Jesus, or of being a Christ-follower, or the collective noun for those Christ-followers cannot be reduced to a single word, phrase, title or attribute.

The outworking of God's mission to and through humanity forms a complex fabric, and the metaphoric threads woven into that fabric are numerous and diverse. Let's try to catalogue them. The following lists are incomplete but show the wide range of images that have been collectively applied to the people of God and their mission in the world. I have tried to leave out metaphors that apply to individual followers of Jesus, though there is an inevitable ambiguity about whether an image applies to us individually or collectively.

OLD TESTAMENT IMAGES

Although the Old Testament predates the formation of the church, it sets up a rich assortment of metaphors to describe God's people and God's work through those people.

The people of God—Exodus 3:7, 10; Exodus 8–10; Leviticus 26:12; 2 Chronicles 7:14; Hosea 2:23; hundreds of other uses of phrases like "my people".
Children—Deuteronomy 14:1; Jeremiah 3:19
Treasured possession—Exodus 19:5; Deuteronomy 7:6, 14:2, 26:18; Psalm 135:4

Chosen—Deuteronomy 7:6 and many other places

Wife, lover—Jeremiah 3:14, 20; Ezekiel 16; Hosea 1–4; Song of Songs

Vine, vineyard—Psalm 80:8–19; Isaiah 5:1–7; Jeremiah 2:21; Hosea 10:1

Remnant—2 Kings 19:30–31; Ezra 9:9–15; Isaiah 10:20–22, 37:31–32

Sheep, flock (see Matthew 26:31)—Jeremiah 23:1–4; Ezekiel 34

NEW TESTAMENT IMAGES

Virtually all those metaphors for Israel are co-opted by the New Testament writers and applied to the church. But many more are added ...

The people of God—Romans 9:25–26; Hebrews 4:9, 11:25; 1 Peter 2:9–10; plus about 30 uses of the phrase, "God's people" or "the Lord's people"

The Israel of God, the twelve tribes—Romans 2:29; Galatians 6:16; James 1:1

Abraham's descendants—Romans 4:16; Galatians 3:29

Inwardly circumcised—Romans 2:25–29; Philippians 3:3; Colossians 2:11–13

One body, the body of Christ—Romans 12:4–5; 1 Corinthians 10:16–17, 12:12–31; Ephesians 4:12, 4:16, 5:22–33; Colossians 1:18,24

The dwelling place of the Holy Spirit—1 Corinthians 3:16; Ephesians 2:22

God's house, household—1 Timothy 3:15; Ephesians 2:19; Hebrews 3:6; 1 Timothy 3:15

Brothers and sisters—Over 100 verses, e.g. 2 Thessalonians 2:13

Brotherhood—1 Peter 2:17

Family—Mark 10:29–30; Galatians 6:10; 1 Thessalonians 4:10; 1 Timothy 5:1–2; Hebrews 2:11; 1 Peter 4:17

Bride, wife—2 Corinthians 11:2; Ephesians 5:22–33; Revelation 19:7–9, 21:9

God's loved ones—Romans 9:25

Pure virgin—2 Corinthians 11:2

Citizens—Ephesians 2:19; Philippians 3:20

Inheritors, heirs—Acts 20:32; Romans 8:17; Galatians 3:29, 4:7; Ephesians 1:14, 18, 5:5; Colossians 1:12; Hebrews 9:15; 1 Peter 1:4, 3:7

The pillar and foundation of the truth—1 Timothy 3:15

Temple, spiritual house—1 Corinthians 3:16–17; Ephesians 2:21–22; 1 Peter 2:5

Altar—Revelation 16:7

Building—1 Corinthians 3:9; Ephesians 2:21–22

God's dwelling—Ephesians 2:21–22

Sheep, flock—Matthew 25:31–46, 26:31; Luke 12:32; John 10:1–18, 21:15–17; Acts 20:28–29; Hebrews 13:20; 1 Peter 5:2–4

New creation—2 Corinthians 5:17; James 1:18

Fellowship, community, communion, common sharing—Acts 2:42–47; 1 Corinthians 1:9; 1 John 1:3, 7

Letter—2 Corinthians 3:1–3

Army—2 Corinthians 10:3–5; Ephesians 6:11–17; 2 Timothy 2:3–4

City on a hill—Matthew 5:14

Branches of the vine—John 15:5–8

Vineyard—Matthew 21:33–45; Mark 12:1–9; Luke 20:9–16

Olive branch—Romans 11:17–21

God's fellow-workers—1 Corinthians 3:9

God's field—1 Corinthians 3:9

God's workmanship/handiwork—Ephesians 2:10

God's elect/chosen—1 Peter 1:1, 2:9

Built on a rock—Matthew 16:18

Servants of the groom—Luke 12:35–38

Clothed with Jesus—Romans 13:14; Galatians 3:27

Clothed in fine linen—Revelations 19:8

Clothed in armor of light—Romans 13:12

Clothed with compassion, kindness, humility, gentleness, patience—Colossians 3:12

Strangers, aliens, exiles—1 Peter 1:1, 2:11; Hebrews 11:13

Scattered—John 11:52; James 1:1; 1 Peter 1:1

Ambassadors—2 Corinthians 5:20

Sons of God, children of God—John 1:12–13, 11:52; Romans 9:26; Galatians 3:26, 4:7; 1 John 3:1–10, 5:19

The first-born—Hebrews 12:23

First fruits—James 1:18

Priesthood—1 Peter 2:9; Revelation 1:6, 5:10

Holy nation—1 Peter 2:9

Buried and raised to life—Romans 6:4; Colossians 2:12

People of the light—Luke 16:8; John 8:12; Ephesians 5:8; 1 Peter 2:9

Sons of light, sons of day—1 Thessalonians 5:5

Shine like stars—Philippians 2:15

Lampstands—Revelation 1:20

The way—Acts 9:2, 19:9, 19:23, 22:4, 24:14, 24:22

NEW TESTAMENT IMAGES OF WHAT THE CHURCH DOES

I have separated the following because they relate less to our identity as the church, and more to the outcomes of us being that church. That is, they evoke ideas about what we *do* rather than what we *are*.

Salt—Matthew 5:13
Light—Matthew 5:14–16; Acts 13:47; Romans 13:12
Aroma of Christ—2 Corinthians 2:15
Fishing—Matthew 4:19; Mark 1:17; Luke 5:1–11; John 21:1–14
Bowl of incense—Revelation 5:8, 8:3
Enters a Sabbath rest—Hebrews 4:1–11
With unveiled faces we reflect God's glory—2 Corinthians 3:7–18
Offering spiritual sacrifices—1 Peter 2:5
Carry each other's burdens—Galatians 6:2

NEW TESTAMENT IMAGES OF THE "KINGDOM"

The lists above omit many references in the Gospels to the "kingdom of God" and the "kingdom of heaven" because those phrases refer not so much to the nature of the church as to the vision of a new humanity Jesus commissioned his followers to help him achieve. Jesus says virtually nothing about the church—just two references in Matthew 16 and Matthew 18—but never stops talking about the kingdom and about the values he expects citizens of that kingdom to demonstrate.

This image of a kingdom is itself a metaphor. Jesus makes clear that the work of God in the world is not literally a kingdom in the sense that his hearers would expect but differs radically from any other kingdom people have previously encountered. I expand on that point in Chapter 6.

The church is the conduit through which Jesus intends to bring the kingdom of heaven to earth. Because this goal was so central to his mission, Jesus assembled a bundle of metaphors to describe that kingdom:

Fishing net—Matthew 13:47
Hidden treasure—Matthew 13:44
The search for something valuable—Matthew 13:45
The search for something lost—Luke 15, 19:10
Mustard seed—Matthew 13:31, 17:20; Mark 4:30–32; Luke 13:18–19, 17:6
Ten virgins with their lamps—Matthew 25:1–13
Wedding feast—Matthew 22:1–14; Luke 12:35–40
Yeast—Matthew 13:33; Luke 13:20–21

Other New Testament authors also note the relationship between the church and the kingdom of God, e.g. Ephesians 5:5, Colossians 1:13, and 4:11.

POST-BIBLICAL IMAGES

There is no reason to assume that the only valid metaphors for the church are those found in the Bible. God's creativity has not ended, and God's spirit continues to inspire images that express new understandings of what it means to be God's people in the world.

Some of those new metaphors are more appropriate than others. Some, I think, are quite misguided. Nevertheless, new metaphors quite naturally evolve alongside changes to languages and cultures, such as ...

Mother: In some traditions, especially Roman Catholicism, the church is described as the mother of our faith—a metaphor that dates back at least to St Augustine.[7]

Empire: Once Christianity became the dominant Roman religion—after the conversion of Emperor Constantine in about 312 CE—the church quickly aligned itself to the aspirations of the Roman Empire. With that change came an understanding that the church was itself like an empire, one that would grow through colonial expansion.

Business: A more recent rethinking of church has likened it to a modern business[8]: with a CEO (who is sometimes portrayed as Jesus and sometimes as the senior pastor), a board, recruitment strategies, income streams, marketing department, etc.

MAKING GOOD USE OF METAPHOR

Lakoff and Johnson point out that metaphors both highlight and hide.[9] Their role in highlighting is obvious. In the most effective metaphors, the "known" end of the arrow (the source), evokes an obvious and small set of important attributes that the author intends the audience to transfer to the "unknown" end of the arrow (the target). "She runs as fast as lightning" very obviously highlights the well-known truth that lightning travels very quickly. But by drawing attention to the fact that she runs quickly, the metaphor claims center stage so that her other attributes are hidden at the back of the stage, obscured by the metaphor. In that example, running like lightning obscures that she can also run slowly when she wants to and that she can run quickly for several minutes rather than just the split second of lightning.

When we use a metaphor repeatedly, the hidden aspects can easily fall out of mind and be ignored or forgotten. What's more, the constant, unconscious use of a metaphor—such as Lakoff and Johnson's example of "arguments as war"—hides assumptions that affect our beliefs and behaviors. To avoid that, a good practice is to identify metaphors and ask whether they are appropriate. When we become aware of the "arguments as war" metaphor, for instance, we can then make conscious decisions about whether that is how we really want to frame our disagreements with the people around us. We might consider other alternatives. What would the world be like if we did not conceptualize arguments as war? What if, for instance, arguments were thought of as a dance?[10] That would not only change our word choices but our whole attitude to the flow of an argument and its relational purpose.

Even when a metaphor is appropriate, we need to ask which attributes can usefully be transferred. It is never the case that every attribute of the source can be applied to the target. When Burns wrote "My love is like a red, red rose" he did not intend the metaphoric calculus to transfer the thorns across to his love. When Jesus compared himself to a door, he did not intend us to infer some spiritual meaning from doorknobs and hinges.

BEWARE OF CHOOSING A SINGLE METAPHOR

Whole books and sermons can—and have—been formed around single metaphors. That's a dangerous practice because it leaves the impression that the metaphor is the only one available. If we keep repeating X is like Y, X is like Y, X is like Y, eventually we all start thinking that Y is the only way to understand X. We may even start thinking that X *is* Y rather than just *like* Y.

I think this has happened with our conception of the church. We have applied the metaphor of a church being a gathering so often many have come to think that is the definition of a church. In doing so we lose the richness of the many other metaphors listed in the previous section.

What's more, focusing on a single metaphor continually emphasizes one set of attributes while continually hiding other attributes. Only by drawing on many metaphors can we create the whole picture. Each metaphor reveals something that another might hide.

For instance, when we consider what it means for the church to be the body of Christ, we will recognize that each member has a specific role that is necessary to the proper functioning of the whole. Did you sing "The Body Song" back in Sunday School?[11] One line says, "A body can't walk on its nose, and a body can't eat with its toes." That of course simply echoes what Paul wrote in 1 Corinthians 12, in which he emphasizes the variety of spiritual gifts, all given by the same Spirit to equip the church for service.

From that metaphor, one person might conclude that their role is to preach (the mouth?) and another might conclude that their role is to support the body's financial needs (the hip pocket?).

On the other hand, when we consider what it means for the church to be a family,[12] we are more likely to see our roles as shared and changing. Anyone can put out the rubbish bins. Everyone takes turns washing the dishes. A dependent child grows up to be a parent and then still later to be cared for as a frail great-grand-parent.

The two visions are not contradictory but complimentary. If you focus on the church as a body you are likely to think in terms of how the various components work together to get the task done efficiently, about the differences between members, and the demarcation of duties. You will tend to label specific roles and provide training in how to be the best possible eye/ear/nose and (probably unconsciously) assign each role a relative importance. You will think about those personalized skills and aptitudes as God-given. This is understandable as they are the types of attributes the "church as a body" metaphor highlights.

You might think about your role within the body as fixed. I have seen church councils where the treasurer is never allowed to break out of that role. It becomes their identity within the body.

On the other hand, if you focus on the church as family, you are more likely to think in terms of relationship—that we are all "brothers and sisters in Christ." You will recognize the need to simply be together rather than to achieve some specific task. You will think about being born into a family and of being an heir. Those attributes, highlighted by the "church as a family" metaphor, would remain hidden if we over-emphasized the "church as a body" metaphor.

The Biblical writers almost seem consciously aware of the danger of fixating on a single metaphor. As they struggle to make sense of their experience of God and of this new community of the kingdom, they say "well, it's like this ..." and "Yes, but it's also like this ... and this ... and this too."

THE STORY SO FAR ...

All this talk about metaphors is important groundwork for how we read the Bible. If it wasn't for our dependence on metaphors, we might read the Bible as though it analytically documents the one and only true definition of church. We might read the Bible as though it proscribes exactly what to do in all situations or as a fixed script to be followed to the letter.

But such a reading is literally impossible. The very process of reading, not to mention translation, is interpretive. The way language and communication work, in fact the way our minds work, leans heavily on the transfer of ideas across the metaphoric calculus. Because of this, a clear understanding of how metaphors work is essential if we are to understand God's intentions as conveyed through the words of the Bible and through the life of Jesus.

The Bible provides an amazing wealth of images to help us understand the nature of the church, and the nature of the church's mission. I've touched on over 60 metaphors relating to church in this section.

A central claim of this book is that we have mistaken the nature of church because we have unconsciously emphasized one metaphor above all others. We have emphasized the metaphor of church as a gathering so much that we can conceive of church in no other way, and we have built an institutional church that reflects a mistaken belief that the church by definition must gather. My intention is to consider what the church would look like if the equally Biblical metaphor of scattering were taken seriously.

In the next chapter I explain more fully what I understand the Bible says about gathering and describe the extent to which that idea has influenced the shape of the historic church.

[2]

GATHERING

SINCE JESUS FIRST COMMISSIONED the community of his followers to enact the kingdom of God on earth, that community has been called "church."

The English word "church" is related to the Dutch "kerk" and German "kirk," and historically derived from the Greek κυριακός (*kuriakos*), meaning "of the Lord."[13] That's a fascinating etymology which emphasizes not what the church *is*, how it is structured, or what it does, but rather on the founder of the church. Whatever the church is, it is *the Lord's* church.

The Greek word *kuriakos* only appears twice in the New Testament, and in both places it is an adjective—"the Lord's supper" in 1 Corinthians 11:20, and "the Lord's day" in Revelations 1:10. *Kuriakos*, from which we derive the English word "church," is never translated as "church" in the Bible.

On the other hand, when the word "church" appears in modern English versions of the Bible, it is virtually always a translation of the Greek ἐκκλησία, whose meaning is simply "an assembly." It relates closely to ἐκκλητός, meaning "summoned" or "called out." Over time, ἐκκλησία was Latinized to *ecclesia*.[14]

In English we still carry that Latin root in words like *ecclesiastical*—an adjective for anything related to the church—and *ecclesiology*—the academic study of the church.

Ecclesia, in various grammatical forms, occurs 114 times in the New Testament. In the New International Version, all except five[15] of those occurrences are translated as "church."

THE IMPOSSIBILITY OF EXACT TRANSLATION

Translating is a strange business! How can you faithfully render a word from one language, with all the grammatical, semantic, and social context surrounding it, into another language that has different—perhaps radically different—grammar, semantics, and social context? A translation is always a paraphrase, because there cannot be an exact one-to-one correspondence of meaning between words in different languages.[16]

We read "church" through our 21st century English eyes and immediately impose all sorts of assumptions onto that word. Perhaps we imagine a certain style of building. Perhaps robed clergy. Perhaps rows of seats all facing the same way. Perhaps a familiar set of beliefs. Perhaps an accepted style of liturgy and music. Perhaps images drawn from our personal experience of preaching, of mission, of youth groups, and choirs, and council meetings, and Bible studies.

A moment's reflection is enough to see through those first assumptions and realize that the church around the world and through the centuries has taken many forms, encompassing a huge diversity of beliefs and practices. Whatever the church is, it is not limited to our own experiences or specific examples.

So let's try to look at church with fresh eyes, beyond the experiences of the institutional church we may have grown up with.

Even if we take away the modern Western connotations of "church," don't you find it interesting that Bible translators have consistently chosen to use the English word "church"—which is derived from "of the Lord"—as the translation of *ecclesia*—which derives from "summoned"? On the surface it doesn't seem like the most direct translation!

The linking concept that makes it reasonable to translate *ecclesia* as *church* is the idea of gathering.

Six centuries before Jesus, Solon reformed the Greek political process to give ultimate authority to a general assembly of citizens called the *Ecclesia*.[17] According to missiologist Alan Hirsch, calling local political assemblies an *Ecclesia* was still common in the first century across the Roman Empire.[18]

By co-opting the word *ecclesia* in this way, the New Testament writers made a political statement. Jesus intended this new community of his followers to create a new political structure in which Jesus was Lord rather than

Caesar. That new political structure—which Jesus called the "kingdom of heaven" or the "kingdom of God"—differs radically from the Roman Empire and every other "kingdom." The political nature of this new "kingdom" is shown in John's account of Jesus' interaction with Pilate (John 18:28 – 19:16). The accusation that Jesus was competing with Caesar for authority became the final factor that convinced the reluctant Pilate to crucify Jesus.

WHO SUMMONED THE ASSEMBLY?

If the church is an assembly, it makes sense to ask why they are assembled? By whom were they summoned?

In the New Testament it is clear the *ecclesia* is not just any assembly but an assembly "of the Lord." The fact that they assembled was much less important than the reason why they were summoned.

From the very early chapters of Matthew, the notion of being called, or summoned, plays a central role. In chapter 4, Jesus summons the fishermen Peter and his brother Andrew with the playful words "Come, follow me and I will make you fishers of men" (Matthew 4:18–19). As this summons is extended to others, a community of followers is formed.

Later, Matthew documents the moment when Jesus explains his intention for this new community: "On this rock I will build my church, and the gates of Hades will not overcome it" (Matthew 16:18). Through this foundational statement, the church was called into being by Jesus' summons to be *his ecclesia*, that is, his assembly.

The same view is held by Paul, writing to the church in Rome: "All the churches *of Christ* send greetings" (Romans 16:16). The New Testament writers also refer to the "church *of God*" (e.g. Acts 20:28, 1 Corinthians 1:2 and Galatians 1:13) and the same thinking underpins the use of *ecclesia* in the other cases as well.

The New Testament writers assumed that the *ecclesia*, the assembly, was always the assembly of people summoned by the Lord.

ECCLESIA AS A METAPHOR

It will be clear now that even the word "church" is one of many metaphors.

The root meaning of the English word "church" is derived from the Greek χυριαχός (*kuriakos*), meaning "of the Lord." This derivation emphasizes that however else you may conceive of the church, it is essentially *the Lord's* church—the church called into being by Jesus.

On the other hand, the root meaning of the New Testament word *ecclesia* is a gathering, or an assembly.

Those two verbal derivations together have become the primary metaphor for us. The church is an assembly in the name of Jesus; the gathering of the Lord's people.

That is a powerful idea. It is one that has become so entrenched in our understanding of church that we can easily confuse it with a *definition* of church.

THE ASSUMPTION OF GATHERING

Through much of church history we have emphasized this idea of gathering.

We have created buildings in which to gather. This building process has been so successful that many people confuse the church with those buildings.

We have created other buildings—seminaries—to train people how to gather other people.

We gather in conferences across the globe.

We have scheduled specific times for gathering so as many people as possible can arrange their personal schedules to be present at once.

We have established liturgies to encourage a sense of corporate worship within those gatherings.

We use those gatherings to collect money to support the infrastructure required to maintain the gathering.

We have created institutions with offices and bureaucracies to manage the church's assets, to document who is part of the gathering, to create a leadership hierarchy and to define appropriate policies to bring consistency of belief and practice across the organization. These institutions have become powerful political players who influence public policy and lobby for laws that are more in keeping with the church's values.

The very word "congregation" to describe a body of believers reflects the centrality of the gathering metaphor.

To be called, however, does not necessarily mean to be assembled. An individual may be called or summoned without implying a gathering. Even when many are called, the summons may be to scatter or spread rather than to congregate.

WHAT'S HIGHLIGHTED? WHAT'S HIDDEN?

Like all metaphors, the metaphor of church as a gathering both highlights and hides. To the extent that the metaphor has evolved into a core set of assumptions about the church, we should be aware of which aspects of Jesus' intentions have been highlighted and what aspects have been hidden.

The concept of an assembly, or gathering, suggests large numbers. I say "suggests" because it does not have to be that way. There can be small gatherings, but when we hear the word "gathering" our natural inclination is to assume that *the purpose is to gather* and that gathering in itself is a sign of success. If the purpose is to gather, then of course we need to manage the gathering process. We tend to think that the more people assembled the more successful the assembly.

In contrast, Jesus notes that it only takes two or three to gather (Matthew 18:20), at least in the context of relational discipline within a church. If you are on your own it is hard to call that a gathering! So it seems that in Jesus' mind, the number of people is not the important factor: any number in the gathering is sufficient. That's in sharp contrast to the Jewish principle in Jesus' time that a synagogue could only be established if there were at least ten men present.

Consequently, the idea of gathering reveals something important: that there is a sense of being summoned to something. But the idea of gathering also hides something important: that the number of people gathered is irrelevant. The emphasis on gathering also hides an important aspect of being summoned: although gathering requires multiple people, a single person can be summoned.

The concept of a gathering also suggests—once again it doesn't require, it just suggests—that there is a *place of assembly*, a location for the gathering. Sometimes a gathering point is important, but this metaphor hides an equally important truth that the church does not rely on any specific place of assembly. In Jesus' kingdom there is no need for a central temple because Jesus is the Temple (John 2:18–22). We are united *in Christ*, not because we are in one location. In the modern world of cyberspace an assembly can be geographically as remote as the communications infrastructure allows. I think it is clear that Jesus did not intend to create a single assembly centered around specific locations. Rather, he intended the message, and the summoned people, to be spread far and wide (e.g. Matthew 24:14, 28:19, Acts 1:8).

Thirdly, the concept of a gathering suggests there is a clear boundary around the assembly. There are people in the gathering and people outside the gathering. Some are summoned, some are not.

But it also hides another aspect of Jesus' intention that is equally important. Jesus firmly discouraged the view that there were outsiders. He sat children on his lap, he touched lepers, he spoke with Samaritan women, and he shared a meal with someone he knew would betray him. Jesus came to set the prisoners free—and we should not assume he only came for those imprisoned *unjustly*.

When the first disciples wanted Jesus to stop "outsiders" from casting out demons, Jesus challenged their boundary assumptions by saying, "Do not stop him, for whoever is not against you is for you" (Luke 9:49–50). Jesus understood that some of the summoned people will not turn up, and in one parable he affirms the servants who "went out into the streets and gathered all the people they could find, both good and bad" (Matthew 22:10).

In these and many other ways, Jesus demonstrated that his goal was not an exclusive club with a sharp definition of who was in and who was out. Jesus came for the sake of the whole world, with a comprehensive vision of gathering a new humanity that encompasses us all.

The assumption that the church is a gathering has dominated the church's self-image for most of its existence; and that assumption has influenced the doctrine, structures, internal practices and mission of the church, both positively and negatively. Attributes inferred from the gathering metaphor have under-girded the creation of an institution that has changed the course of human history.

I believe the over-emphasis on the metaphor of gathering has misdirected us. The metaphoric calculus has encouraged us to transfer ideas such as the importance of the number of people, the importance of a location in which to gather, and the importance of defining who's in and who's out. These are ideas that naturally spring from the gathering metaphor but they are not the features Jesus intended us to incorporate into the church.

On the other hand, Jesus encouraged other characteristics in his followers that are outside the scope of the gathering metaphor. An over-emphasis on this single metaphor has effectively hidden some of those other important characteristics.

I am not saying the metaphor of gathering is invalid. No, it does bring important features into play—especially the idea of being summoned, and as we shall see later, the idea of community. But it does not paint the whole picture. The church as a gathering is only one of many metaphors that should inform our understanding.

THE CHURCH AND A CHURCH

This label "church" can be applied both to the universal *ecclesia* of Jesus Christ and to a localized expression of that *ecclesia*.

The first sense points to the invisible collection of Jesus' followers across all time. This aligns to the "communion of the saints" mentioned in the Apostles' Creed, and to Paul's view that the diverse followers of Jesus all form a single entity (e.g. Romans 12:5, 1 Corinthians 12:13). In the Catechism of the Catholic Church, section 946 says "What is the Church if not the assembly of all the saints? The communion of saints is the Church."[19] By that definition, the church universal encompasses those living, dead and still to come, and includes followers who may not attend or belong to any local gathering.

The second sense points to the visible collection of Jesus' followers within a specific location in the present. Many of the letters included in the New Testament are addressed to such churches: "To the church of God in Corinth" (1 Corinthians 1:2), etc. As is well documented, the church need not occupy a purpose-made building but may be simply a small group of followers who meet in someone's home (see for instance Romans 16:3–5). Depending on how you define it, the local church may include people who are not part of the universal church, since people who attend the visible church meetings, and even be confirmed members of those churches, may nevertheless not in fact be followers of Jesus.

In this book I switch between those two senses with perhaps less concern or precision than some people would like. Most of the time I use "the church" for the first sense and "a church" for the second, but many times I use the unadorned "church" because my main emphasis is on our underlying attitudes towards being church and the dynamics of God's mission in the world, regardless of whether those attitudes and dynamics relate to the universal church or to a specific local expression of that universal church.

RITUALS

One of the obvious features of the historical church is the use of rituals. Many other cultural groups also use rituals in similar ways. In fact, probably every group of people employs rituals in one form or another, but I wish to focus on the way we rely on rituals in the context of church gatherings.

By ritual I mean the collection of elements that make up the normal process of a church gathering. It includes the setting aside of a time and place for the gathering, the atmosphere created by décor (whether stained glass windows or a raised stage in a warehouse), smells, lighting, and music. It also includes the liturgical structure of the meeting: welcoming, singing, bible readings, financial collection, sermon, prayers, benediction, etc.

Some of this liturgical structure is fairly common across most church gatherings, though each denomination or local group adds their own components, like the ritual of shaking hands with the pastor on the way out of the church building in many Western Protestant gatherings. A core aspect of our traditional church ritual is the use of specific symbols and symbolic events: candles, icons, crosses, incense, the celebration of Communion or Eucharist, and baptism.

In the gathered church we are used to these rituals and their familiarity makes us feel at home. They are honored and repeated. They constitute the "proper" way of doing things. They bring back rich memories and instill a sense of belonging.

The flip side, however, is that rituals make others feel that they don't belong. They confuse, isolate, and even cause embarrassment to the newcomer who is unfamiliar with the ritual. That discomfort highlights an important consequence of this traditional form of ritual: it can become an identifying feature that defines who belongs to a group and who doesn't.

In some contexts, this consequence is explicitly the primary purpose of the ritual: to mark the boundary of who's in and who's out. That's the case, for instance, in various rites of passage like baptism, weddings and ordination. But any ritual, regardless of how welcoming and inclusive its intention, can exclude.

I remember inviting a work colleague to church on a Sunday when I was the preacher. I thought he would be interested in the topic, which I think might have been based on the invitation to people who are thirsty in Isaiah 55. The church was a small Uniting Church in suburban Sydney, and we were a very informal group. We dressed casually, encouraged everyone to participate, and ran the weekly services with minimal supervision of any ordained minister. We were young and excited about the opportunity to experiment with how church services were organized. There were several severely disabled people in the regular congregation and one of them, Murray, loved to play the organ. Murray was a wonderful man, but he was not noted for his musical ability! Nevertheless, part of our ritual was for him to play an improvised postlude after the benediction.

My work colleague was not a church-goer and based on some guesses about what to expect, he arrived dressed up in a full business suit. In some churches that might have been a good guess, but in our church that made him stand out as the obvious outsider. I mentally kicked myself for not letting him know more about what to expect beforehand. The very casualness of our ritual which was intended to make everyone feel welcome marked him as not belonging. Was it that, or my preaching that discouraged him from coming again?

Ritual plays a second important role in traditional churches that I believe also springs from the focus on gathering. Ritual seeks to anchor the gathering in something beyond.

This is most clearly seen in what mainstream churches refer to as sacraments: ceremonies such as Baptism and Eucharist. Rituals use the physical elements present in the gathering to remind us that something transcendent is also occurring. The physical elements act symbolically: they represent something other. For example, the bread and wine in the Eucharist represent (in some traditions they actually become) the body and blood of Christ.

The symbolic dynamic within a sacrament means the sacraments themselves act according to the metaphoric calculus. Sacraments juxtapose something that is known— water, bread, wine, a wedding ring etc.—with something else that is the real focus of the ceremony—new birth, res- urrection, the making of a lifelong commitment etc. In or- der to understand and emotionally resonate with the real focus, we are invited to transfer some of the attributes of the physical elements to their spiritual counterparts. For instance, in the Eucharist, the physical nourishment of bread that we understand so well is transferred across the metaphor to remind us that our spirit is nourished by Christ.

I think the term "transcendent" has two connotations in this context. First, the rituals of the gathered church are designed to remind us of something supernatural, some- thing of spiritual importance that is not physically present. The Eucharistic bread symbolizes the body of Christ. The steeple reaching to the sky symbolically points us towards heaven. The cross devoid of a body reminds us both that Christ has died, and that Christ has risen.

Second, the common description of sacraments as "an outward and visible sign of an inward and spiritual grace" points to an inward experience of transcendence. The external physical elements of the ritual somehow reflect, or cause, or supervene, on an inner spiritual experience. That inward spiritual experience involves opening our awareness to a greater truth or mystery beyond ourselves and beyond the physicality of the ritual.

Through these two avenues—the transcendence of what a ritual points to, and the transcendence of our inner experience during the ritual—traditional rituals create a link with, and a yearning for, a deeper spiritual reality. That valuable outcome would be hard to achieve without the symbolic element.

In many cases, however, this sets up a dualistic conflict between the concrete physical present and the desired yet abstract spiritual reality. As I've noted before, every metaphor both highlights and hides. There are important truths that a traditional approach to ritual distorts or obscures. By anchoring the gathering in a yearning for a connection to some transcendent Other, a ritual easily generates a disconnection between normal daily life and spiritual life. It suggests that the concrete physical present is insufficient and less valuable than the goal of some transcendent reality. It also suggests that the gathering, and the ritual employed during the gathering, is the way to achieve the spiritual goal.

THE STORY SO FAR ...

Following the metaphoric calculus, this section has considered the importance of gathering as a metaphor for the church. A clear and compelling case can be made from the Biblical text that aspects of gathering apply to the identity and operational model of the church. Despite challenges of translation, the process of being summoned to an assembly can be seen as an essential component to understanding what Jesus intended to build.

I have pointed out several limitations to that picture. I have suggested that more important than being summoned to an assembly is the real cornerstone of the church: that we have been summoned *by the Lord*, that we are *the Lord's* assembly. We can too easily retrofit our modern understanding of church back onto the New Testament picture. Let's resist the assumption that the church we see today—with its dependence on purpose-built meeting places, a certain style of liturgy and ritual, etc.—is the church Jesus intended.

One area where the metaphor of gathering has influenced the practice of the church is our understanding of rituals. Rituals in the gathering church create belonging, but also exclude outsiders. Rituals point us to spiritual realities, but at the risk of undermining the important connection to the here and now. In Chapter 14, I describe another way to frame rituals that retains the advantages while avoiding the disadvantages.

Focusing on the church as a gathering has blinkered our thinking. It has emphasized some aspects of Jesus' intention but hidden others. In the next section, I start to question whether the idea of the church as a gathering is as essential as many have assumed. Despite the dominance of gathering as the goal of the church, the historical reality does not match the ideal. For several reasons, the church has also scattered.

[3]

Scattered

ALTHOUGH GATHERING HAS BEEN a core assumption underlying how the shape of the church has evolved, various forces, internal and external, have caused the church to be scattered. In this section I outline how the scattered reality throughout church history has augmented the core assumption of the church as a gathering.

There has been both synergy and tension between the ideas of a scattered church and a gathered church.

Diaspora

The Greek word διασπορά, Latinized to *diaspora*, refers to dispersion or scattering, especially of a group of people.[20]

Diaspora is applied historically and in modern writings to the Jewish people following the destruction of the Temple in AD 70. In the Greek version of the Old Testament it is used in Nehemiah 1:8–9 with reference to the removal of the Hebrew people from their homeland. A similar meaning is found in John 7:35, where Jesus' Jewish audience discuss the fact that "our people live scattered among the Greeks."

In the introduction to his letter in the New Testament, James writes "to the twelve tribes *scattered* among the nations" (James 1:1). Peter uses the same word in the introduction to his first letter—"To God's elect, strangers in the world, *scattered* throughout the provinces of Pontus, Galatia, Cappadocia, Asia and Bithynia ... " (1 Peter 1:1). In both of those verses, the writers see forced scattering as a significant aspect of the early church's self-image. James' reference to the "twelve tribes" metaphorically links the experience of Israel in exile with the experience of first-century Christians. James wrote to followers of Jesus within the scattered Jewish community, drawing on what they already knew about the Jewish diaspora, and implicitly invites them to think about their first-century Christian experience in the same way.

What aspects of the Jewish diaspora can be transferred across the metaphoric calculus to the experience of the young church? Certainly the idea of persecution and exile. Perhaps the idea of disruption to a stable group identity and the feeling of not belonging. Certainly also an understanding that as God's "chosen people," the church, like Israel, is called to be a blessing for all nations. This theme is founded in Genesis (e.g. 12:3, 18:18, 26:4) and Paul explicitly applies the same purpose to Christians in Galatians 3:7–9.

GEOGRAPHICALLY SCATTERED

The forced scattering of the followers of Jesus started within the first generation of believers. The early church historian, Luke, records that immediately after the martyrdom of Stephen—perhaps in 34 CE—"a great persecution broke out against the church in Jerusalem, and all except the apostles were scattered throughout Judea and Samaria" (Acts 8:1). Successive rounds of persecution followed, authorized by Roman emperors from Nero in 64 CE to Maximinus right up to 313 CE.

Christians also scattered as a result of a strong missionary urge. That outward impulse finds its basis in the whole tenor of the Biblical account of how God interacts with human history. Through both Israel and the church, God seeks to bless all humanity. This is why Jesus said to the disciples, "As the Father has sent me, I am sending you" (John 20:21). In Matthew's account, the commission to "go" constituted Jesus' final instruction to his followers (Matthew 28:18–20).

More than any other early follower, Paul understood the imperative of Jesus' commission. He wasn't the first or the only example—Philip's interaction with the Ethiopian eunuch (Acts 8:26–40) shows that he felt the same urge—but Paul's example of sustained missionary zeal and his personal theological reflection on the importance of that outward movement established the paradigm of missionary activity that drove the expansion of the church around the globe.

So, it was through both forced dispersion by persecution and the missionary urge that the early Christian church spread across the Roman empire. They travelled on the coat-tails of Roman expansion, relying on the convenience of Roman-built roads and the safety of Roman security forces.[21]

This same combination of external and internal forces has continued to scatter Christians up to the present day. While the church has expanded by deliberate missions to new population groups, it has also scattered to escape persecution, even persecution by other Christians. The church has often scattered on the coattails of colonial expansion, such as the British conquest of Australia.

In most cases, this scattering is accompanied by a strong intention of re-gathering. Sometimes that intention is an unstated assumption, but it is often an explicit principle. Scattering is viewed as a strategy for establishing new gathering points: a strategy which is foundational to the whole church-planting movement. We start with a successful gathering, then send people to other places in order to build a new gathering in our own image. To some it can seem as though this is the only way of thinking about mission, as though the mission of the church is to establish more churches. As you'll read later, I'm not a fan of that way of thinking about mission.

There are notable exceptions—groups that scatter because scattering is a good thing by itself, rather than the majority who scatter in order to gather. I have always been impressed with the way Mennonite's from the USA established a network in Australia and New Zealand. They sent missionaries in 1990, but after listening to local voices they determined that a better approach than creating Mennonite churches was to influence the life of faith communities already in Australia and New Zealand.

Since 1995, the resulting Anabaptist Association of Australia and New Zealand (AAANZ) has implemented that vision by providing resources to inform the church about the Anabaptist tradition and encouraging people in the network to bring an Anabaptist perspective to their own churches. This is an excellent example of a mission-oriented movement scattering globally to equip people for ministry wherever they are, rather than seeking to plant new churches in the image of the sending church.

Another example is the approach to mission taken by the 19th century Lutheran pastor, Christoph Blumhardt. His son-in-law was a missionary in China, and Blumhardt wrote over 100 letters to him between 1898 and 1914, encouraging him in his work.[22] Blumhardt warns about simply transporting a European church into China and sees the importance of scattering as a means of discovering how Christ is already incarnated in the mission field.

THEOLOGICALLY SCATTERED

The church is scattered not only in terms of its location but also in terms of its doctrines and practices. We may be one in Christ, but the global church is extremely varied in terms of what each gathering believes and how they enact those beliefs.

The major divisions of Catholic, Orthodox, and Protestant each have their own sub-divisions: Evangelical,

Pentecostal, Liberal, Progressive, Charismatic, Pre-millennial, Post-millennial, Amillennial, Pre-trib, Post-trib, etc. We have differing emphases on the foundations of our faith: the centrality of the Bible, the role of the Spirit, the importance of church tradition in contrast to personal experience. We have differing understandings of mission, as exemplified by ongoing debates about the relative importance of evangelization and social justice.

In part, this diversity springs from a decision by church leaders in the generation immediately after Jesus' ascension.[23] Acts 15 records the outcome of a council meeting in Jerusalem in response to the growing number of non-Jewish converts. The experience of the church up to that point, and the example by Jesus, lay within the theological and cultural norms of Judaism. Rather than impose those theological and cultural constraints, however, the church leaders gave the Gentile converts permission to develop their own distinctively Hellenistic (i.e. Greek) way of living as followers of Jesus without being circumcised or needing to submit to the Law of Moses.

As a consequence, they developed a practice of faith in their own language, incorporating their own cultural symbols, and drawing on the best of their own history, literature, and philosophy. That same pattern has been repeated countless times over the past 2,000 years. There is no universal "Christian culture," and that itself is a distinguishing feature of Christianity as a social movement.

The diversity of beliefs and practices within the church is a direct consequence of this non-tribal approach, which is at the heart of our faith. Expressing our allegiance to

Jesus, under the continuing guidance of the Holy Spirit, we are radically free to find a path of faith within whatever tribe we find ourselves.

These differences divide us and question the reality of our underlying unity. They also inspire a good deal of pride and arrogance, as though our small expression of the church universal is the only true and right remnant. This is shown with wonderful clarity in the following cartoon.[24]

I need to be careful not to fall into this same mistake in this book. So let me be clear that I am not claiming that the traditional wisdom about how the church should operate is wrong and that I have finally discovered the true way. No, I affirm the broad expressions of church that have been crafted in response to both the Spirit of God and the varied cultural contexts around the world and across two millennia. What I hope to do in this book is re-awaken an under-appreciated aspect of being church, and to suggest that the idea of a deliberately scattering church is more suited to our current cultural context.

The differences between churches in terms of organizational structure, decision-making processes, liturgy, membership conditions, and beliefs are many and significant. Underlying those differences is often a foundational difference in how we understand the source of authority: the relative weight given to personal experience, the Bible and tradition.

I firmly believe that some expressions of church are more on track than others: that some more accurately follow Jesus' vision for the kingdom of God than others. But many of the distinctive flavors are valid expressions of sensitivity to personal preferences and cultural context. Given the diversity of people's musical tastes, for instance, there is good reason for different churches to use different music in their gatherings. If someone has grown up with rock bands, why torture them with organ music on Sundays— and vice versa? Given the historical beliefs of Australian Indigenous people that the land is the source of the sacred, there is good reason for Australian churches to emphasize the God who is grounded and present here on earth rather than the remote God-in-the-heavens metaphor of the traditional European churches. That is a faithful outworking of Paul's principle to "become all things to all people so that by all possible means I might save some" (1 Corinthians 9:19–23).

What interests me though, is the vehemence generated by the differences between the many varied expressions of church. There is not just pride within each faction, but serious animosity between factions. This is nicely parodied in the Emo Philips joke quoted below. The fact that this joke was listed in CQ Magazine's "75 Funniest Jokes of All Time"[25] shows how broadly the truth of this joke is understood. It would not be funny if we didn't recognize it to be true.

Once I saw this guy on a bridge about to jump. I said, "Don't do it!" He said, "Nobody loves me." I said, "God loves you. Do you believe in God?"

He said, "Yes." I said, "Are you a Christian or a Jew?" He said, "A Christian." I said, "Me, too! Protestant or Catholic?" He said, "Protestant." I said, "Me, too! What franchise?" He said, "Baptist." I said, "Me, too! Northern Baptist or Southern Baptist?" He said, "Northern Baptist." I said, "Me, too! Northern Conservative Baptist or Northern Liberal Baptist?"

He said, "Northern Conservative Baptist." I said, "Me, too! Northern Conservative Baptist Great Lakes Region, or Northern Conservative Baptist Eastern Region?" He said, "Northern Conservative Baptist Great Lakes Region." I said, "Me, too!"

Northern Conservative Baptist Great Lakes Region Council of 1879, or Northern Conservative Baptist Great Lakes Region Council of 1912?" He said, "Northern Conservative Baptist Great Lakes Region Council of 1912." I said, "Die, heretic!" And I pushed him over.[26]

Why is there so much animosity between factions? What arrogance fuels that anger? Surely it doesn't spring from the spirit of Jesus.

SYNERGY AND TENSION

I am certainly not the first to contrast the gathered and scattered movements within the church. The synergy and tension between those two movements has been a driving force throughout church history.

From one point of view, as noted in Chapter 2, the defining purpose of the church is to gather—to assemble the people of God. From another point of view, the only way to gather is to go out and call people in: a missionary dynamic through which we scatter in order to gather. From yet another point of view, the very purpose of gathering is to equip the people of God to go out into the world: an equipping dynamic through which we gather in order to scatter.

Two recent books have discussed this in detail,[27] both seeking in their own ways to show how the two dynamics work together—or should work together—within the modern institutional church. I want to summarize and comment on those two books because they both capture important wisdom about the current state of the church and encourage us to see opportunities in the tension.

I also want to summarize those two books to contrast them with the more untamed approach to being church that I develop in later chapters.

But first, a practical example ...

ANNABELLA'S SOAKING GROUP

My wife Annabella was part of an expression of church in the form of a dozen people who met in homes and occasionally at the local pub. The group was not affiliated with any other church, had no assets, no paid leadership, no mission program, and no children's ministry. The group didn't even have a name. Nevertheless, they gathered together most weeks on Wednesday night for more than twelve years.

There would always be some light food and unstructured discussion about each other's lives, but the group's primary form of liturgy revolved around the idea of soaking in God's presence using music. In each meeting, the people would sit comfortably in the lounge room, or more usually lie on the floor and listen to some inspirational music, normally without words, for about 30 minutes. Annabella compares the practice to the way a cucumber soaks up flavor as it sits in pickling juices. In the same way, the people in this group were infused with the Holy Spirit. This was a form of prayer through which they could relax, process the recent activities of their lives and release their burdens, creatively imagine God in their midst, and listen to whatever God revealed. In this gentle way they individually met God within the context of a small community who valued each other and valued the way God nurtured each of their lives together.

At one point in the group's history a relative newcomer suggested that the group should consider taking on a more outward, missional focus. They thought the group shouldn't be so wholly inward looking but do something that presented God's message to the world and called others into a relationship with God. As that idea was discussed, the group saw it was not just a suggestion to add one more task to the list of things they did together but a rethinking of the nature of the group. Why did they meet? What was their mission? Was God calling them as a group into a new outreach orientation?

Through the discussion, each person talked more about what they did during the rest of their week. At that time, Annabella worked as a teacher's aide with disabled children. One person ran a counselling business, one was a GP, and another was a radiologist. One was a cleaner at a local school who saw her ministry as praying over the people in the school as she cleaned. Another connected with high-school students and their parents in the context of being a tutor while still another worked in the disability sector. One volunteered with a more structured Christian women's organization. Another owned an accountancy business, and one fostered children from traumatic backgrounds. These varied vocations are virtually all service-oriented roles through which the people each expressed their faith in public. When you add up all that ministry, what became clear was that the group was already extensively engaged in outward-focused mission.

There was no need for the group to feel tension or spiritually inadequate. Their inward focus and soaking liturgy did not conflict with the mission urge. Nor were the small group gatherings an escape from the world. No, the very strength of the small group and the value of deliberately setting time aside to rest in God's embrace, was that it enabled the scattered ministries that shared God's presence with the world.

Now, onto an examination of what some other authors have written about the synergy and tension between gathering and scattering.

EDWARD H. HAMMETT

The American Baptist Edward H. Hammett published *The Gathered and Scattered Church: equipping believers for the 21st century* in 1999 (with a second edition in 2005).

In the Foreword, Findley B. Edge poses the question "Can our kind of church save our kind of world?" and answers with a definite "No." "Our kind of church" is typically large, relatively rich, with strategically located real estate. But it is also selfish and irrelevant.[28]

For the most part, I think that is an accurate observation.

Hammett's book is an attempt to diagnose the cause of that problem and suggest a remedy.

His starting point is that the church must gather. That is essential because "being scattered means losing power and identity."[29] But his primary concern about the congregations with which he is familiar is their tendency to focus on gathering to such an extent they are missionally ineffective. Hammett's vision is a church in which the gathered and scattered emphases form "one vital, continuing double-movement of the people of God."[30]

The New Testament presents an "image of a church gathering itself in order to propel its people outward to the

world,"[31] yet he observes that "in our churches we have
learned the gathering part of the equation, but have continually fallen short when it comes to being scattered."[32] In
contrast, in Hammett's ideal church ...

> *The believers who meet as the gathered church for worship,*
> *praise, and equipping on Sundays fulfil their mission as the*
> *scattered church when they intentionally live out their faith*
> *in Christ throughout the week in the world. The scattered*
> *church is where 90 percent of the church's work can be ac-*
> *complished.[33]*

In this book, Hammett tries to encourage a change of
thinking among church leaders so they in turn will encourage their church members to take hold of this outward mission. "The church that will survive in the future will be the
church that sees itself as a 'mission outpost' from which the
gathered church scatters."[34]

I applaud Hammett's work in providing motivation and
resources to achieve that goal. For church gatherings stuck
in that insular, inward-looking, self-protective, institutional mindset, his advice is likely to be a fruitful way to
broaden the congregation's horizon towards real mission
in the world.

The book gives numerous examples of individuals,
churches, and para-church organizations who effectively
engage with the needs and culture of their surrounding
communities. But this summary bothers me deeply:

> *These committed Christians and others like them have*
> *learned that the church is not restricted to four walls. They*

*have realized that being a Christian involves more than at-
tending church on Sunday morning. Christ calls his people
out of the church building and into kingdom work. Certainly this concept of church is radical, but we must break
the mold of doing church the traditional way.*[35]

How can this possibly be seen as a "radical" approach
that breaks with "the traditional way"? This sending out of
people into the world has been the core of church life since
the Great Commission! Are there really whole gatherings
where the people do not understand that being a Christian
means to be called into God's service to the world? Do people really think they can be followers of Jesus by warming
the pew rather than actually following?

If this is a radical message, then it reflects a far worse
situation in the modern evangelicalism of North America
than I had imagined.

One key cause of the problem, which Hammett rightly
identifies, is the tendency towards institutionalism where
"the driving issues become territory and survival rather
than purpose and renewal."[36] My primary criticism of
Hammet's approach is that he does not follow the implications of that observation far enough. If institutionalism is
part of the problem, why continue founding the activities
of the church in a gathered institution? Sure, he promotes
a change of focus so the gathered institution supports the
scattered work of mission, but Hammet pre-supposes that
the gathered church is the foundation of mission and identity. I question that assumption. I disagree with his assertion that "being scattered means losing power and

identity,"[37] and I wonder whether he has rejected the very thing that is most valuable about scattering.

HUGH HALTER AND MATT SMAY

Like Hammett, Hugh Halter and Matt Smay reflect on the state of the church they know and find that, "we need to do a better job of scattering our gathered bodies back into the world, a world that desperately needs to know the truth about God."[38] Their book *AND: the gathered and scattered church*, published in 2010, is a call for the institutional church to transform into something more missional, with a focus on spiritual formation that encourages all church members to connect their faith to daily life in the world.

As the title of their book suggests, Halter and Smay are convinced that the tension between the gathered and scattered movements can be turned into a synergy; that the church should not be formed around just one movement or the other but both.

Halter writes:

> *I was reminded of the creativity and power of God. I wondered what God could do with an entire generation who loves him but won't settle for stale church anymore. What could God do with an army of kingdom peasants who have no interest in safety, religion, money, but who want to help people experience the presence of the kingdom in the here and now? While denominations struggle to survive, what might God do with relational networks of kingdom leaders who long to see something new happen in this generation?*[39]

Those questions inspire me tremendously.

I believe there is indeed a yearning among "kingdom peasants" to work relationally rather than programmatically, committed to Jesus rather than an institution, willing to live the Good News in the world. If you step outside the institutional church for a while, you will find grassroots kingdom building all over the place as followers of Jesus, frustrated with the strictures of traditional church-ianity, allowing the wind of the Spirit to blow them where God wills.

Halter and Smay recognize there are already many different expressions of church, from the mega-church to the informal house church, along with the vast majority of churches in the middle with perhaps 100 members. Each have their benefits and their challenges.

Their own church expression is a "congregational network of incarnational communities"[40]—a structure that reminds me of the Dove House Fellowship I belonged to for several years in South Africa. In this model, the main life of the church occurs in small groups meeting across a city in people's houses. In contrast to many house churches, this model also includes regular larger gatherings. This bi-modal approach promotes a high level of participation and shared ownership. The large gatherings can generate a lot of excitement along with a sense of belonging to something substantial, visible, and influential. The small gatherings emphasize nurturing relationships and provide the context for a day-by-day presence through normal life connections to neighbors, friends, and work colleagues.

In many churches, I think most of the internal work and external ministry is carried out by 20% of the people, while the remaining 80% warm the pews. In contrast, a typical outcome of the network-of-small-communities model flips that around with 80% of the people being deeply engaged participants, committed to each other and to working together in mission. At least that's the hope.

Halter and Smay note the importance of passionate followers of Jesus (they coin the wonderful term "passionaries") being connected to a "viable faith collective".[41] That's a useful phrase, and I am glad they chose the word *viable* rather than *visible*. A lot of their book reflects a desire for the church to be visible and more relevant to our modern society, but the visibility of a faith collective is not what makes it viable. There's only a couple of letters different between the two, but whether or not a faith collective is viable does not depend on having a large membership or a prime piece of real estate with a prominent steeple in the center of town, or a large following on social media. A viable faith collective depends on relationships with each other and a shared set of values derived from a common allegiance to Jesus. What an *invisible* church could look like is a thought I will develop further when I unpack the implications of Jesus' metaphor of us acting like yeast.

In "AND," Halter and Smay turn the typical model of church mission on its head. Most missional movements, they claim, start with a structured church that attempts to build community, and from that position reaches out to engage the culture outside the church. In contrast, they promote the same three steps in reverse order. Start by engaging the culture in which you live. As you connect with people and live out your faith among them a community develops in which discipleship and evangelism can occur. The final phase, rather than the first, is to provide a church structure for people's "continued growth, connection and common vision."[42]

This third phase is where I depart from the shape of church espoused by Halter and Smay. I disagree with the inevitability or necessity of creating formal structures to contain and control growth, connection, and vision. The message of this present book is that containing, controlling, and centralizing are less effective strategies than an approach that releases and radically decentralizes. As I'll argue later, the role of community is core to Jesus' kingdom-building strategy rather than just as a transitional stage to the "structured congregation" that many people presume is a *real* church.

Halter and Smay are dismayed at the number of people who leave a church after consuming a huge amount of the church leaders' time. "Looking back over twenty years of pastoral ministry, I can add up thousands of hours spent trying to get people to come with us or be a part of us, only to have them leave us later, some after another hundred hours invested in trying to work out some values or vision differences."[43]

Rather than being frustrated with that dynamic, what if people leaving constituted the very shape of success? What if people leaving was the result of a deliberate goal of scattering?

Putting that aside, there is much I admire about their dedication to drawing followers of Jesus back into the world. They locate spiritual formation at the very center of "kingdom DNA"[44] and their outline of how to promote spiritual formation is well worth reading.

I have often been troubled by the hymn, "I have decided to follow Jesus." The verse that bothers me says, "The world behind me, the cross before me; no turning back, no turning back." This proposes that the path of discipleship, of spiritual formation, requires a rejection of the world so we can get to the cross. But if we are following Jesus, isn't he going in the opposite direction? Isn't the incarnation about God coming *into* the world? While engaging with the death of Jesus on the cross may be the beginning of discipleship, what is it that we hear Jesus say once we get there? Surely he tells us to turn around and join him in his mission to the world. The cross is the foundation stone of spiritual formation, not the destination.

When I sing that hymn, I change the words—sometimes quietly, sometimes more challengingly—and sing "the cross behind me, the world before me; no turning back, no turning back." I believe Halter and Smay would approve.

THE CHURCH HAS ALWAYS BEEN AT ITS BEST WHEN IT HAS BEEN IN THE MINORITY

In a world where "bigger is better" we can easily fall into the belief that the success of a church—and even more sadly, the success of *the* church—is measured by its size and power. We can believe, perhaps unconsciously, that to be effective, the church needs to be big and visible so it can influence people and nations. We can believe that the mark of real success would be wielding significant influence over public policy, using legislation in the impossible[45] attempt to impose "Christian" morality and to create a "Christian country."

That seems contrary to Jesus' approach which values relationship over numbers, individuals over institutions, freedom over coercion, and solidarity with the marginalized over power. He notes that the meek are blessed by God (Matthew 5: 5), not the powerful.

Jim Palmer makes a good point when he observes that, "Jesus, as a homeless man with a handful of confused followers and no budget, had more of a revolutionary impact in three years than the entire Christian church has in three centuries."[46]

If that is true, we should not be despondent about the demise of the church as a dominant political force. The period of "Christendom" may be over, but that does not mean the influence of Jesus is diminished.

THE ANABAPTIST TRADITION

To make sense of why I believe that, I need to say some more about a stream of Christian thinking and practice that may be unfamiliar.

My own faith has been influenced by multiple streams of church tradition: protestant, evangelical, charismatic, social justice, and what has more recently been labelled "progressive." But the core of my theological understanding comes from the Anabaptist tradition. I will write more about the Anabaptist conception of church as a witnessing community later. But for now, a brief overview of that tradition will suffice.[47]

Anabaptism started in the sixteenth century as part of the Radical Reformation movement in Europe. The more well-known Reformation leaders, such as Luther, Calvin, and Zwingli, challenged the Catholic church on many issues both theological and political. But the Radical Reformers considered that those leaders had not gone far enough. The Anabaptists denounced infant baptism and called for a more complete separation of the church from state control. In response, both Catholics and Protestants persecuted the Anabaptists, imprisoning and executing many.

Anabaptists tend to emphasize—more strongly than Catholic or Protestant groups—an ethical framework built on the life of Jesus, the shared life of a worshipping community, and a commitment to reconciliation and peace-making.

Multiple church groups identify with the Anabaptist tradition, the largest being the Mennonites and the German Baptists. Through those, and smaller groups such as the Hutterites, Church of the Brethren, and Amish, there may be between 2 and 4 million Anabaptists in the world today.

The Anabaptist Network lists the following "core convictions"[48]:

> 1. *Jesus is our example, teacher, friend, redeemer and Lord. He is the source of our life, the central reference point for our faith and lifestyle, for our understanding of church and our engagement with*

society. We are committed to following Jesus as well as worshipping him.

2. *Jesus is the focal point of God's revelation. We are committed to a Jesus-centered approach to the Bible, and to the community of faith as the primary context in which we read the Bible and discern and apply its implications for discipleship.*

3. *Western culture is slowly emerging from the Christendom era when church and state jointly presided over a society in which almost all were assumed to be Christian. Whatever its positive contributions on values and institutions, Christendom seriously distorted the gospel, marginalized Jesus, and has left the churches ill-equipped for mission in a post-Christendom culture. As we reflect on this, we are committed to learning from the experience and perspectives of movements such as Anabaptism that rejected standard Christendom assumptions and pursued alternative ways of thinking and behaving.*

4. *The frequent association of the church with status, wealth and force is inappropriate for followers of Jesus and damages our witness. We are committed to exploring ways of being good news to the poor, powerless and persecuted, aware that such discipleship may attract opposition, resulting in suffering and sometimes ultimately martyrdom.*

5. *Churches are called to be committed communities of discipleship and mission, places of friendship, mutual accountability and multi-voiced worship.*

As we eat together, sharing bread and wine, we sustain hope as we seek God's kingdom together. We are committed to nurturing and developing such churches, in which young and old are valued, leadership is consultative, roles are related to gifts rather than gender and baptism is for believers.

6. *Spirituality and economics are inter-connected. In an individualist and consumerist culture and in a world where economic injustice is rife, we are committed to finding ways of living simply, sharing generously, caring for creation, and working for justice.*

7. *Peace is at the heart of the gospel. As followers of Jesus in a divided and violent world, we are committed to finding non-violent alternatives and to learning how to make peace between individuals, within and among churches, in society, and between nations.*

I introduce the Anabaptist heritage here to make a point about the size and influence of the church, but you will see that these seven convictions underpin many other themes in this book.

Anabaptism has always been a minority view within the overall church. Anabaptists would see that as an advantage rather than a failure. Being in a minority allows those in the Anabaptist tradition to identify with other minorities, and to speak prophetically to the more powerful groups within the church and in the broader society.

From this point of view, the fact that the church is scattered geographically and theologically, whether by external or internal forces, is to be celebrated. The church—not just the Anabaptist branch but the whole church—will always be a minority in the world. As leading Anabaptist theologian John Howard Yoder[49] notes, that "is not a statistical but a theological observation." Now that the Church has become weak in a socio-political sense we should "recognize with joy that her calling is [has always been] to be weak."[50] The church is not called to dominate the world but rather "Our witness is in being a new humanity in which all our social relationships demonstrate to the world how life is to be lived."[51]

WHEN WE WERE IN POWER

Anabaptist theology questions the nature of power and our persistent drive to gain power. Since its inception, Anabaptism has been critical of the way the church has historically aligned itself to secular power.[52] With the conversion of Emperor Constantine, the church may have gained socio-political legitimacy but it also acquired an empire-building mentality that obscured the vision of Jesus for a kingdom that was radically different from the world's kingdoms.

The rise of Christendom meant that the church looked just like any other earthly kingdom. We felt good about being a powerful actor on the world stage with the ability to direct things using our temporal power. Now, with the power of Christendom fading, many feel threatened and defensively build up the walls to protect our "Christian" way of life.

During that period of our ascendency, when the church was in a position of social power, we misused that power just as thoroughly as any other ideology. The church, as an institution, acted like every other institution: seeking above all else to protect itself, to ensure its own survival, and to maintain its own power. We coerced and oppressed just as much as we released and uplifted. We abused and destroyed just as much as we nourished and created. We sowed hate and fear just as much as we sowed love.

Compare that to what William Temple, Archbishop of Canterbury during World War 2, is often quoted as saying: "The church is the only society that exists for the benefit of those who are not its members." Dietrich Bonhoeffer echoed the same thought: "The church is the church only when it exists for others."[53] We cannot achieve that purpose by focusing on gathering. The gathered church is self-serving, risk averse, and constrained by inertia.

While gathering is a thoroughly Biblical metaphor for the church, and serves important purposes, we need to also be a scattered church if we are to be a blessing to the world.

If we don't choose to scatter, God has a habit of forcing us to scatter. The rapid growth of Christianity in China is a modern example of how persecution can cause the church to scatter and how effective that scattered and largely invisible church can be.

THE STORY SO FAR ...

What I have tried to show in this chapter is that although the dominant conception of the church is founded on the metaphor of a gathering, the historical reality has been that the strength of the church arises from being scattered.

As Edward Hammett, Hugh Halter, and Matt Smay have each noted, the two movements have some tension between them but can work in synergy. It is possible to draw insights from both metaphors and weave them together into a model of church that values both gathered and scattered modes of operation.

So far, we have moved from a concept of church that relies solely on gathering to a concept that accepts the reality of being both gathered and scattered. I have pointed out some difficulties with both those conceptions, particularly the assumption that the only reason we scatter is as a strategy to enable bigger and better gathering.

In the next chapter, I describe four key aspects of the modern Western context that pose major additional challenges to the gathered church model.

It seems to me that the idea of the church as a Great Gathering is no longer working. Perhaps it never really worked. There is no sound theological reason to think that it should. In fact, the institutional church—which promotes gathering and encourages scattering only insofar as it enables more gathering—actually holds us back from our true mission. The effective church in our world today is one that must deliberately scatter.

[4]

THE WORLD WE LIVE IN

I ASSUME THE MAJORITY OF THE READERS of this book will live in the English-speaking so-called "first world" and share a lot of cultural similarities with my experience.

An obvious observation is that we have not always thought about life, the universe and everything in the way we do now. There are many and varied worldviews, and the human social cultures that both nurture and reflect those worldviews change over time. That observation is easy to forget. Because we live and breathe in one specific time and culture, we can easily fall into thinking that everyone thinks—or should think!—just like us.

Not being a social scientist, I will not attempt to write in detail about changes in Western cultures, and because this book is written specifically for a culturally Western audience, I will say nothing at all about non-Western cultures. Instead, I will briefly describe a handful of cultural features that impact the effectiveness of the church and help to explain the ineffectiveness of the institutional, gathering church model in our current social context.

THE PERCEIVED IRRELEVANCE OF CHURCH

Research driven by the Bible Society of NSW in 2003 sought to understand Australian attitudes to the church, the Bible, Christianity, and Jesus. Although they found positive opinions about Jesus and Christian values, it was difficult for the research participants to separate them from their negative opinions about the church. "Essentially the Church was an almost insurmountable problem for most people."[54] They saw in the church hypocrisy, intoler-ance, judgementalism, rule-driven rigidity, and pedophilia. More recent research "reveals an alarming gap between how the church and the community perceive each other."[55]

As Simon Smart once quipped about the attitudes of Australians to the church, "It's a thin layer of resentment over a sea of apathy."[56] One can easily find similar attitudes in the UK, where "To say that you are a Christian is 'to declare yourself intolerant, naive, superstitious and back-ward'"[57] and in the USA where the number of people with a "great deal" of confidence in the church has more than halved over the past 45 years.[58]

In Australia, the percentage of people who attend church at least once a month decreased from 36% in 1972 to 15% in 2014.[59] The biggest reason Australians cite for not attending church is that it is "irrelevant to my life."[60] In the USA, the figures for monthly church attendance are much higher than Australia but follow the same trajectory, dropping from 58% in 1992 to 42% in 2018.[61]

Leaving the institutional church does not mean that people are less spiritual, nor even that they have lost faith in Jesus. American market researcher George Barna has commented extensively on this movement of Christians exiting the established church and he notes: "The core issue isn't whether or not one is involved in a local church, but whether or not one is connected to the body of believers in the pursuit of godliness and worship."[62]

American social researchers Josh Packard and Ashleigh Hope describe a population of about 30 million "Dones"— people with continuing faith in Jesus but who no longer attend any church.[63] They note that:

> *The two most important macro-level trends are undoubtedly the loss of trust in social institutions in general and religious leaders in particular and the perception that religious institutions are no longer tied into the daily life of individuals as intimately as they once were. In other words, they're increasingly considered irrelevant.*[64]

Similar research in Australia found that of the 45% of Australians who identify their religion as Christian, more than half attend church less than monthly.[65]

Recent research from the USA, titled "How We Gather" shows where the increasing number of "unaffiliated millennials" find meaning. This growing group hold no conventional religious affiliation but nevertheless continues to own a sense of spirituality and seeks community and shared meaning. "When they say they are not looking for a faith community, millennials might mean they are not interested in belonging to an institution with religious creed as the threshold. However, they are decidedly looking for spirituality and community in combination, and feel they can't lead a meaningful life without it."[66]

So where do people look for spirituality and community? The answer highlighted in *How We Gather* can be found in the growing importance of fitness clubs (perhaps especially the CrossFit movement), groups that meet on trains, adult adventure camps, and organizations that encourage shared meals.

Many aspects of the modern Western world contribute to this perception that the church is irrelevant. Four aspects that seem important to me are personal mobility, increased reliance on digital technologies, the dominance of postmodern assumptions, and the movement towards a post-institutional social order. I'll explain each of those below.

PERSONAL MOBILITY

Although I grew up in a stable family in a rural area of Australia, at 17 I went to the city of Newcastle to study at university. After graduating, I moved to Sydney for work. I stayed with that company for six years, including a three-month internal transfer to another state and another three-month transfer to Boston in the USA.

In my 35-year working life I have been employed by eight different companies for at least a year as well as doing short-term contract work in between those major jobs. Like most people I know, I have not only changed *jobs* more frequently than our parent's generation, I have re-trained and changed *careers* several times.

I have lived in 20 different houses for at least six months each.

The circle of my friends during the formative years of undergraduate university study are now scattered in terms of career and location. One of my children lives in South Africa while the other is currently spending a year in England.

I consider my life thus far to be fairly stable compared to my peers, and all of that movement is typical of a highly mobile social environment that is a key characteristic of the modern Western world.

The enormous advantages of this social mobility are counter-balanced by a fragmentation of community and a loss of the sense of belonging that in earlier centuries could be taken for granted.

RELIANCE ON DIGITAL TECHNOLOGIES

I doubt that I need to quote any statistics showing the importance of computers, mobile phones, and the Internet on our 21st century lives. We spend more time interacting with devices than with people, and an increasing amount of our interaction with other people is via some electronic device.

Our relationships with each other and the natural world have become intermediated, that is, rather than interacting directly, we interact via intermediary technologies. This has the dual effect of making us appear highly connected while we are ever more isolated. We can communicate with people all over the world. We can see what they see. Through virtual reality technologies we can increasingly immerse ourselves in contexts where we are not physically present. Yet this global connectedness often leaves us locally isolated. We do not know our neighbors.

Digital, electronic, communications technologies have resulted in the formation of virtual communities. Groups with similar interests can meet in cyberspace to share information, buy, sell, and swap products, play games together, support and encourage each other, learn together, and form lobby groups to pressure social policy.

These communities include many virtual churches. Not only do established, physical churches have an online presence, some churches exist only, or primarily, in cyberspace. Life Church (https://www.life.church/online) and the Living Stream Church of the Brethren (http://www.living-streamcob.org) are two quite different examples.

One of the consequences of global communication technology is almost anyone can contribute to the conversation. The ease of self-publishing and social media has not only upset the traditional processes of publication and journalism, it has changed the way we manage truth and authority.

In social media and the new digital economy, online reputations become incredibly important.

In a world where information is power, it used to be that the power was vested in those who could control access to information: large media and publishing companies, governments, university research centers, and the editors of academic journals. Increasingly, it is not those who hold the information to themselves and impose conditions on access (such as a monetary payment) who have the power or gain reputation and status. No, the one who first releases the information gains reputation and status. In the digital economy, the quick release of information is more powerful than imposing conditional access.

DOMINANCE OF POSTMODERN ASSUMPTIONS

The cultures in which Christianity have traditionally thrived (or one could equally say the cultures that Christianity has traditionally enabled to thrive) are in a period of rapid change, and this rate of change is likely to continue to increase. Many assumptions about progress, truth, and authority that used to be rock-solid are now either questioned or discarded completely by both academics and the general public.

Back in the 17th century, the Age of Enlightenment elevated reason as the primary source of authority and scientific rationalism as the driving force of progress. In the 18th century, the Industrial Revolution changed our approach to production and consumption and moved large portions of the population into cities. At the same time, Romanticism reacted against both the Enlightenment and the Industrial Revolution by re-emphasizing nature, awe, emotions, and the heroic element of human aspirations.

Arising out of that period of social transformation was a philosophical shift that rejected the certainty of Enlightenment thinking but continued to be optimistic about progress through science and technology. During the 19th century, this became known as Modernism. Modernism noted that many traditional aspects of culture (including social and political structures, faith, art, and architecture) no longer made sense in a rapidly changing world. Modernism promoted a confidence in our power to create and improve the world—a confidence that led to a belief that new was better.

Although those Modernist attitudes continue to influence us, they have been supplanted in the past 50 or so years by a loosely-connected set of ideas collectively labelled "Postmodern." Postmodernism is not just a direct response to Modernism, but a critique of everything in social theory and philosophy that has come before. Postmodernism is notoriously difficult to define but has quickly and pervasively influenced today's Western cultures. Postmodernism has changed the way we think about and practice every part of our individual and social lives, including art, education, communication, entertainment, research, politics, and religion.

Rather than attempt a comprehensive definition, I will just pick out five core features that highlight how postmodernism has undermined confidence in the church.[67]

First, the postmodern critique notes that there is no neutral point of view. Whatever we think, we are biased. Biased by our personal experiences. Biased by the limitations of our language. Biased by the cultural assumptions we grow up imbibing, and by what we have read and been told by authority figures. No one can stand outside those influences and see things "as they really are." We always interpret what we see through the lenses of a particular set of glasses.

To this, Christians may respond "Yes, but *God* knows everything as it really is, and we have the word of God in the Bible." The theological scattering described earlier shows that this defense cannot work. If it did, then all Christians would believe the same things, but clearly we do not. Even given that the original authors were inspired by God, their written words reflect cultural assumptions of the time, and each translation into another language depends on further cultural assumptions. Whenever we read the Bible in our own language, we impose our own lens on how we interpret the words. One cannot read without interpreting—that is simply impossible. Furthermore, any interpretation will be biased by the same factors that underlie all our beliefs, religious and non-religious.

Second, postmodernism claims there is no objective truth, only the truth that each person constructs for themselves. We start life knowing nothing and gradually build mental structures that enable us to understand and interact with the world. A similar process operates on a larger scale when a group of people interact within a community or a larger society. We agree to use certain symbols (e.g. words, colors, icons), and their meanings are built out of the way we use them. People who live in different parts of the world with different languages, different climates, and different religions will construct what is true for them in ways that are barely even comprehensible to people in other situations.

This leads to a relativism that stands in opposition to any personal or cultural arrogance. None can claim they know absolute truth and that others who disagree must be wrong, for there is no absolute truth to know. This also applies to morality: if our knowledge and beliefs are constructed and relative, then so too are our beliefs about right and wrong, what is good and bad. Morally laudable behavior in one social context may be morally reprehensible in another.

Postmodern relativism undermines any moral high ground the church might have previously held (even before we lost that high-ground through hypocrisy, greed, and abuse) by denying there *is* any high ground from which one can look down on others.

Third, postmodernism rejects the "grand narratives" that have formed the basis of social meaning in past philosophies and ideologies. Every life and every society is full of stories: the story in my family about how I nearly drowned at a primary school swimming carnival before a teacher dived in to save me; the story of the arrival of Captain Cook in Australia in 1770; the story of Little Red Riding Hood, ad infinitum.

But we also rely on grand narratives (also called metanarratives) to help us interpret the meaning of those stories, indeed, to interpret the meaning of history and progress. Examples may be the Biblical grand narrative of humanity's fall and redemption; the Enlightenment confidence that rationality would explain everything; and the Capitalist grand narrative that links progress to the free market.

Postmodernism not only rejects these historical grand narratives but claims there cannot be any universal grand narrative. The aim is not to replace the foundational stories of our society with another story, but to reject the idea that there can be any foundational story underlying meaning in our society. Instead, every story is multi-valent, that is, open to many meanings.

Fourth, postmodernism says we should treat with skepticism any claim that there is a neutral point of view, or that there is an objective truth, or that there is some narrative that will explain the meaning of life. When faced with such claims, we should look below the surface with suspicion. Did the claimed events really happen? Is the reporting biased by an underlying agenda? Rather than accept the surface meaning of a text, read between the lines to identify internal contradictions and make explicit what's deliberately or unconsciously *not* being said.

As an example, when the Bible frequently claims, "thus saith the Lord," did God really say that? Did God really command genocide (e.g. in Deuteronomy 20:16–17)? Or should we read such passages as reflecting the view of *people who thought* God's will was clear?

This "hermeneutic of suspicion" leads to a fifth core feature of postmodernist thinking: the continual need to deconstruct. Deconstruction is perhaps postmodernism's primary mode of analyzing any idea, whether expressed in a work of art, a novel, a newspaper report, a political speech, a phone call, or religious scripture. Deconstruction *as a principle* questions whether language in any form can adequately represent reality. Deconstruction *as a process* pulls apart the role that power and presuppositions play in belief through questions like who wrote this, what bias did they bring, what is assumed or left unsaid, what authority is claimed or implied by these words, what's the social-political-cultural-intellectual context in which this was written, and what's the social-political-cultural-intellectual context of the reader?

In a detailed survey of Australian attitudes to religion and spirituality in 2017, one question was "To what extent would the following attract or repel you from investigating religion and spirituality further?" The item in the list of options that was most selected as one that somewhat or strongly repelled the non-Christian respondents was "Hearing from public figures and celebrities who are examples of that faith."[68] That is, they considered hearing from Christian leaders the biggest turn-off of all!

I think that response most likely arises from the five postmodern attitudes I have described. Non-Christians see public religious figures as speaking from a specific point-of-view, who assume they know the truth and look down morally on others, and who spout a grand narrative of salvation. The non-Christian hears that with skepticism. If they bother to deconstruct what the public figure says, they see internal contradictions and self-serving arrogance. As a result, the actual message becomes irrelevant and they quickly switch to another channel.

TOWARDS A POST-INSTITUTIONAL SOCIAL ORDER

A common observation within churches I know is that it is now difficult to rely on members' loyalty. People may or may not turn up for church programs and may or may not continue as members next year.

I don't think that challenge is limited to the established church. I find it increasingly difficult to arrange a weekend barbecue where I know more than two days ahead of time who will attend! That makes planning difficult, but it seems that many people today make last minute decisions rather than commit themselves to anything.

That same lack of commitment is seen in the challenges facing retailers. Consumers no longer remain loyal to one brand, whether cars, clothes, food, or services. We shop around for the best deal rather than trust any specific brand or retail chain. Quite often, the "best deal" means the lowest price. We tend to think less and less about quality, environmental impact, after sales service, or our personal connection with the business owner or staff.

Of course, there are many exceptions but the modern economy tends to operate through impersonal financial transactions based on short-term decisions rather than through relationships of trust built over a lifetime.

This lack of long-term loyalty affects not only churches and commercial brands, but other community organizations and governments. It acts as a sign of changing attitudes to institutions in general.

The term "institution" can apply to several quite distinct ideas.

In one sense, an institution is a specific organization such as the Royal Institute of British Architects, or the University of Karueein.[69] The Anglican Church of Australia is an institution in this sense, as are every bank we deal with, every supermarket we buy from, and every sporting club we support.

In another sense, an institution, or perhaps more appropriately called a meta-institution, organizes or controls other organizations. A national government is an example. Perhaps the global Anglican Communion[70] is another.

An institution can also be a generic system. For instance, we can talk about capitalism as a kind of economic institution. Religion as a whole may also be called an institution,[71] as may family, schools, and banking.

Some sociologists and economists include a broader range of informal rules, roles, and social norms under the label "institution." So, for instance, they would call language an institution, as well as fatherhood, driving on the left side of the road, and taking off your hat when inside.

Lastly, we can also use "institution" as a verb, as in when we talk about "the institution of the Lord's Supper," by which we mean Jesus' act of establishing that sacrament.

In my use of the word "institution" I am more interested in the earlier connotations in that list than the later ones. What I want to focus on may be called *the institutional mindset*, that is, the way of thinking that drives large organizations, governments, and institutional systems. The institutional mindset emphasizes control, bureaucracy, and regulation. It is task-oriented and goal-driven, dictating clear boundaries around who is inside and who is outside. The institutional mindset ensures that the rules are clear and maintains strict controls over standardization and authority.

Above all else, an institution is systematically structured to ensure its own survival. This core urge for self-preservation is expressed through a reluctance to change and an almost medical response to any threat. A threat is like a virus which the institution must protect itself against. The institution favors equilibrium, and if there is any pressure to change from either inside or outside, powerful mechanisms are activated to restore the equilibrium. Defensive barriers keep the threat outside, and if the threat is identified internally it is expelled.

Many church structures succumb to this institutional mindset. Most people within those structures cannot conceive of an alternative. Many leaders apparently believe the institutional mindset is the optimal and God-ordained formula for an effective church.

But this institutional mindset is a long way from the approach of Jesus as he wandered the roads of Judaea, Samaria, and Galilee with his first followers.

What I think we are currently seeing is a powerful social movement away from this institutional mindset, driven by a deep mistrust of traditional institutions, leading us into a post-institutional society.

The description "post-institutional" is my own invention, but I predict it will become a significant topic of social research over the coming decade. I use the term in a similar sense to "post-industrial," which was coined by Alain Touraine in 1969.[72] With the Industrial Revolution, the driving force of the economy and the locus of control moved from agricultural production to industrial manufacturing. But in the last 40 or 50 years, the industrial powerbase has given way to the service sector, forming an economy where information is the central commodity. This does not mean agriculture and industry no longer exist or no longer serve important functions, just that they no longer form the basis of economic or political power.

In the same way, when I apply the term post-institutional to our 21st century context, I don't mean there will be no institutions or that they serve no useful purpose. But in a post-institutional world, they no longer play the central role they once did. We are often unaware of them and when we are aware of them we don't trust them. We increasingly reject the institutional mindset and achieve what we need to without reference to them.

We often find reasons not to trust a specific organization and when that happens enough, we start generalizing and stop trusting the whole institution. Banking is a good example. A generation or two ago people opened a savings account as a youth, got a cheque account with the same bank once they start working, took out a home loan from the same bank, and continued saving and borrowing from the same organization their entire life. This is a rare sequence today. More likely we have a bad experience somewhere along the way and change to another bank. We listen with disgust as investigations by journalists and government commissions uncover hidden fees, misleading advice and devious practices.

Out of all those experiences, we gradually lose trust in banking as a social institution. Will they manage our money wisely? Will they make decisions and give us advice that is in our best interest? Should we perhaps go back to hiding our money under the mattress?

We apply our post-modern hermeneutic of suspicion to institutions and wonder whether they ever have our best interests at heart. We feel no loyalty to them because we doubt whether they have any loyalty towards us. Our distaste of grand narratives makes us reject institutions who claim some special authority. We don't believe any institution has more access to the truth than we do, because we reject the possibility of objective truth or a neutral point of view.

In the institutional mindset, the locus of power is centralized. In the post-institutional world, power becomes decentralized.

To a large extent, this change of attitude has been enabled by information and communication technology. The first example I noticed of this was the widespread availability of desktop publishing software in the 1980s. Prior to that, everyone used a typewriter for simple documents but typesetting that required complex page layouts or multiple fonts could only be achieved with expensive equipment and professional skills. But in the 80s a few thousand dollars could equip anyone with a Macintosh computer, PageMaker software, and a printer you could use to format a magazine or a book yourself. Of course, many people produced visually awful designs, but the institutional centralization of phototypesetting was broken.

About the same time, the Internet started, with a key consequence being the ability to disseminate information by almost anyone. Not only could anyone from their home write and format a document without professional help, they could distribute it around the world without the need for a traditional publishing institution. The whole shape of the media industry has changed in the last three decades as central, controlling institutions continue to lose ground to a decentralized anarchy through the self-publishing of books and blogs.

Something similar is happening with various service industries as individuals continue to become empowered, through technology, to offer their services outside any institutional control. I'm thinking of the various websites that facilitate ride-sharing, couch surfing, and house swapping. The heartbeat of these initiatives stands in opposition to the institutional mindset. They despise control, bureaucracy, and regulation and instead foster connection through a decentralized model.

The same heartbeat can be seen in crowd-sourced websites where thousands of people willingly contribute their time and knowledge for the common good. Wikipedia is a prominent example. More technical sites like StackOverflow and OpenStreetMap are perhaps even more substantial examples of altruistic, non-institutional projects.[73]

There is always a danger that these non-institutional initiatives will become reinstitutionalised. That happens when a government steps in to regulate the market and forces the formation of some controlling body. In Australia that happened to Meals on Wheels, a grassroots community service where volunteers cooked and delivered meals to the homebound. In the 1990s, ostensibly because of concerns over food safety, government regulation required such services to be commercialized.

Reinstitutionalisation (biggest word in the book so far!) also happens when the success of a non-institutional service attracts commercial interest, and a new institution is formed to control and profit from it. Ride-sharing is a current example: the taxi industry, a regulated institution, was disrupted by ride-sharing options, but then ride-sharing became a new institution through businesses like Uber and Lyft. AirBnB is another, with the generous sharing of rooms being reinstitutionalised as a massive global commercial venture.

Given the loss of trust in institutions, the post-institutional move creates a new need to rethink the basis for trust. In non-institutional modes of operation, trust has its own challenges. When anyone can contribute or offer a service, how do you know if they can be trusted? That's a crucial question and one that is actively being worked on through various techniques for tracking data integrity and establishing personal online reputations.

The same applies with government decision making. We are close to having the technology to enable direct democracy, that is, a system where people can vote directly on matters of concern rather than electing a representative who votes on their behalf. There is already a political party in Australia whose core policy is to enable that option.[74]

This may all seem like a large detour, and I've hardly mentioned "church" for five pages, so let me summarize the key point. Our economy and society are moving into a post-institutional stage. In the last 40 years we have seen the rapid demise of trust in institutions and the corresponding rise of non-institutional structures, largely enabled by information and communication technologies such as the Internet. In the next 40 years, we will see that trajectory continue at an increasing pace. If we want the church to be effective in this context, we cannot continue to position it as a centralized, authoritative institution.

CONSEQUENCES FOR THE CHURCH

In a world that is socially mobile, digital, postmodern, and increasingly post-institutional, we cannot expect that maintaining the traditional model of the gathered church will continue being an effective strategy for building God's kingdom.

Large numbers of people simply don't think about the church or the message of the Gospel because it is irrelevant to them. They have no interest in even considering an invitation to join an institution marked by large buildings, strange rituals, and what is perceived to be arrogant and judgmental attitudes. They find far more interesting and life-giving things to do on a Sunday morning.

Others have become consciously disillusioned with the church. In our group, "The Escape Goats" we have met many in that situation. Some were actively abused by the church, by church leaders, and by God. Others find it impossible to speak honestly in church about their doubts or struggles with life because they will be patronized, sidelined and told to simply have more faith. Church seems like a place where you mustn't rock the boat.

An important step in many of those people's journey is to separate the church from faith.

Alice, a frequent customer at Annabella's coffee cart is a good example. She was raised in the traditional church but has since become disillusioned and thrown away her whole faith in God.

Alice was born in Germany and inherited a Catholic faith from her parents. But that faith has been undermined by the global spate of reports about sexual abuse by church leaders. In particular, the revelations of the Australian Royal Commission into Institutional Responses to Child Sexual Abuse[75] made Alice feel she had no choice but to reject Christianity entirely.

She spoke of rejecting "my faith" with a degree of sadness and loss. Annabella commented to her that it was sad she could be robbed of the deep feelings of connection she used to have with God. As the conversation developed, Annabella asked whether there might have been any way to separate that disappointment with the church from her understanding of God? Did the loss of trust in the one need to result in the loss of trust in the other?

Annabella says, "She looked at me with quizzically, but with hope and delight, as though I had given her back something precious." Alice said, "I've never thought of that" and went away, extra-hot cappuccino in hand, pondering whether there was a possibility of reclaiming the good things about her faith that had been stolen from her by institutional corruption.

Let's think more about what options we have for the future shape of the church. In this current social context, how can the church best achieve the purpose for which Jesus called it into being?

One option is to circle the wagons and defend our traditional way of doing things. There are several important roles the institutional church continues to play. The institution often curates important historical locations and events. Cathedrals and memorials around the world, owned and cared for by the institutional church, maintain public awareness of important historical moments that underpin cultural identities. Another important role for the institutional church is to facilitate various rites of passage that mark important times in our personal journeys. To maintain control over such roles, we can double-down and refuse to change. We can even write self-serving treatises about how standing our ground reflects our faithfulness to the Gospel. But seeing those roles as the core reason for the church's existence is a very limiting ecclesiology. Thinking that the world needs us because of those roles is ill-conceived arrogance with no relationship to the hope of being God's blessing to the world. It is a recipe for slow suicide.

Even in a post-institutional world there will be many institutions that serve their purpose and can succeed within the bounds of their metric-driven goals. So another option is to co-opt (or be co-opted by?) the latest business management trend and define our success in terms of the seductive metaphor "big is better."

We can continue building churches in the image of other modern institutions. We can revamp the marketing message, update our branding, play more contemporary music, invest in our own radio stations, provide decent coffee in the foyer and hand out loyalty cards. With the right mixture of professionalism and a strategic emphasis on efficiency, those initiatives might even result in growing numbers of people who hear the message and give some passing allegiance to that organization or to its charismatic leader.

Alternatively, we can stop being a traditional, self-serving institution and start engaging with people relationally and authentically, positioning a shared desire for all of us to flourish on center stage. That would require us to deal with people's transience, not expecting them to stay in one place or make long-term commitments. It would require us to draw on interest-based and virtual communities rather than solely geographic communities. It would require us to maintain connection within those communities through electronic channels as well as face-to-face. It would require an acceptance that everyone has to make sense of their own experience and construct their own faith. Certainly, people will draw on traditions, other people's experiences, and the authority of significant people in their lives. But they will not simply be told what they should believe.

This option would also require us to re-establish trust. In a post-modern, post-institutional culture we need to ask how trust can be earned outside of the institutional mindset. People used to trust ministers of religion and the integrity of the institutional church, but in general they no longer trust either. Australian social research shows the action that most repels people from considering Christianity is when church leaders speak in the media. On the other hand, that same research shows that the action most likely to attract people to Christianity is the life example of Christians they know personally.[76] Trust is much more a result of personal relationship than institutional authority.

That sets the stage for the real work of this book, which is to describe a church with deliberate scattering at its core. I flesh that out in the Part 2 by clarifying what the church is for and explaining seven key attributes of a scattering church.

Part 2:

Scattering

I HAVE DESCRIBED HOW the idea of the church as a gathering became the dominant metaphor. I've also shown that throughout the reality of church history, the church is also extensively and repeatedly scattered. The two directions of movement often interact, but in the common conception of church it is the gathered church that is fundamental. Even when a specific expression of church places high value on scattering—for instance the churches and para-church organizations with strong missional focusses—the goal is virtually always to establish new gathering points and draw converts back into the gathered church. The scattering is a tool to enable the gathering. The success of the church is not seen in its effectiveness in scattering but in its ability to accumulate large numbers in the gathering.

Now it is time to describe more explicitly an approach to being the church where scattering is a deliberate goal.

There is a conscious ambiguity in the way I use "scattering" as both a verb and an adjective. As a verb, *scattering* church is a process through which internal and external forces scatter the seeds of the Good News throughout the world. As an adjective, the *scattering* church is one that views those internal and external forces not as secondary or in conflict with the church's goal, but as the primary mode of operation.

I want to describe a form of church that is not scattered by chance or as a side-effect of some other interest but, as part of its core constitution, chooses to scatter. Such a church may still gather at various times and for specific purposes, but these occasional gatherings no longer hold the fundamental position that we are used to. After all, Jesus' final instructions to his disciples after the resurrection was to "*Go* and make disciples" (Matthew 28:19), not to "Stay here and build an institution."

I hope to convince you of the value of a scattering church on two grounds: that it is aligned to our current cultural context, and that it is aligned to core New Testament metaphors about the nature of church. After that, I draw out seven key principles that can inform the shape and practices of a scattering church.

[5]

PARABLES OF SOWING

J ESUS WAS APPARENTLY FOND of agricultural metaphors. Among the many parables recorded by the Gospel writers, three are based on the idea of scattering
seeds, all of which were intended to help his hearers
understand the dynamics of the kingdom of God.

I don't want to give a full exegesis of these passages but
only call attention to two aspects. First, the importance of
understanding these, and other, parables as metaphors.
Second, to highlight what the scattering metaphor might
mean for the way we conceive of church.

For two of these three parables, Jesus offers his own
commentary. But those commentaries themselves do not
provide a full exegesis. Jesus' approach to parables seems
to be that their meaning needs to be left open-ended.

SPEIRÓ AND SKORPIZÓ

We saw in Chapter 1 that the Bible uses many words,
phrases, and metaphors to describe the people of God. This

113

rich texture of ideas together forms a picture of the church summoned into being by Jesus.

In Chapter 2 we saw that one theme in that picture, captured powerfully by the Greek word *ecclesia*, is the gathering of people. The idea of gathering has dominated the way most people conceive of the church and has guided the practicalities of church structure throughout Christian history.

In Chapter 3 we saw that another theme, captured by the Greek *diaspora*, reflects the way the church is scattered. Sometimes the church becomes scattered by external forces, while at other times the church has chosen to scatter as part of its mission to the whole world. For the most part, however, that scattering is seen as a technique to support the more primary goal of gathering.

Diaspora is not the only Biblical model for scattering. The NIV translates several other New Testament Greek words as "scatter." For instance, *bale* in Mark 4:26, *ekcheo* in John 2:15, and *katastrónnumi* in 1 Corinthians 10:5. But the more common words are *speiró* (σπείρω)[77] and *skorpizó* (σκορπίζω).[78] These two words both mean to sow, spread, scatter or disperse. In the intensified form *diaskorpizó* the word can even mean to waste or to squander[79] (e.g. the son who squandered his inheritance in Luke 15:13).

Rather than the process of gathering, or the process of being scattered in order to gather, these words *speiró* and *skorpizó* suggest a different metaphor for the church. They suggest the possibility of a church that is thrown up into the wind to be blown to who-knows-where by the Spirit of God.

PARABLE OF THE GROWING SEED

In Mark 4:26–29, we read of a man who scatters seeds and then does nothing to tend to his crop. The plants grow by themselves. It doesn't matter whether the sower is there to watch or is asleep somewhere else. The sower doesn't even need to understand how it all happens! The seeds just germinate and grow by themselves until they are ready for harvesting.

Jesus says the kingdom of God is like that.

Metaphorical seeds are scattered—by God, or by God's servants—but the scatterer does not need to interfere, understand, or control how those seeds flourish.

In this parable there is no indication of what the seed represents, but we will find out more about that from the other parables.

PARABLE OF THE WEEDS

A second sowing parable is recounted in Matthew 13:24–30, followed by a commentary in verses 36–43.

In this parable, a man sows good wheat seed, but while he is asleep an enemy sows weed seed among the wheat. The original sower recognizes what happened and is asked by his servants whether they should pull out the weeds. The surprise in this parable is that the sower says, "No! If you pull out the weeds you'll probably disturb the roots of the wheat as well. Better to let them both grow together and we'll sort them out at harvest time" (my paraphrase of 29–30).

Jesus says the kingdom of heaven is like that.

In his explanation of the parable, Jesus makes explicit the first component of the metaphoric calculus: he draws our attention to the ideas being juxtaposed within the metaphor. One side of the metaphor is a set of agricultural ideas: a sower, a field, good seed, and weeds. On the other side are aspects of the kingdom: the Son of Man, the world, the sons of the kingdom, and the sons of the evil one. The trajectory of the metaphor goes from the agricultural ideas with which the listeners would be familiar to the new concept of kingdom that Jesus is hoping to reveal to those who will listen.

Jesus equates the sower with himself (37) and the field with the whole world (38). The good seed metaphorically represents the "sons of the kingdom" (38) and the weeds represent the "sons of the evil one" (38). As verse 41 makes clear, the "sons" do not just mean people but everything that springs from the respective sowers—"everything that causes sin" that springs from the evil one and everything promoting kingdom values that spring from God.

Notice the implication for us, if we consider ourselves to be among the "sons of the kingdom" represented by the good seed. From the beginning we are scattered as seed and should expect to grow up side-by-side with weeds. The sower knows and accepts that. Neither the sower nor the growing wheat try to create a weed-free wheat-ghetto.

Even if we write ourselves into this parable as servants of the good sower rather than the seed, the instruction to us is *not* to remove all the weeds to make the crop pure. The instruction from Jesus, the good sower, is to leave things be and trust that whatever separation is required will be dealt with at harvest time.

This links nicely with the "parable of the growing seed" mentioned earlier. In both parables a person scatters seeds in a field, representing the good influence of the kingdom in the world. In both parables the sower seems unconcerned about what happens next but is confident about the harvest.

I believe we too can be confident about the harvest—that is, about the end results, the lasting value, of our ministry—without needing to control how the plants grow. Following Jesus' example, we can scatter the seeds and let go. We do not have to worry about the outcome, whether there will be sufficient rain or fertilizer for the seeds we have planted to flourish. In the kingdom of heaven that growth happens under the influence of the God who pours out rain and sunshine on the unrighteous just as much as on the righteous (Matthew 5:45). We do not have to worry about the weeds in the field growing alongside the seeds we have planted. We have been instructed to allow "everything that causes sin and all who do evil" to co-exist beside the "sons of the kingdom."

This kingdom that Jesus invites us to help create is patient and hopeful. It is organic rather than tightly controlled. It allows the influence of the good news to grow at its own pace rather than through coercion. This is true at the personal level in the lives of Christians and non-Christians who are exposed to the kingdom. It is equally true at the societal level, the whole field in which these parables are set. Throughout the world, wherever the influence of the good news is scattered side-by-side with the influence of evil, our job is not to pull out the weeds or force the whole field to be "Christian." No, the mission of the church is something else: to scatter seeds and demonstrate a radical alternative to "everything that causes sin."

PARABLE OF THE SOWER, PART 1

Both of the previous parables follow on from the so-called "Parable of the Sower," which is included in the gospels of Matthew (13:1–23), Mark (4:1–20) and Luke (8:4–15).

> *That same day Jesus went out of the house and sat by the lake. Such large crowds gathered round him that he got into a boat and sat in it, while all the people stood on the shore. Then he told them many things in parables, saying: 'A farmer went out to sow his seed. As he was scattering the seed, some fell along the path, and the birds came and ate it up. Some fell on rocky places, where it did not have much soil. It sprang up quickly, because the soil was shallow. But when the sun came up, the plants were scorched, and they withered because they had no root. Other seed fell among thorns, which grew up and choked the plants. Still other seed fell on good soil, where it produced a crop—a hundred, sixty or thirty times what was sown. Whoever has ears, let them hear.' (Matthew 13:1–9)*

The first thing I notice about this parable is the wastefulness of this approach to planting a crop. The sower just throws seeds all over the place! He seems to have no concern about where they land.

Now please bear with my mathematical personality for a few minutes. What exactly is the level of wastage here, and what is the expected yield?

Suppose in the random scattering that each of the four landing places received equal quantities of seed. Then three quarters of the seed yielded nothing!

It must be noted that one quarter of the seed did succeed in feeding some birds, and perhaps that is also an important outcome that deserves further theological reflection. Feeding birds is a natural purpose of seeds in the ecology God created and a valuable outcome of the scattering process. Who might be the birds who pick up the message of the Gospel after it has been scattered on pathways where they can see it easily? People who are not part of the "Christian" crop, but are nourished by the seed cast far and wide by our profligate God.

What happens after birds eat the seed? That is not mentioned in this parable, but it seems natural to extend the metaphor this way—the birds fly to other fields, other countries, and poop the seeds far more widely than the sower could cast them alone. That deep truth reflects something core to the way the kingdom of heaven is spread. All sorts of people are nourished by the kingdom and become unwitting agents in the scattering process.

Nevertheless, the main arc of the parable is that three quarters of the seeds yielded nothing: only a quarter of them landed in fertile soil and produced a harvestable crop. Each of those seeds resulted in 30, 60 or 100 harvested grains. If we make another assumption that those three outcomes happened in equal proportion, then ...

- If the sower had a kilogram of wheat to start with, about 25,000 seeds are scattered
- 6,250 seeds fall onto the good soil
- A third of them yield 100 grains—a total of 208,333
- A third yield 60 grains—a total of 125,000
- A third yield 30 grains—a total of 62,500
- Adding that up gives an overall yield of 395,833
- The multiplication factor—turning 25,000 seeds into 395,833 harvested grains—is just under 16.

In other words, for the first-century sower following Jesus' method, each seed sown brings in 16 at harvest time.[80] In today's management lingo, Jesus has described a project with an ROI (return on investment) of 1,483%, which is quite phenomenal.

PARABLE OF THE SOWER, PART 2

This story has the same three-movement dialectic structure as most parables. First, there is a familiar setting—"A farmer went out to sow seeds." Second, there is a counterintuitive surprise, an almost unbelievable twist—the seeds are scattered randomly with no regard for where they land. Third, after working through the implications we find that the original intention is actually achieved by the counterintuitive twist—the random sowing results in a massive crop.

Jesus told the parable of the sower to the general public, but later adds some commentary for the benefit of his closer circle of followers.

Listen then to what the parable of the sower means: when anyone hears the message about the kingdom and does not understand it, the evil one comes and snatches away what was sown in their heart. This is the seed sown along the path. The seed falling on rocky ground refers to someone who hears the word and at once receives it with joy. But since they have no root, they last only a short time. When trouble or persecution comes because of the word, they quickly fall away. The seed falling among the thorns refers to someone who hears the word, but the worries of this life and the deceitfulness of wealth choke the word, making it unfruitful. But the seed falling on good soil refers to someone who hears the word and understands it. This is the one who produces a crop, yielding a hundred, sixty or thirty times what was sown. (Matthew 13:18–23)

From this commentary we learn some key information about how Jesus expected the metaphoric calculus to work. The two juxtaposed ideas are the seed and a person "who hears the message about the kingdom." As with the other sowing parables, the trajectory is from agricultural ideas that the listeners already understand to the new concept of the kingdom of heaven. Jesus implicitly invites us to transfer attributes from the sowing process to help us to understand the dynamics of the kingdom.

What is it that gets scattered? Most sermons I have heard interpret the seed as the message of the kingdom. God, Jesus, or Jesus' followers spread that message in the same way the sower spreads seeds. That's a meaningful starting point, supported by Mark 4:14 and Luke 8:11, and it teaches us something about how we might spread the kingdom message.

If the seed is the message, then one of the transferable attributes of the metaphor is that we do not need to be selective in how we sow the message of the kingdom. Jesus could have said, "The kingdom of heaven is like a gardener who carefully prepares the soil, digs a hole, adds some compost to provide nutrients, plants a seed, covers it firmly and sprinkles liberally with water." But he didn't. He noted that in the kingdom of heaven the sower scatters across all types of ground.

A church that followed the model of Jesus' sower would be open-handed, scattering seeds of influence across every social context, regardless of the expected outcome. We wouldn't just nurture relationships with the rich and powerful or with the "good soil" where we expect high yields. We would not be concerned with efficiency. We would not be results-driven. We would not be side-lined by the modern corporate philosophy that aligns strategy to "bottom-line" outcomes.

A closer reading of Jesus' commentary suggests another interpretation of what the sower scatters. Rather than equating the seed with the message, Matthew records Jesus as saying "what was sown ... is the man who ... " (13:20,22,23). Mark remembers "some people are like seed ... " (Mark 4:15,16,18,20). Luke's recount is a bit more ambiguous but still includes phrases like "the seed that fell among thorns stands for those who hear ..." (Luke 8:14), which implies that the seed is the person rather than the message to that person.

If a seed is a person, then another implication of the metaphor is that God scatters people into varied environments. Some of us are eaten by birds and carried to another field. Some of us are cast onto barren ground or into contexts where we continually struggle with thorns. Some of us fall into fertile contexts where our lives and the lives of those around us flourish. But all are part of the ecology of the kingdom.

The scattering by the sower turns out not to be so random after all, but a deliberate strategy.

MEANWHILE, BACK AT THE COFFEE CART ...

A wonderful example of seed scattering walked into Annabella's coffee business one day in the form of a man and his young son. The boy wore a t-shirt emblazoned with the one word: "Loved."

Annabella told the father that in our Sunday discussion group we had been speaking about human flourishing— what it looked like and how it could be fostered. She said that for her, one of the bedrocks underpinning flourishing is the sure knowledge that you are loved.

The man picked up his boy and hugged him and said, "Yes, this one is well loved. What's more, I used to wear this very t-shirt when I was his age. My father bought it for me. He kept it to give it to me much later and I have passed it on to my son."

What an amazing example of seed planting with fruit that continues from one generation to the next. That t-shirt is good seed. It was planted and nurtured by two generations of fathers. But it was also designed by some t-shirt manufacturer, whose motives we will never know. Did they realize that by scattering the seeds of a t-shirt with the word "Loved" they were drawing people into the kingdom of God? Into what varied soil did the hundreds or thousands of other "Loved" t-shirts fall?

Another, more public example is the recent baptism of 85-year old Bill Hayden, formerly a senior Australian politician and later Governor-General. Through his career, Hayden was clear about his atheist position[81] but was nevertheless influenced by his Catholic upbringing, and in particular a couple of Catholic nuns.

Sister Angela Mary Doyle had been a inspiration to Hayden for many years through her advocacy of health care for the poor. Hayden said, "Without her, there would have been no Medibank and no Medicare today."[82] That is a remarkable testimony to the seeds she scattered: seeds from God's heart for the marginalized, for the "orphan and widow." Undoubtedly, some of those seeds fell unheard on stony ground or were choked by the thorns of political opposition and social inertia. But some of those seeds germinated and changed the shape of Australian health care with the introduction of a universal public health care system in 1975 that continues today.

Other seeds of faith scattered by Sister Doyle fell into the heart of Bill Hayden where for many years they grew as weeds in his atheist garden. Eventually, at age 85, Hayden seems to have realized that the weeds were the better part of the garden, and now says, "From this day forward I'm going to vouch for God."

We all scatter seeds in our individual lives: some good and some bad. We rarely see the outcome.

Sometimes the good seed we scatter turns out badly, like the death of my friend Don.

In the late 1980s I lived in a house in suburban Sydney that was owned by the local Uniting Church. Several single members of the church lived together with the aim of providing a safe place for troubled youth. Don had recently been released from jail and moved in with us while finding his feet. After migrating from Vietnam he had lost touch with his family. He was in his early twenties and trying to break a drug habit.

We helped Don's English, learnt some Vietnamese cooking from him and taught him a bit about Australian etiquette. Don came to church with us and soaked up the ideas of Jesus with enthusiasm.

At the time, I was part of a program to give street kids an alternate access path into university. Various homeless and often abused youth, addicts, and prostitutes were in the program and I arranged for Don to join as well. He started some foundational courses in the hope that after a year he would be eligible to enroll in a normal university course.

Don also made awesome chả giò, a Vietnamese version of spring rolls. He took samples to cafes around our suburb and soon had a list of orders. That didn't last very long though, because one of the café's offered him part-time work and he had no spare time for his own cooking.

Shortly afterwards, Don and his father contacted each other. His father was so excited to hear from his son that he travelled from Vietnam to visit us. Their joy in seeing each other was a highlight of that whole period of my life.

All good seeds, germinating in rich soil.

One week later, after being drug free for six months or more, Don decided to visit the area he lived in before going to jail. The police found him the next morning, dead of a heroin overdose. I doubt that he went there intending to find drugs. More likely he met some old friends who cajoled or forced him to take a shot, and who probably didn't realize that his previous dose would be too much for him.

Does this mean the seeds were wasted? Should we choose more carefully where the seeds are scattered? By no means! The sower in Jesus' parable consciously and confidently scatters those seeds knowing full well the risks.

One of the principles I take from Jesus' parables on sowing is that we need not be too concerned about the harvest. We can be part of the sowing and then release the outcome into God's hands. We are called to be part of the scattering. We do not need to worry if some of the seeds are wasted, nor do we control the plants' growth or fear the weeds.

Seeds hold potential life. The process of sowing initiates the germination of something new out of that potential. One of the problems with the modern, large, gathered church is that, like a single-cropping strategy in modern farming, it is unsustainable. Farmers who plant huge paddocks with a single crop year after year can gain high yields in the short-term but in the process, they damage the environment. What's more, they must use massive volumes of artificial fertilizer, herbicides, and pesticides to manage the crop. That is a high-risk strategy in both agriculture and ecclesiology.

Of course, there are also times when each of us sows bad seed, seed that chokes and kills rather than gives life. I'm too embarrassed, too ashamed, to give examples but that too must be embraced as part of life. I pray that the bad seeds I have scattered are at least neutralized by the grace of God and hopefully turned around, redeemed.

[6]

What is the Church *for*?

S O MUCH HAS BEEN WRITTEN about the nature, or
the essence, of the church that another book—this
one—might do little more than add to the landfill!
Perhaps there is so much written because the
church is so varied that its common essence is difficult to
distil. Perhaps there is always more to say because the cultural context and audience is constantly changing.

One well-regarded book on the subject is Veli-Matti
Kärkkäinen's *An Introduction to Ecclesiology*, which
neatly summarizes the views of the church as held by seven
traditions. Although he attempts to answer the question
"What *is* the church?," he notes in passing another question—"What is the church *for*?"[83]—which strikes me as the
more important issue.

The question of what the church is *for* can be interpreted in two ways: on the one hand what is the purpose of
the church, it's *raison d'être*, and on the other hand what
beliefs and practices does the church promote as distinct

from what it is *against*. Both have implications for the identity and the structure of the church, and both underpin my approach in this book.

Different traditions express varied and sometimes conflicting views on the essence of the church and answer the question, "What is the church for?" quite differently. For some, the focus is *upward* (the glory of God, or the sacramental communion with God), for some *inward* (a pilgrim community or a fellowship of God's people), and for others *outward* (faithful preaching and witness as part of God's message to the world).

ECCLESIA REVISITED

In Chapter 2, I pointed out that the word *ecclesia* only occurs twice in the Gospels. In the memories of the four Gospel writers, Jesus did not speak much at all about church. On the other hand, Jesus spoke incessantly about the kingdom of God and the kingdom of heaven.

It is easy enough to assume that building an *ecclesia* (that is, a church) requires gathering people together, because as we have seen, the core meaning of the noun *ecclesia* is "an assembly." In the light of everything else I have said so far, however, it should be clear that the fact we are summoned by Jesus is more important than the size or shape of the assembly. The summoned people of Jesus are called many things apart from simply *the assembly*. In the New Testament, providing a gathering point is only one of many attributes of the church.

But now, as we consider what the church is for, two other re-arrangements of thought about the meaning of *ecclesia* become important.

The first is to reconsider what we mean when we say things like "going to church" or "attending a church." Such phrases are implied metaphors. They only make sense it you already understand the church as a place that you can "go to" or a meeting you can "attend."

In my culture, when people meet for the first time, the introductions often start with exchanging first names. After that one might ask, "Where are you from?" and "What do you do?" If the people know they are each Christians, then the next question is almost inevitably "What church do you go to?" or perhaps "Where do you worship?"

If you dig down in a more serious discussion, most Christians probably know a church is not the building but the body of believers. But at the surface of our conscious assumptions about church, we mostly still think about church as a named gathering point. "I go to St Luke's, Toowoomba" or "I go to Hillsong."

Again, if you dig down, most Christians will know that you can worship God anywhere and at any time. But on the surface, most still think worship is about singing as part of a gathering at a particular place on a Sunday. We know church is about following Jesus whenever and wherever we are, and that worship is a whole-of-life dedication of ourselves to God (Romans 12:1–2), but we seldom think that way or talk about church that way.

I agree with George Barna, founder of the Barna Group, who wrote, "We are not called to *go* to church. We are called to *be* the church."[84] We do not *attend* a church, we *are* the church. Being church is a full-time calling. There should be no compartmentalization of our lives into the church part, the family part, and the work part as though we "give" God a couple of hours a week along with a per-centage of our money. Rather than trying to "balance" those various interests as though they are in competition, we can see them as integrated components of a whole. We are the church when we interact with co-workers on Mon-day just as much as we were when we interacted with co-worshippers on Sunday. We are the church when we share a tense Christmas meal with estranged family members. We are the church when we discuss our child's progress in a parent-teacher meeting. We are the church when we're travelling to the snow fields for a holiday. We are the church when we vote on whether marriage should be legal-ized for homosexual couples.

The essence of *ecclesia* is that we are the summoned people of God wherever we are and whatever we are doing.

A MEANS OR AN END?

The second re-arrangement of thought that arises from questioning what the church is *for* is whether the church is a means or an end. If Jesus intended the church to be an end in itself, that is to say a goal, then of course it should become our primary pre-occupation as followers of Jesus. But what if building a church is not the goal of following Jesus in the first place?

Given the balance of what Jesus had to say about the church compared to what he had to say about the kingdom, ought we not assume that the church is intended to be a tool rather than a goal, a means rather than the end? There will be no church in heaven. Jesus did not come to build a church but a kingdom. As Howard Snyder explains in depth is his book *Community of the King*, "The Church is God's *agent* for establishing his kingdom."[85]

In that case, the answer to the question "what is the church for?" has to be something like "To work with Jesus to build the kingdom."

If we follow that line of reasoning, then we need to spend a lot more effort understanding the type of kingdom Jesus envisages. It is a weird sort of kingdom! Jesus' kingdom is not a colonizing military force. It does not coerce. It reverses the normal hierarchy of value by putting the last first and the first last, and by making servanthood the defining characteristic of leaders. It is a kingdom "not of this world" (John 18:36) because it differs so radically from every other kingdom humans have ever experienced.

It is a weird kingdom because it has a weird king. In Jesus' teaching, little is said directly about the king. But we feel the presence of a king behind the scenes, even when, according to some of Jesus' parables, the king or landowner is absent (e.g. Matthew 21:33, Matthew 25:14–15, Luke 20:9, and even the direct reference to Jesus' departure in John 16:7). The head of Jesus' kingdom prefers to be called "father," even "daddy," rather than "king." This kingdom leader is powerful yet forgiving, patiently waiting (e.g. Luke 15:20) because of a desire that all may be saved (1 Timothy 2:4, 2 Peter 3:9). This king values the dispossessed and outsider (Luke 4:16–19, Matthew 20:1–7, Matthew 25:31–46).

In fact, the king looks remarkably like Jesus.[86]

MISSION

A kingdom-building ecclesiology has important implications for our understanding of mission. If the church is a vehicle rather than the destination, then how do we change our thinking from church-building to kingdom-building?

If we are co-workers with God, acting as agents of change in the world as ambassadors of God, then aligning the mission of the church to the mission of God is a crucial task.[87] Through an appreciation of God's intentions for the world, we come to an understanding of what the church's posture should be in relation to the world. "To be missional is to understand that our deepest identity is that we are children of God sent into the world to cooperate in the mission of God."[88]

Agents are summoned by their master or employer and commissioned to perform some task as their representative. In the same way, Jesus called the church into being to "be my witnesses in Jerusalem, and in all Judea and Samaria, and to the ends of the earth" (Acts 1:8). The church's calling is to scatter Jesus' invitation to all people—including the marginalized (Luke 14:21) and those loitering on the street corners, whether they are good or bad (Matthew 22:10)—an invitation to recognize, acknowledge, join, and revel in the new kingdom. As Paul describes this announcement to the followers in Galatia, it is a continuation of God's promise to Abraham in Genesis 12 that "all nations will be blessed" (Galatians 3:7–9).

One further adjustment is required to this picture of what the church is for. To say the purpose of the church is to deliver an invitation is not quite correct because that over-emphasizes the proclamation of an abstract message rather than an incarnational identity. That's why Jesus, in the verse quoted above, did not say "you will announce ... " but, "you will be my witnesses ..." (Acts 1:8). Mission is not something that the church *does* but something the church *is*, and the core of that mission is to act as a witness.[89] The new thing God is doing in the world through the church is the visible embodiment of a witnessing community.

The church is not simply the bearer of the message of reconciliation, nor the result of the message, but an integral part of the message.[90]

The scattering church, as an agent of change in the world, takes this mission as central to its identity. The church is "a letter from Christ, ... written not with ink but with the Spirit of the living God, not on tablets of stone but on tablets of human hearts" (2 Corinthians 3:3). We exemplify, through our way of relating to God, to each other, and to the created world, what the kingdom of heaven looks like on earth. Through that example, we act out God's invitation for others to come to the banquet as well.

MODALITIES AND SODALITIES?

In some missiological circles, Ralph Winter's terms "modalities" and "sodalities" are used to distinguish between two aspects of the church.

> *A modality is a structured fellowship in which there is no distinction of sex or age, while a sodality is a structured fellowship in which membership involves an adult second decision beyond modality membership, and is limited by either age or sex or marital status. In this use of these terms, both the denomination and the local congregation are modalities, while a mission agency or a local men's club are sodalities.* [91]

Many think of the local congregation meeting in a recognizable church building as the modality that forms the foundation of the church, and the various para-church and mission organizations as the sodalities through which the church extends itself by outward mission. In Winter's view, these are not opposing structures but co-operating components of the church as a whole.

On the surface, it may seem that my suggestion of a scattering church is simply a greater emphasis on sodality, or even a rejection of the role of modalities.

Winter situates the Anabaptist model of church "midway between a modality and a sodality." Although the ideas of a scattering church draw some inspiration from the Anabaptist model, I don't think Winter's distinction applies to the scattering church.

The scattering church is neither modality nor sodality, nor midway between them.[92]

Both modalities and sodalities are expressions of an institutional way of thinking about church. But central to the hope of this book is that we can discover a *non-institutional* expression of church.

The scattering church encompasses both the nurturing of Jesus' followers and the mission to the world. The scattering church is not a modality in a fixed geographic location, nor is it a separate missional structure that requires a second commitment. The scattering church is also not the composite of one structure that gathers and another that goes out to draw in more people to the gathering. Instead, the scattering church is a more loosely structured—even unstructured—movement, a way of life that builds the kingdom by constant scattering.

[7]

INSTITUTIONLESS CHRISTIANITY

MANY OF US WHO GREW UP "in the church" will find it difficult to separate what we know of church from what we know of its expression in various institutions. But let's see what would happen if we stripped away the outward signs of an institution, along with the underlying elements of an institutional mindset.

Consider a church without ...

- Large investments in buildings set aside for church meetings
- A hierarchy of ordained priests, pastors, and bishops who lead the church
- Weekly meetings each Sunday in which those leaders bring God's word to the congregated members within a structured one or two hour liturgy

- Programs for children, youth, evangelism, overseas mission support etc.
- Constitutions that prescribe how the organization will be governed
- Written rules about who is accepted as a member
- Central committees who control what is allowed to be done and who is allowed to do it
- An administrative bureaucracy that manages the properties, investments, national decision making, and regulates training and certification
- The need to protect itself from internal and external threats to ensure its own survival
- Financial metrics and membership counts that are inherited from the business world to measure success.

Is there anything left?

My answer is YES! What's left when all that is taken away is the real church!

What's left is a group of people who, under the direction of the Holy Spirit, seek to work with Jesus to build the kingdom of God.

What's left is people going about their daily lives in fellowship with each other, and in dependence on God.

What's left is people who find their identity as dearly loved humans through their allegiance to Jesus.

What's left is a missional heart to serve rather than to gain, to demonstrate rather than to coerce, to empower rather than to control, to release rather than to hoard.

What's left is God-given creativity and a summons to use that creativity to bless the whole world.

What's left is a movement rather than an organization.

TEMPLE OR TABERNACLE

Back in the early 1980s I enthusiastically read Howard Snyder's book *The Problem of Wine Skins*. He drew on the Biblical metaphor that compares Jesus' new orthopraxy to wine storage. Jesus notes that no one would pour new wine into old wine skins because the container will burst and you'd lose both the new wine and the old skins (Matthew 9:14–17, Mark 2:18–22, Luke 5:33–39). So it is, says Snyder, with the new things God is doing in the world: it is foolish to contain it within the old structure of the church.

Although I think Snyder does an excellent job of diagnosing key problems with the modern church, I have now come to quite different conclusions about the remedy— though maybe this is simply because the new wine skins we need today differ from those needed when he was writing in 1975.

In chapter 4 and 5, Snyder makes some helpful insights about the symbolic roles of the tabernacle and the temple in the Bible. In early Jewish history, God instructed Moses to make a tent—a tabernacle—as a sign that God dwelt among them (Exodus 25:8–9). It takes six chapters for God to describe the design of the tabernacle and how it should be used!

An essential element of the tabernacle, like any tent, was that it had to be mobile. It could—and frequently was—pulled down, packed up, and re-pitched somewhere else. Even the Ark of the Covenant inside the tabernacle was designed—by God—with rings into which poles were inserted to carry it (Exodus 25:12–15). The poles were not to be removed: a double emphasis that the presence of God had to be always ready to move on.

In the New Testament we find that Jesus is metaphorically the tabernacle. John writes that Jesus pitched his tent, or tabernacled, with us (John 1:14[93]). The letter to the Hebrews indicates that the need for the earthly tabernacle has been superseded by the work of Jesus (Hebrews 9).

In contrast, the temple in Jerusalem was David's idea (2 Samuel 7:1–2). God did not seem overly impressed with the idea (2 Samuel 7:5–7), for God cannot be contained or limited to a specific building (1 Kings 8:27, Isaiah 66:1, Acts 17:24).[94]

The fundamental difference between a tabernacle and a temple is that the latter is fixed in one location. A temple is a sure sign of institutionalism, and as Jeremiah warned, it is deceptive to simply repeat "This is the temple of the Lord, the temple of the Lord, the temple of the Lord!" (Jeremiah 4:4) as though our commitment to the institution will please God.

Which metaphor has the church traditionally followed? Unfortunately, it has usually chosen to build temples rather than tabernacles. The gathering church needs somewhere to gather, so it builds a "church" in every suburb and town, and it builds cathedrals in major cities. It builds the management frameworks that buildings require, including offices to house the resulting bureaucracy.

The tabernacle "emphasizes God as dynamic not static, as mobile, as a God of surprises. And it thus shows God's people—the church—as mobile and flexible, as pilgrims. But the image of the temple is strikingly incompatible with the idea of a pilgrim people."[95]

There is no theological reason why the church needs temples or tabernacles, for Jesus has fulfilled the need for both. God no longer needs any symbolic dwelling because Jesus *is* God dwelling with us.

We should also consider the role church buildings play sociologically. That is, what connotations do they arouse? What attitude do they convey, or as Snyder asks, to what do they bear witness? By his analysis, "our church buildings ... witness to the *immobility, inflexibility, lack of fellowship, pride* and *class divisions* in the modern church."[96]

From my observations, this has not changed for the majority of the gathering church since Snyder wrote that 40 years ago. These negative social consequences are not simply a problem caused by the church being tied to buildings, rather the buildings are the symptom that reveals the underlying institutional disease.

INSTITUTIONLESS COMPARED TO RELIGIONLESS

A great deal is sometimes made about Dietrich Bonhoeffer's suggestions about the possibility of religionless Christianity. Back in 1944, while in a German prison and near the end of his life, Bonhoeffer questioned the relevance of the traditional shape of Christianity in a changing world.

Bonhoeffer understood that, "The time when people could be told everything by means of words, whether theological or pious, is over, and so is the time of inwardness and conscience—and that means the time of religion in general. We are moving towards a completely religionless time."[97] Our past proclamation of Christianity has been based on the presumption that people have pre-existing religious tendencies. But now, what seemed like obvious and innate religious beliefs appear more and more to be "historically conditioned and transient."

If that is so, then who is Christ and what is the church to a religionless society? He wondered what Christian faith could look like if its connection to religion was severed. Could Christ become the Lord of the religionless as well? Could there be such a thing as a religionless Christian? "If religion is only a garb of Christianity ... then what is a religionless Christianity?"[98]

Perhaps we who are called by Christ would no longer see ourselves "from a religious point of view as specially favored, but rather as belonging wholly to the world. In that case Christ is no longer an object of religion, but something quite different, really the Lord of the world."[99]

Unfortunately, Bonhoeffer was killed before being able to flesh out answers to his own questions. We are left to guess where he might have taken those ideas.

I do not wish to conflate the idea of an institutionless Christianity with Bonhoeffer's religionless Christianity: they are different proposals, but I do think there is a substantial overlap between the two. The backdrop to Bonhoeffer's questions was a state-supported church in Germany in which people of faith were co-opted by the Nazi regime to accept and largely approve of the most horrendous of sins. Bonhoeffer did not reject the importance of the gathering church, though he called for its thorough reform. He wrote that "our church, which has been fighting in these years only for its self-preservation, as though that were an end in itself, is incapable of taking the word of reconciliation and redemption to mankind and the world."[100] As I have noted, this fight of self-preservation is one of the primary features of institutionalism. He thought that Christians needed to continue in prayer and "righteous action" until a day comes when the world can again be renewed by the word of God. "It will be a new language, perhaps quite non-religious, but liberating and redeeming—as was Jesus' language; it will shock people and yet overcome them by its power; it will be the language of a new righteousness and truth, proclaiming God's peace with men and the coming of his kingdom."[101]

His questions reflect a concern about how the institution of religion could become so corrupted, and on the other hand, whether a rejection of God and of institutionalized religion necessitated a rejection of Christ. Now, over 70 years after Bonhoeffer's death, we live in a world that is not only post-religious, but increasingly post-institutional. Whereas Bonhoeffer responded to his social context with a call to decouple Christianity from religion, my invitation to rethink the church in terms of scattering is largely a call to take Bonhoeffer further by decoupling Christianity from institutionalism.

The difference today, as noted back in Chapter 4, is that many faithful followers of Jesus have already left the institutional church and are already discovering how Christ can be the Lord outside.

THE ANARCHY OBJECTION

Some people may criticize a non-institutional approach to church on the grounds that it will breed anarchy. That's an interesting charge, but one that may reflect a misunderstanding of anarchy. I think what most people disparage about anarchy is that it promotes a free-for-all chaos, as though the essence of anarchy is a society without any order or rules. Avoiding dependence on institutions, however, does not mean there can be no order or rules.

The linguistic roots of "anarchy" come from the time when Athens had no Archon, that is, no governing leader. The core meaning is hence a social structure without a ruler, not one without rules.

It is easy to conflate the two ideas. An anti-anarchist with a Biblical background might quote Judges 21:25 and incorrectly claim that society—or at least a godly society—cannot survive without a king bringing order because without that top-down control everyone will just do whatever they want.

In popular usage, anarchy has become synonymous with lawlessness, but as a political philosophy that is not what the term signifies. The essence of anarchy has more to do with a lack of external, hierarchical control than with a lack of laws. It should be interpreted in terms of non-domination rather than disorder. A society modelled on anarchistic principles will still have rules that mold behavior so that people can collaborate and hold each other to account. But those rules will be derived from peer pressure and social convention rather than by a king, government, or police force.

In this sense, anarchy is consistent with Christianity. If you search, you can find scattered historical examples of Christian Anarchists who emphasized the importance of the authority of God and autonomy of individuals rather than the authority of any human government.[102] Biblical support can be found in verses like Jeremiah 31:31–34 (which was important enough to be quoted in Hebrews 8), stating that God's intention is for a new covenant in which laws are written on everyone's mind and heart by God rather than learnt from, or imposed by other people. The rules are internal rather than externally imposed, and everyone has equal access to God because all are classified as God's people.

I'll pick up that issue of where authority comes from in Chapter 10. But regardless of one's definition of anarchy, its perceived or potential problems arise not because we reduce the power of institutions, but because of an extreme individualism. The way the scattering church counters that tendency to individualism is described in the next chapter.

[8]

THE PRIMACY OF RELATIONSHIP

A CHURCH THAT THRIVES in a mobile, digital, post-modern, post-institutional world, and works with Jesus to co-create God's kingdom will have relationship at its core.

I am painting a picture of a church that scatters into the world while rarely gathering in a holy huddle. This does not mean everyone is on their own without deep connections to other followers of Jesus. On the contrary, in the scattering church, relationships—relationships with God and with each other—are far more important than they are in the gathering church.

In the gathering church, rules, programs, and structures can mask the fact that we need each other. We can get our sense of belonging and ethical guidance from the institution rather than our relationship with God. We can be satisfied that the person sitting next to us on Sunday morning believes the same creed as us, rather than deeply knowing them or being deeply known.

In the scattering church, for theological and sociological reasons, we depend on healthy and life-giving relationships to provide us with that sense of belonging and to help us grow.

THE THEOLOGICAL NECESSITY

Building relationship into the foundation of the scattering church is a theological necessity because the kingdom and its king are relational. The Christian understanding of God as trinity places relationship at the heart of deity. The Father, Son, and Spirit are separate, yet inextricably linked together. They communicate and co-operate together in relationship with each other.

We believe in a personal God. This does not mean we believe in a God who is just ours in the way we might have referred to a "personal computer" in the 1990s. By "personal God" we mean that God is a person as distinct from an amorphous life force. Both through creating us and through living with us, God knows exactly what it is like to be a human.

We run the risk of simply projecting human attributes onto God, but the Bible certainly depicts God as changing in response to human interactions, having emotions, regret, having compassion on us, etc. This risk is countered by the recognition that these attributes, and any other attributes we assign to God can only apply metaphorically, as I noted back in Chapter 1.

One thing that stands out in the Biblical narrative is that God wants to relate to us, and repeatedly takes the initiative to do so. Ultimately, God took on human form in

Jesus, and invites people into the kingdom in order to expand the relational embrace of the Trinity to us. As Luke notes in the so-called "parable of the great banquet" (Luke 14:15–24), many guests are invited, and if some of them cannot or will not attend then the host invites others and still more others until the house is full. Paul understands this relational and inclusive heart of God when he writes that God "wants all people to be saved and to come to a knowledge of the truth" (1 Timothy 2:4).

Dietrich Bonhoeffer notes that the Christian life is defined by our relationships, not with each other, but with Jesus.[103] The essence of transcendence, our connection to the divine image, is shown in the Incarnation where we see a reversal of all human life in the fact that Jesus is there only for others. "Our relation to God is not a 'religious' relationship to a highest, most powerful, and best Being imaginable—that is not authentic transcendence—but our relation to God is a new life in 'being there for others,' in participation in the being of Jesus."[104]

In other words, the outworking of God's relational essence is seen in the way Jesus lived among us: *for us* rather than for himself. We can experience that human-but-more-than-human relational essence only insofar as we share that vocation of Jesus through being for others ourselves.

Jesus' approach while on earth was to build close relationships with a small band of followers. Sure, he spoke to crowds and met many others as he travelled, but his primary mode of operation was to interact with people one-on-one or in small groups. The "master plan of evangelism"[105] was based on what we often call personal discipleship: he entrusted his message and way of life to his close followers so they could replicate the model to others, who could in turn replicate it to still others. This was the pattern of church that Jesus demonstrated, and the strategy is essentially relational.

THE SOCIOLOGICAL NECESSITY

Apart from being a theological necessity, the relational core of an effective church is also a sociological necessity.

Even the sociology starts with a theological truth: that our personal, relational God created humans with the same personal and relational nature. All societies arise out of the desire, the in-built need, to relate to each other.

Australian social researchers have noted that our youth do not see themselves as being born into a pre-existing community in which they have responsibilities. Rather, they create the community (or communities) through which they nurture the friendships they need. Even though there is a strong individualistic ethos, that does not mean friendships and community are unimportant.[106]

The mobility of our population, and the increase in digital interactions instead of face-to-face meetings impact the shape of relationships in the modern world.

In Chapter 4 I introduced some research from the USA on the millennial generation (i.e. those born around 1981–1997). The researchers noted that:

Millennials are less religiously affiliated than ever before. Churches are just one of many institutional casualties of the

internet age in which young people are more globally con-
nected yet more locally isolated than ever before.

Against this bleak backdrop, a hopeful landscape is emerg-
ing. Millennials are flocking to a host of new organizations
that deepen community in ways that are powerful, surpris-
ing, and perhaps even religious. [107]

This research found that American Millennials keenly feel the lack of community and are looking for that deeper sense of connection with other people with increasing urgency. When they cannot find it, they create it through CrossFit and SoulCycle fitness clubs, structured discussion groups around a dinner table, shared life coaching groups, summer camps for adults, and creative arts collectives.

Of course, it is not just Americans or Millennials who yearn for friendships, deeper relationships with peers and mentors, belonging, connectedness, and community. That need is embedded in us all, yet it is a need our Western individualistic culture has not been able to provide. In many cases the church has not been able to provide it either.

COMMUNITY

I've used the word community multiple times in this book, so it is about time to describe what that means. Rather than give a single formal definition, I will describe four types of community: geographical communities, communities of interest, virtual communities, and intentional Christian communities. The scattering church interacts with all four of those forms of community.

Community is the middle ground between individualism and institutionalism where you find the sweet spot for relationships. A community-oriented mindset avoids the selfish and isolated extremes of individualism while also avoiding the controlling rigidity of institutionalism.

Community can mean a local area. The "community of Denman," for instance, consists of 1,800 or so people within the geographical boundaries of that rural town in Australia's Hunter Valley. Historically, geographic communities[108] were quite stable and provided the primary backdrop for each person's role and sense of belonging. Today, population mobility and the impersonal nature of many urban and suburban locations mean that geographic communities have far less impact on our social connections and personal identity than they used to.

Today, we invest more energy in communities of interest than geographic communities. Those communities of interest may be social clubs, sports clubs, political parties, justice lobby groups, unions, Rotary International, a bike gang, a school, a church, etc. A community of interest brings people together around a shared topic or activity. They are often more homogenous than a geographic community, tending to bring together people with similar ages, cultural background, educational level and beliefs. Within those communities of interest, you may build a friendship that extends beyond the confines of the community, but in most case you probably have only a very slim commitment to the well-being of other community members. With the exception of groups that specifically meet for mutual support—Alcoholics Anonymous for instance—communities of interest do not actively promote that deeper level of inter-personal engagement.

Increasingly, communities of interest use digital tools to communicate with each other. Groups that meet face-to-face may have a Facebook group to stay in touch between meetings and to announce details of coming events. But since we no longer need to be in the same room at the same time, a community of interest can exist online without the members ever meeting each other. The growth of these virtual communities is an important sociological change. It also has significant commercial implications as businesses attempt to create online self-help communities for their customers. There are now hundreds of jobs for online community builders.

A traditional local church where geographically proximate people congregate regularly in a dedicated building, and even the new breed of virtual churches, are a bit different from most communities of interest because they *do* emphasize a sense of commitment to one another.

That relational emphasis, however, is often secondary to the church's mission. I know there are many traditional gathering churches with a heart that truly cares for their members, encouraging their spiritual growth, providing mentoring, and building strong networks between people to support each other through difficult times, but often that "caring" is a later add-on. "We've got this huge gathering and people don't feel it is very welcoming, so we'd better set up small groups to foster something that feels more intimate."

It seems to me that the gathering church also often views relationship as a means to another end, which can loosely be described as getting bums on seats. In this instrumental view, encouraging relationships is a tool rather than a core value. That attitude is clearly seen in some "friendship evangelism" programs.

Annabella has some friends who experienced that type of evangelism. The way it looked to them was some church-goers they knew were saying to them, "We want to be your friends" and soon afterwards, "Will you come with us to church?" and then, after Annabella's friends declined that invitation, the church-goers said in effect, "Oh, well we might go and find someone else to befriend instead." A rapid end to the instrumental friendship which left the "targets" feeling manipulated and used.

The scattering church brings relationship to center stage rather than as a peripheral afterthought and rather than a coercive means to some other end. This is nothing new, so I don't think I'm proposing anything radical here.[109]

When Bonhoeffer notes that the Christian life is defined by our relationship with Jesus, he goes on to say that as a consequence, we live in community with each other "through and in Jesus Christ."[110] Our community is a spiritual rather than human reality.[111] The goal of all Christian communities is to "meet one another as bringers of the message of salvation."[112]

Bonhoeffer takes a broader view of "salvation" than simply escaping the struggles of earth for a place in heaven. I do think he over-emphasizes the dichotomy between "spiritual" and "human" in this passage. In my view, there is no conflict between being spiritual and being human. A human community is a spiritual expression of the relational image of God within us all. This is true regardless of whether the people in that human community acknowledge it. There is no doubt that the church is founded on the call of Jesus, but it is also a community of humans who seek to discover through their relationship with Jesus the spiritual truth of what it means to be fully human.

Like Bonhoeffer, the scattering church recognizes that we bring God's message to each other, and that Christ may come to us through the seemingly weak or insignificant[113]—even from the outsider. That is why we bear "the message of salvation" not with arrogance, coercion, and control but with empathy, openness to see God's message in others, and through lives that demonstrate God's reality.

Many types of church structure can place relationship at the core, but a great example is the home church movement.[114] A home church is a small gathering that does not aspire to be a large gathering. It is not the first step of a vision that later hires a school hall and then funds a new building project as the church "grows." In the home church movement, small is beautiful. If there are too many people to fit in one lounge room then start another home church in someone else's lounge room. A home church is not a "home group" that provides some extra intimacy within a larger church; not a Wednesday night bible study group that augments the "real" church meeting on a Sunday. A home church is a complete church on its own. It can exist without a larger denominational structure, without a building fund, and without an ordained priesthood.

In a home church, people get to know each other well. Although the composition will change over time, there is sufficient time spent together to build deep relationships of care, support, and discipleship. People will drop around to each other's homes for coffee and prayer, eat meals together and share ideas about a Bible passage over the washing up, celebrate life's ups and downs regularly, and baptize in the backyard pool. Home churches both reach inwards to encourage the faith journeys of their members as well as reach outwards to their neighbors.

Lastly, there is also a form of community that is more intentional and committed. This approach to practicing faith together has a long history in the shape of monastic communities, and in the past decade has seen a revival under the label "the new monasticism."

This form of intentional Christian community—the idea of deliberately living together—has been an important element of my approach to church since I started university in 1980. During university Orientation Week I met Mike, who was a member of the Cornerstone Community and a recent graduate of their discipleship training program.

Mike inspired me to think about a style of life that broke away from the individualism around us and the common assumption that a household should be limited to a nuclear family. Two parents and their children living together as an isolated social unit is a very recent but dominant idea, and maybe kingdom values are better displayed by households with more open boundaries. Maybe there is a kingdom way of relating where faith is shared with each other and demonstrated to the watching world in our day-to-day life together. Maybe a community in which we shared our living space, cooked, ate and washed up together, only owned one lawn mower and one washing machine, shared child-minding so parents could go out occasionally, prayed together—maybe that was closer to what the kingdom of heaven was like.

Inspired by books like *Living Together in a World Falling Apart,*[115] about the experience of the Reba Place Fellowship in Chicago, we thought we'd give it a go ourselves. Since then, probably half my life has been spent in houses that included people other than my immediate family. Sometimes it has been a family house with one or two additional people, other times it has been a more deliberate multi-family adventure. I've visited many other similar communities, read other books[116] and even published a directory of intentional Christian communities in Australia.[117]

Some community purists will see my involvement as too transitory; that I have not been committed to one location or one group of people long enough to really appreciate the depth of this counter-cultural lifestyle. I think they are quite right, but I would respond that long-term communities—perhaps with a well-defined rule of life and clear stages of membership—run the same risks as other institutions. They can become exclusive and hierarchically controlling. They can separate from society rather than engage with it.

What drives my interest in intentional community is not a desire for a cloistered, stable existence, but the building of relationships that both nurture each other and demonstrate grace to all. Those relationships might grow intensely as you spend time together—a few weeks or a few years—and then the winds of change might blow you in separate directions. But the relationships can continue across geographical distance and across time.

The monastic model of intentional community is a form of sodality—an organizational structure running in parallel to the traditional church—which requires a second decision.

The community mindset that I would advocate, however, is just as intentional but more open-ended. You can foster community wherever you are by creating spaces that invite people to experience something nourishing for all. This mindset is neither individualistic nor institutional, but relational. It values connectedness but does not impose membership conditions. It holds on to relationships lightly, knowing that people will move on.

THE HEBREWS 10 AND MATTHEW 12 OBJECTION

In this context, addressing a possible objection to the idea of a scattering church might be helpful.

"Isn't it true," one might say, "that the Bible commands us to meet together? What about Hebrews 10:25 for instance?"

The writer to the Hebrews encouraged readers to "consider how we may spur one another on toward love and good deeds, *not giving up meeting together*, as some are in the habit of doing, but encouraging one another." (Hebrews 10:24–25)

I agree with that entirely. As this chapter on the primacy of relationships should make clear, the community of the scattered church does not mean we live as individuals, never meeting each other or sharing fellowship with other followers of Jesus.

Those verses, however, do not say, "spur one another on to meet together." They do not imply that the purpose of mutual encouragement is to increase the size or frequency of gathering. No, it is the reverse: we meet each other and build encouraging relationships with each other *in order to* "spur one another on towards love and good deeds."

Scattering church is not a refusal to gather but a reduced emphasis on the role of gathering. When gathering is the focus, it is often *not* the case that we spur each other on to love and good works. Instead, we sit in the pews expecting the leaders to do all the work. We gather but hardly know each other. We give our money to the institution, thinking that counts as "love and good works." We shake hands as we leave and call that fellowship. We sing a couple of songs and call that worship.

On the other hand, scattering church fosters strong relationships across time and distance through community building rather than by virtue of "attending a church" together. We don't bump into each other because we all attend the same church service at the same time of a Sunday morning. We do not build relationships with each other just because we go to the same church. No, the opposite is what happens in the scattering church: we build relationships in community with each other because we live and work and play and worship together, and because of those connections we sometimes meet together in order to "spur one another on."

"But," my hypothetical critic might add, "what about Matthew 12:30 where Jesus clearly says, 'Whoever is not with me is against me, and whoever does not gather with me scatters'? Doesn't that mean we have to gather together to work with Jesus? This idea of scattering is actually *against* Jesus."

There are three points I'd make to redirect the thinking about that verse. First, in line with my comments on Hebrews 10:25, I am not saying that we never gather together, only that we shift the focus away from a controlling institution to a decentralized relationship-based mission.

Second, the context of that verse (Matthew 12:22–37[118]) is Jesus' public defense of the accusation that he is in league with demons. In response to that accusation by the Pharisees, Jesus first points out that it is crazy to think that Satan would deliberately empower anyone to cast out demons. Satan's kingdom would already have destroyed itself if that were the case! On the contrary, Jesus claims his power comes from the Spirit of God, in which case the correct interpretation of the events is that Satan has been disempowered (the strong man tied up, v. 29) because the kingdom of God has arrived. In this confrontation between two kingdoms, Jesus challenges the Pharisees to reconsider which side they are on. They think they are following the Spirit of God, but the fruit of their actions indicates otherwise. In context, the verse about gathering and scattering has nothing to do with the structure of church or the nature of mission, rather it is a call for the Pharisees to rethink their kingdom allegiance.

Third, to what does the contrast between "gather" and "scatter" refer? In this context it does not refer to whether the followers of Jesus gather together or spread out as individuals. The focus is on Jesus and the Pharisees, not the disciples. Jesus is asking the Pharisees whether they are with him (and with the Spirit of God) or against him; whether they are drawing people towards him or making them run away. In effect Jesus is saying to them, "Don't imagine that you are living in line with the Spirit of God if you charge me with blasphemy in an attempt to scare people away from me."

Nothing I am proposing about the importance of the church scattering throughout the world in any way contravenes either the passage from Hebrews or the passage from Matthew.

EXPRESSIONS OF RELATIONSHIP

Positioning relationship at the core of a scattering church will be seen in many ways but let me note a few examples.

In the scattering church, inter-personal relationships are more important than doctrine about correct belief and rules about correct behavior. I am not saying those things are unimportant, just that they are less important than relationships.

Those inter-personal relationships will include peer relationships between friends, as well as mentoring relationships. They also include our relationships with God as we seek to understand God's character and follow the call of Jesus. In all cases, the relationships develop and deepen over time. Actively allocating time to those relationships is essential because out of those relationships we develop our beliefs and ethics.

In the scattering church, relationships are more important than "church growth" or other quantitative goals. If there is a choice between the needs of a specific relationship and increasing the number of people "brought to Christ," the institutional gathering church will always opt for the latter, but the scattering church will always opt for the former.

The scattering church recognizes and accepts transience. Rather than feeling betrayed, rejected or abandoned when someone leaves, we celebrate because the seeds we have sown in each other's lives will be spread more widely where they can bless others as well.

The scattering church protects each person's dignity in the knowledge that we are equally loved by God. As Dietrich Bonhoeffer wrote: "Because Christ has long since acted decisively for my brother, before I could begin to act, I must leave him his freedom to be Christ's; I must meet him only as the person he already is in Christ's eyes. ... Spiritual love recognizes the true image of the other person which he has received from Jesus Christ; the image that Jesus Christ has embodied and would stamp on all men."[119]

This means we do not coerce people, whether they be followers of Jesus or not, to become like us. The scattering church will not try to impose "Christian" laws so that a whole society is forced into right behavior. Instead, valuing the image of God already present in each person, we demonstrate respectful and nourishing relationships and invite people into a kingdom where such relationships are normal.

The scattering church makes great use of community builders: people who are good at encouraging connection, engagement, conversation, mutual support, sharing, and honesty; people whose smile puts others at ease; whose warm hospitality invites people to join in; whose creative use of décor, color, humor, music, and food creates spaces that are both grounded and sacred. Those abilities are equally important in the physical world and the virtual/digital world. They are not everyone's gift, but they are important abilities within the body of Christ.

Even when followers of Jesus are not living in some intentionally shared community, we can foster these types of deeper relationships, and practice openness and hospitality. We find ways to share life with other people, whether they are family members, geographic neighbors, work colleagues, the stranger we pass in the local shopping center, or someone we encounter through internet gaming.

Through sharing life together, we share the overflowing love and grace of God. We share a vision of hope based on what God is doing in our midst. We share in the common joys and struggles of being human. We demonstrate a way of relating to God, to each other, and to our environment that invites people to taste the kingdom of heaven.

[9]

EMBRACING/INCLUSIVE

THE SCATTERING CHURCH HAS a permeable boundary that enables all to come and to go. It willingly embraces everybody and creates spaces that are inclusive. It actively seeks what can be learnt from the outsider.

One of our favorite books is *Room on the Broom* by Julia Donaldson. It's a book that should be in the theological section of the bookshop, but you usually find it in the children's section!

A witch—the stereotypically scary "other," the outsider—gathers an assortment of companions on her broom: a frog, a bird, a cat, and a dog. There is always room for one more until, overloaded, the broom snaps and the passengers plummet to the ground. Once there, the witch has lost her companions but is attacked by a dragon. She is about to be barbecued by dragons-breath when ... well I can't wreck the whole story for you can I?

Of all the books I reference in this book, *Room on the Broom* is the one I most recommend that you read.

The book is about open-hearted hospitality and our dependence on life's travelling companions. It is about loss and struggle and fear. It is about redemption and creating something amazing out of the synergy each person is able to bring. It is about living in the knowledge that there is always enough to give away. It is about knowing that when you give, you will always receive far more.

Just as a pot of soup can always be extended for one more guest, the scattering church is open and inclusive, welcoming the insider as well as the outsider. "I'm just a dog. Is there room in the kingdom for me?" Jesus' response is always a resounding, "YES," and we echo that with our "Amen!" (which means, simply, "we agree" or "we affirm that truth") knowing there is always enough room on the broom.

Who are our companions? How do we choose them? Are we open to them being an odd assortment of misfits? Can we invite people onto our broom, or into our homes, with no guarantee of what might happen next? They may be socially awkward, self-centered, angry, greedy, unthankful, literally unclean, rich, scared, scarred, judgmental, atheist, Moslem, or pedophiles. But then again, they may also be angels (Hebrews 13:2) or Jesus (Matthew 25:40).

THE VOLF EMBRACE

In his amazing book *Exclusion & Embrace*, Miroslav Volf presents the idea of a physical embrace between two people as a metaphor for God's posture towards us, and for the church's posture towards the world. I hope I can do justice to his key insights in this brief summary.[120]

The movement of embrace has four essential components: a four-act drama. For a proper embrace, all four acts must happen in order.

Act 1: Opening the arms. One person starts by opening themselves to reach out for the other. This has an inward as well as an outward effect. Inwardly, it signals a yearning beyond oneself, a desire to connect with someone else and opens up a space into which the other may come. Opening your arms creates a gap in your personal boundary as you move towards the other. Outwardly, open arms display the desire for connection and convert that desire into an invitation.

Act 2: Waiting. The open arms reach out but do not touch the other. An embrace is not an act of invasion. The invitation may or may not be reciprocated. "The other cannot be coerced or manipulated in an embrace; violence is so much the opposite of embrace that it undoes the embrace. If the embrace takes place, it will always be because the other has desired the self just as the self has desired the other."[121]

Act 3: Closing the arms. If the invitation is accepted, and the other opens their arms as well, then the two can move together into the embrace proper. The two enter through the gaps in the others' boundaries and clasp each other. A soft touch is necessary so the embrace is not perverted into a bear hug. The embrace is not intended to assimilate the other, nor to lose our own identity by being absorbed into the other. In the embrace we recognize that we are still two individuals: individuals who largely do not understand each other.

Act 4: Opening the arms again. The embrace must always end with a release of each other so that both people's identity is preserved. The embrace does not turn two "I"'s into one undifferentiated "we." Through the embrace we leave a scent of each other behind while remaining individuals.

Can you hear the implications of this metaphor for the church?

Can you see God, eternally standing with open arms, inviting us into the embrace of love? Can you see Jesus, with arms outstretched on the cross, inviting us to follow his example? This is God's posture towards all, for God "wants all people to be saved and to come to a knowledge of the truth." (1 Timothy 2:3–4)

God invites but waits for us to respond. God does not coerce us into the embrace, nor absorb us through the embrace. God releases us to be ourselves and to carry the God-scent away with us.

God calls us friends, children, and heirs, but as Volf notes, "For the self shaped by the cross of Christ and the life of the triune God, however, embrace includes not just the other who is a friend but also the other who is an enemy. Such a self will seek to open its arms toward the other even when the other holds a sword."[122] We take that posture because it is the posture of God, and because we are called to be children of that God. It is the posture of the father in Luke 15 who is always waiting, looking and hoping for his son to return.

As Volf observes, this posture holds no guarantee of any outcome. We invite and wait without knowing whether the invitation will be accepted. We enter the embrace of the other without knowing their intentions. Even when a proper embrace occurs, we cannot know how the experience will affect us or the other person, nor can we know what either of us will do with that experience after the release. This is the risk God always takes. It is the risk God asks the church to take. For "embrace is grace, and grace is gamble, always."[123]

This is also the appropriate posture of the church. Within the scattering church we follow God's pattern by opening our arms to all, whether friend or foe. We respect the decision of the other about whether they return the embrace or not. We respect the autonomy and dignity of the other as we embrace. We embrace without coercion and without smothering. And we release each other.

OTHERING AND SCAPEGOATING

A long-standing human social pattern is to create group identities that separate "us" from "them." If we are to treat each person as equally loved by God and bearing God's image, the scattering church must resist this deeply engrained pattern, not by denying the importance of group identities but by refusing to use those identities to exclude other people.

A word that describes this pattern of thinking is "othering." Othering is "a set of dynamics, processes, and

structures that engender marginality and persistent ine-
quality across any of the full range of human differences
based on group identities."[124] In other words, othering emphasizes the differences between groups of people in order
to establish a power structure between "us" and "them."

Identifying an "other" is not always a negative process,
nor does it always imply some hierarchy of power. The negative concept of "othering" is not the same as the process
of differentiating our personal selves from other selves.
Any understanding of personhood requires that differen-
tiation. It is one of the first psychological moves of a young
child as they realize there is a "self," distinct from the rest
of the world. Indeed, one is not truly a person, not a self,
before that realization.

The flip side of becoming a self is the knowledge that
there are others who are not the self. There is me and there
is you. I am not you, and I am not God. By necessity, if there
is a me, then there is an other. That essential process is not
what "othering" refers to.

Nor is othering the same as the desire we all have to belong, or the sense of belonging that forms the bonds within
a social group.

Othering excludes and divides on the basis of some
identified difference of race, religion, language, gender,
sexual orientation or any other attribute, to create and
maintain a belief in our superiority and consequently the
others' inferiority. Othering pushes the other outside the
circle of what we admire about ourselves. We are civilized;
they are not. We are intelligent; they are unreasonable. We

have been chosen by God; they were not. We are moral and righteous; they are sinners.

By treating people based on some group stereotype, we dehumanize them. We don't approach them as another person, another individual. Othering is never about whether we like or dislike someone personally—there is no relational basis for the process and we rarely know the people we are othering.

In the kingdom of God, however, the distinctions on which othering is based become irrelevant. As Paul declares in Galatians 3:28, there is no racial or religious divide—"neither Jew nor Greek." There is no socioeconomic divide—"neither slave nor free." There is no gender divide—"neither male nor female."

In the scattering church, all tribal identities are put aside. This does not mean that we ignore the differences. To move away from othering does not mean that we treat everyone as the same. Instead, we recognize and value the differences between us and the other, and set aside those tribal identities so that we can embrace as equals.

One of the key purposes of othering is to identify someone to blame. This happens on both a personal and group level. When something goes wrong or we feel threatened, we find comfort in casting the blame onto someone else or some other group of people. By casting out the cause of the problem, externalizing it from within our self or from our group, we can maintain the cohesion of the group. We can even *increase* the cohesion by finding a new thing in common—the rejection of the people we choose to blame. The group feels stronger when we stand together against a common foe. The initiating problem can even go away, for a while at least.

This process is rarely conscious to the people in the process of othering. Some leaders may use othering as a deliberate strategy to generate distrust and hate in order to enhance their own political power-base. But in general, othering is not a conscious process. In fact, the effectiveness of othering is largely negated if the process is made visible.

Othering is closely related to scapegoating. The idea of a scapegoat is that guilt can be laid onto a chosen victim who is then cast out to take away the guilt. Our use of that word is derived from the Jewish ritual described in Leviticus 16, in which a real goat is randomly selected, prayed over in a communal confession of sin, then accompanied into the desert where it is abandoned.

Interestingly, this Jewish ritual is not the original instance of scapegoating—it is just the ritualized example from which we gain the name "scapegoat." The process pre-dates that Jewish ritual. In fact, as Rene Girard documents,[125] the process of scapegoating to avoid internal crises is the founding mechanism of all human culture and hence as old as civilization itself.

Scapegoating always needs a victim, though of course that victim is rarely an actual goat! Usually, the victim is a person or group of people selected on the basis of some arbitrary difference: they are the richest or poorest, ugly or the most beautiful, gay, transgender, homeless, or drug-addicted.

After a scapegoat has been selected, the casting out can take many forms. The person or people may be sidelined from decision making, muted, vilified, shunned, excommunicated, imprisoned, deported, or even killed.

Often the victim belongs to a minority group, and through the process of othering, one group can make a scapegoat of the entirety of another group.

An Australian example is the vilification of asylum seekers who arrive by boat. Back in 2013, the Australian Government initiated a policy that no person arriving by boat without a pre-existing visa would even be considered as an asylum seeker. The government and various media influencers pursued scare tactics to ensure that the general population would support this policy. They promoted the idea that the people arriving by boat were uneducated and undesirable trouble makers, terrorists and queue-jumpers who were taking advantage of Australian generosity; that the security of our borders, our national sovereignty, and our "Australian way of life" would be severely compromised if the boats weren't turned away.

Australia's inability to co-exist with the other in our midst led to the scapegoating of this particular group, boat-arriving asylum seekers, in a vain attempt to assuage our fear and guilt.

Some fact checking would show that immigration into Australia exceeds 450,000 per year[126] and that the arrival of asylum seekers by boat in the five years leading up to the new policy averaged less than 9,000 per year,[127] that is, 2% of our total inflow. Thus, a minority group, almost arbitrarily selected, is blamed for Australia's perceived multicultural problems.

Fact checking would also show that the success rate for asylum seekers who arrived by boat was far greater than for those who arrived by plane.[128] This implies the people arriving by boat are more likely to meet Australia's immigration criteria than those arriving by plane, revealing the lie that those arriving by boat are the undesirable ones.

The embracing posture of the scattering church stands in direct opposition to othering and scapegoating. The scattering church is an incarnational church, reflecting the movement of God who came from heaven to earth to live in solidarity with the broken world.

We recognize that in Jesus' kingdom the last are made first (Matthew 19:30, Matthew 20:1–16, Mark 9:35–37, Mark 10:31, Luke 13:22–30, Luke 14:7–14). Consequently, rather than dismissing or castigating the marginalized, oppressed, disempowered, or abused minorities, we stand with those who are "last" in the world's rankings. Rather than separate ourselves from the perceived otherness of "them," we dwell in their midst.

We refuse to be so tightly bound to our own group identities—whether that be our national identity, skin color, sexual orientation, cultural identity, or even our identity as followers of Jesus—that those identities are placed in opposition to other group identities.

Of course, we value the groups to which we belong. But at the same time, we value the differences between those groups and the other groups to which we do not belong. Our own personal identity and boundaries change over time, as does the identity and boundaries of every group to which we belong. We hold those group identities loosely, allowing the boundaries to be open and flexible—what Miroslav Volf refers to as permeable or porous boundaries.[129]

At first glance, one may think that permeable boundaries are the result of a weak or insecure identity. There is a type of pathology where a person has no clear boundaries and is easily manipulated by others. We say they have no backbone.

On the other hand, hard, impenetrable boundaries are often a sign of insecurity and fear. I often think that much of the modern church's posture is deeply defensive because of that insecurity. The triumphalist corners of the church, and even those who promote rational apologetics, seem scared of what might happen if we were too open to the influence of "the world."

In contrast to those two positions, a third option is demonstrated by Jesus and the early church. At a personal level, Jesus' supreme confidence in his own identity was precisely what enabled him to be vulnerable, even to the point of death. As the beloved disciple noted, it was because Jesus knew his own authority and his relationship to the Father that he could wash his disciples' feet (John 13:3–5). He did not need to prove he was the master, nor did he need to distance himself from others or defend himself, because he was neither threatened nor controlled by social status. His clear personal boundaries enabled him to take on the role of a servant.

Similarly, confidence in their own group identity was the basis of how the early church was called to engage with the world. Volf shows how this attitude underlies the structure of 1 Peter. Peter reminds the reader of their collective identity—we are scattered but chosen and sanctified, we have a living hope, heirs with an imperishable inheritance, shielded by God's power, refined through suffering, we are already receiving salvation, we are the envy of angels, like living stones being built into a temple, a royal priesthood, etc. Precisely because of those things, Peter says we can live in submission (not just to God and to each other but also to our bosses and secular authorities); we can live without deceit or hypocrisy; we do not need to retaliate when others hurl insults at us, nor do we need to show off with worldly riches or beauty; we can offer hospitality and treat others with gentleness and respect.

In short, the church can be different from the world around us, and yet not build a hard, defensive barrier between ourselves and the world. With a secure identity, we can reflect a "soft difference" between the church and the world.

A decision for a soft difference ... presupposes a fearlessness which 1 Peter repeatedly encourages his readers to assume (3:14; 3:6). People who are secure in themselves—more accurately, who are secure in their God—are able to live the soft difference without fear. They have no need to subordinate or damn others, but can allow others space to be themselves. For people who live the soft difference, mission fundamentally takes the form of witness and invitation.

> *They seek to win others without pressure or manipulation, sometimes even 'without a word'.* [130]

Volf's concepts of soft difference and permeable boundaries are the positive flip side of not othering or scapegoating.

Many people from a secular perspective could agree with the importance of not othering and scapegoating on purely humanist grounds. But followers of Jesus have an additional and compelling reason for doing so, because one of the essential purposes of the incarnation was to end the need for sacrifice. Jesus became the ultimate scapegoat and dismantled the need for any future scapegoating. [131]

At one level, the murder of Jesus was a typical example of sacrificial scapegoating. He stood out as different, and in the midst of a communal crisis he was selected as the victim whose expulsion could prevent a greater disaster (John 11:47–53). But at a deeper level this was not an ordinary sacrifice. This was not a lamb being offered *to* God, but the lamb *of* God (John 1:29, 1:36).

To understand that, note that we use the word "sacrifice" in two quite different ways. In one context, someone sacrifices a victim without that victim's permission. It is an act of coercive violence. In another context, a person can choose to make a sacrifice for some greater good. An example is when a parent forgoes their own pleasure to meet the needs of their child, or when a person gives up a kidney for a relative whose own kidneys have failed. These are rightly called sacrifices but they are neither coerced or violent.

Which was it with Jesus? Was he violently victimized by the people of the day? Yes he was, on the surface. But if we believe that Jesus was God and quite capable of avoiding crucifixion then there must have been something deeper going on. Was he violently victimized by God as a means of redirected retribution? Some would have us believe that. Or did he, as Paul repeatedly claims, "give himself" for us (Galatians 1:4, Galatians 2:20, Ephesians 5:2, Ephesians 5:25, 1 Timothy 2:6, Titus 2:14)?

The sacrifice of Jesus was fundamentally a self-sacrifice, intended to draw attention to and disempower the process of coercive violent sacrifice. Richard Rohr puts it this way: "Jesus replaced the myth of redemptive violence with the truth of redemptive suffering."[132] What Jesus did was emphasize that God does not desire a coercive, violent sacrifice (Psalm 51:16–17, Isaiah 1:11, Micah 6:6–8, Hosea 6:6 which was affirmed by Jesus in Matthew 9:13 and Matthew 12:7), and that no further sacrifice is necessary (Hebrews 8–10).

The scope of this change, which is the heart of the Gospel, is universal. It is not limited to the spiritualized notion of a coercive violent sacrifice to appease God's wrath but lays the scandalous foundation stone of the kingdom of God—a foundation stone that many Christians still trip over—that enables us to stop victimizing anyone. Because of the atoning work of Jesus we no longer need to "circle the wagons" to protect our own turf; we no longer need to disarm or condemn others; we no longer need to find someone to blame; we no longer need to protect God's reputation or see ourselves as agents of God's judgement.

The church can therefore take a more open, generous, merciful, and non-defensive approach to its engagement with the world. Jesus willingly marginalized, disempowered, and offered himself as the sacrificial lamb so we can now build an inclusive kingdom without othering and without scapegoating anyone.

VALUING THE OUTSIDER

Part of the reason why the scattering church takes a posture of embrace and inclusion is the knowledge that everyone belongs to God.[133] In that sense, there is no outsider. If it is already true that everyone belongs to God, then instead of seeing enemies surrounding us—people to fear or to convert—we see opportunities to experience God all around us. God is always and everywhere present. God has gone before us. God is already in the world and at work in the people we meet: they were all created by God, and all bear the divine image. God desires all to be saved (1 Timothy 2:4), and the Cross draws all people towards Christ (John 12:32).

Have you heard about the competition to enclose the biggest paddock with limited fencing materials?[134] Many competitors applied their mathematical and construction skills to the task, creating various sizes and shapes of large paddocks. But one competitor used all the materials to construct a square, just one meter by one meter. When the judges laughed at this hopeless attempt, the builder simply pointed out that *his* paddock was everything *outside* that square!

That paddock is more like Jesus' kingdom than the traditional institutional church! You can box yourself into a theological corner if you like and protect your patch from the "other," but where you'll encounter God is everywhere *outside* that box!

The scattering church expresses a particular honor for the outsider, for minorities, for the marginalized, the poor, those who have been treated unjustly, the disempowered, and the outcast. In Biblical terms, this reflects God's compassion for the leper, the orphan, and the widow.

Such people receive God's attention not because they are somehow more worthy or deserving of it, but simply because they are in greatest need. God is like the shepherd in Jesus' parable who is more concerned over the well-being of the one missing sheep than the 99 who are already safely cared for (Matthew 18:12–14, Luke 15:1–7).

Do not imagine that this involvement with the marginalized is a one-way rescue mission. The scattering church does not hold a paternalistic and patronizing attitude in which we have God's truth and must pass it on so that others may be saved. Our solidarity with the marginalized is as much for our benefit as theirs because the outsider is often the one who brings God's truth to us.

From inside the church we easily hear God's word in a way that reassures and reinforces what we already know. Those on the margins of the church tell us more about ourselves than those in the center. Those outside the church can, and often are, prophetic voices to us if we have ears to hear.

There are numerous Biblical examples of this: from Balaam's donkey (Numbers 22), to Rahab in the city of Jericho (Joshua 2), Moses' father-in-law (Exodus 18), and the children who shouted praises to Jesus (Matthew 21). The ultimate example is Jesus himself: born into a poor family from the backwoods town of Nazareth ("Can anything good come from Nazareth?" John 1:46), a refugee (Matthew 2:13–15), and killed outside the city in shame. In all these cases, God's message is brought to God's people by an outsider who is able to demonstrate great faith, like the centurion whose servant Jesus healed (Luke 7) and the Canaanite woman who changes Jesus' mind (Matthew 15).[135]

Some call this "mission in reverse,"[136] and it forms the basis of one of the decentering practices of Irish theologian Peter Rollins. Through "The Evangelism Project,"[137] Rollins encourages groups of Christians to visit the home territory of a different religious, political or cultural community. The aim is not to disrupt the group you visit or evangelize them, but to allow ourselves to be disrupted and evangelized.

Some readers may struggle with the idea that we, being followers of Jesus already, need to be evangelized or converted. But it is an important step in our own faith journeys to realize that we do not have a monopoly on truth. To be evangelized means to receive the good news, and even mature and faithful followers of Jesus continually need to hear and receive that good news, however God may choose to deliver it to us.

Annabella and I tried this with the icon-vo group in Sydney. Ten of us went together to a monthly meeting of the Sydney Atheists.

I had contacted the Sydney Atheists' president several months before the meeting to describe our intention and to ask his permission to attend. We exchanged a few emails and met for coffee beforehand. He was open to the idea, though somewhat confused by it.

The evening we attended was an open mic session, where anyone could speak for a few minutes about something controversial and then others had the opportunity to respond. Our group was in the minority—ten of us among about 60 overall—and we experienced what it feels like to be outsiders. The president announced our presence, and we were included in parts of the ensuing discussion. Afterwards, there was an opportunity to debrief with the president and mingle with the other attendees.

One annoying part of the evening was the ease with which some of the Sydney Atheists made assumptions about what we believed. But that had exactly the effect that the Evangelism Project promotes: to see ourselves through their eyes. By being the outsider on their turf, we could more deeply encounter the strangeness of our own beliefs and practices.

Sometimes the outsider is the one who reveals God's truth to us.

Sometimes the bread we need comes from a small boy in the crowd because we don't have the bread ourselves (John 6:9). If we live with closed boundaries, as though we already have all that we need, then we will never receive the bread of life that God is trying to supply us through the "other" whom we keep at arm's length.

THE COMMONS

Andrew and Miriam were founding members of a remarkable venture called The Commons, which operated in Newcastle, Australia from 2012 to 2017. Annabella and I were part of the broader community surrounding The Commons, but the reflections below are largely from Andrew and Miriam.

In an urban area of Newcastle, some members of the Uniting Church were looking for ways to engage in community development beyond the walls of the church building. With support and encouragement from the Minister, they convinced the congregation to turn a building owned by the church into a multi-purpose meeting space, open to anyone.

A huge variety of activities evolved in that space, including Friday night live music featuring local artists, an organic food store, seed library, evenings watching rare movies, and faith discussion groups. "Just Dance" would regularly attract a hundred people who were encouraged to dance without worrying about who was watching. People would dress up outrageously and share amazing food at a Eurovision party. All manner of groups used the space for workshops and business meetings. Annabella and I ran versions of Peter Rollins' Omega Course and Atheism for Lent at The Commons.

Although there was a management team and, later on, a paid part-time coordinator, The Commons depended

primarily on volunteers and an ethos of shared custodian-
ship. The décor was rustic and eclectic, as is necessary
when so many people contribute time, ideas and skills to a
physical space. The result was a relaxed, safe, homelike
space that hosted a lot of fun.

> *As an organisation, The Commons aims to "connect com-
> munities of care and justice and empower people to live lives
> of hope, joy and meaning". It is guided by the values of being
> ethical, creative, inclusive and sustainable. In everything we
> do, we try and meet these values and aims. This is reflected
> in the collective democratic decisions we make about which
> tea and coffee we sell, what we do with the money we make
> and which groups use the space. We try to make The Com-
> mons a safe space that cares for diverse people and our
> world. This is always a dynamic process.*
>
> *So whilst The Commons is a café, a goods store and a com-
> munity hub, it is also more than this. It is ours and yours
> and no ones. The Commons is a common resource, a com-
> munity space, an idea, a dream and a movement that is chal-
> lenging the dominance of injustice in our world by being the
> change in the world we want to see now!* [138]

The Commons exemplified Volf's embrace in an urban,
public setting that extended the heartbeat of the local
church outwards to its surrounding community. Their
conscientious emphasis on the core value of inclusivity
turned a traditional church space into a diverse and welcoming public space.

For Andrew, an important principle was to locate The
Commons on "the edge of the inside"—a phrase taken from

Richard Rohr.[139] This is a prophetic position to occupy: not throwing rocks at an institution from outside, nor towing the party line from deep inside, but challenging the institution from within by reformulating what happens around the margins. In line with that, The Commons was constituted as a faith community under the auspices of the Uniting Church of Australia.

This "edge of the inside" positioning of The Commons was challenging for both the church insiders and many of those who would have seen themselves as far outside the church.

To those within the church, especially some in the local congregation whose building was being re-purposed for The Commons, the challenge related to whether this community-building project was really missional. The scattering church often raises that concern, because it does not measure success by how many people have "confessed that Jesus is Lord," nor how many attend Sunday church services. The Commons did not host traditional "worship" times, didn't require leadership to affirm any statement of faith, and avoided most religious language. In a sense, the absence of those things are exactly what made the model missional. Singing worship songs, praying publicly, requiring certain theological affirmations, and using Christian jargon all indicate a protection of what the "insiders" already know and feel comfortable with, and an expectation that "outsiders" must conform if they are to be welcome. That stance is inherently isolationist rather than missional. The lack of those elements show the openness of the faith community to step out into the neighborhood to infect the "outside" world with the virus of the Kingdom.

To those outside the traditional church, the challenge of The Commons may have been that it confused their stereotypes of "religious people." They would ask why anyone holding to the values of The Commons would still want to hang around the church or identify as Christian. There was certainly interest in the fact that The Commons was willing to use "church space" to engage in explicitly non-church activities. Many people were attracted to the vision, even if they did not fully understand it. Consequently, they could benefit from the generosity and embrace of the church while still maintaining their distrust and dislike of the church.

Andrew and Miriam saw the diversity of people, activities and points of view as both a complication and a strength. An important part of their role was translating between the two positions and helping both churched and unchurched participants to see the role of authentic Christian faith within the vision.

The questions raised on both sides were perhaps some of The Commons' most significant outcomes, for they reveal many disruptions to people's normal assumptions about church. Although there was frequently an uncomfortable tension, there was also ample opportunity for diverse people to come together and experience life-giving community in which people sought to bless rather than coerce each other.

This type of inclusivity is the polar opposite of what many consider to be missional. The following cartoon[140] is precisely what The Commons was *not*:

"Oh look! There's some unconditional love!"

The idea of inclusion is not to trick people into coming inside so we can make them become like us. Instead, the scattering church breaks down the dividing wall between "insiders" and "outsiders," and actively nurtures shared spaces of mutual respect.

Ventures like The Commons are often—perhaps always—fragile and fleeting. In the form originally envisaged, The Commons lasted about five years. Such initiatives depend a lot on the individuals who carry the vision. They are like boats being rowed against the cultural tide: if you stop rowing or cannot co-ordinate the rowing, then the boat succumbs to the dominant flow. But when done well, the success of counter-cultural ventures like The Commons is marked by ongoing relationships and values that survive far beyond the time-bound and geographically-bound project itself.

[10]

RADICALLY DECENTRALIZED

THE SCATTERING CHURCH HAS NO centralized hub of power and authority but, blown by the breath of God, spreads the power and authority of Jesus throughout the world. Like the sower we found in Jesus' parables, the scattering church releases rather than controls.

This practice of release is impossible for the institutional church because institutions are fundamentally oriented towards centralization and control. When an institution or a business talks of decentralizing, they mean opening regional offices and spreading some of the workload and decision making from the headquarters to those regional offices. But, like a franchise operation, the institution's branding, operating procedures, quality control, appointment of leaders, and training are all dictated from the center. So it is with the institutional church.

Some people conceive of God's operation in the world in that same hierarchical way, as though there is a natural hierarchy of authority and control from God down to Jesus to the Apostles to other believers to unbelievers. But that can only be read into the New Testament with difficulty. Jesus derived his authority from "being in very nature God" (Philippians 2:6), and if we take equality within the Trinity seriously then we cannot think of the relationship between the Father and Jesus as hierarchical.

Certainly, Jesus passed the good news on to a close group of followers so they could pass it on to others, but that organic flow through relationships is not a mandate to create a hierarchy. On the contrary, Jesus demonstrated an egalitarianism that was completely radical in his cultural context. He said to his close followers, "I no longer call you servants ... I have called you friends" (John 15:15). It is through a band of *friends* that Jesus intended to spread his message. He ignored or annoyed the established religious and political authorities, and instead related to those at the bottom of the social pile in ways that demonstrated a complete disregard of any hierarchy. He spoke with women, even non-Jewish outcasts. He allowed himself to be touched by the "unclean." He told people not to sit in places of honor at a banquet. He shared meals with "tax collectors and sinners."

This attitude, demonstrated in the life of Jesus and the life of the early church, is truly radical—it alters the root of social dynamics. It does not question the established hierarchy in order to replace it with a different hierarchy but replaces the whole idea of a top-down power structure with a wild freedom to honor and serve all as equals.

One of Jesus' metaphors for the new kingdom is the way yeast works in a loaf of bread. The metaphor is quoted by Matthew (13:31–33) and Luke (13:18–21), and in both cases it is coupled with a metaphor about mustard seeds. A mustard seed is very small, yet grows into a huge tree that blesses many birds. In the same way, a small amount of yeast can transform a large amount of flour into nourishing bread. Those two metaphors run in the same direction as Jesus' declaration that, "You are the salt of the earth" (Matthew 5:13), with the implication that only a small amount is needed to season the whole world.

Just last week Annabella and I cooked some bread. We made two batches to experiment with how yeast works. We made one loaf with yeast dissolved in warm milk and mixed throughout the dough. For the other loaf we mixed the flour, milk, and other ingredients but left out the yeast. Once the dough was formed in that second batch, we pushed in a thumb to make a small hole and poured the yeast powder into that hole and covered it over.

You can guess what happened. The first batch rose in the oven and become a wonderful damper that we ate with our dinner. The second batch stayed flat and dense and its only value was as chook food the next day.

When we cut open that second loaf, the yeast was still right where we left it, a pocket of powder sitting in one corner. It had done nothing. Not only had the yeast not transformed the flour, the flour had not affected the yeast either. That, I think, is a great metaphor for the gathered church. All the yeast sits in one place where it is totally inert. It is protected from any influence of the surrounding

193

world—which some "church builders" would consider a success!—and conversely has no impact on the world.

There is no other way for the church to be effective as salt or yeast than to be spread around, scattered, and decentralized.

EMBRACING IS NOT CONTROLLING

Thinking back to Miroslav Volf's metaphor of embrace, recall the importance of letting each other go at the end of the embrace. A posture of embrace means that one does not control or seek to control the other.

Consequently, the scattering church becomes adept at letting go. Releasing is more important than controlling. Releasing is a spiritual discipline, that is, a habit that we consciously develop to grow our character towards Christ. We learn to hold on lightly to our possessions, our identity, our relationships with other people, our goals and our reputations. What we don't compromise, however, is our allegiance to Christ and the values that flow from Christ's example: the value of love above all else.

We take on the same attitude as Christ, "who, being in the very nature God, did not consider equality with God something to be grasped" (Philippians 2:5–8). Rather than grasp or cling to divinity and use that status to be master over others, Jesus let go: he emptied himself, released his claim to authority, and humbled himself. Not only was he willing to give up the transcendent otherness of God to become human, he was willing, as a human, to give up his life. In this passage, Paul notes that Jesus is both "in very nature God" and "the very nature of a servant." In Jesus there is no conflict between the two. Jesus shows us that (part of) the very nature of God is to be a servant.

In primary school, I always confused the spelling of "loose" and "lose." One of the challenges for people in the scattering church is the continual grief of letting go. To let something loose often means to lose it. In releasing people and places and habits and religious practices and power, that process of letting something loose often feels like a loss.

School teachers feel that every year. After investing themselves in a class of say 30 children, they must let them go at the end of the year and next year start again with a new group of people to invest in. The scattering church is like that.

It can be difficult and painful. Perhaps the wish to avoid the sense of loss through change is part of the reason we create institutions in the first place. Institutions can control change so we do not experience as much loss.

But you cannot sow with a closed hand.

GOD IS NOT IN CONTROL! HALLELUJAH!

Open-handed release is the fundamental power disruption of the Gospel. It subverts the normal human tendency to control and creates the possibility of a new way of relating to each other based on mutual respect and service. The spiritual discipline of release enables us to give rather than take. It refuses to use power to coerce.

All of this is a direct consequence of the character of God as revealed in Jesus.

In a recent conversation, a friend spoke about the need to trust that God is in control. I've heard it before, often in the context of a reassurance that even if your situation looks bleak, it is supposed to be comforting to know that God is in control.

I don't believe it.

The God I see described in the Bible gives up control rather than always bringing about what God desires. God suffers as much as we do in the brokenness of life. God allows all sorts of personal calamities, disasters that affect millions of people, and horrendous evils like genocide. It would be blasphemous to say God is in control of such things.

Was the genocide in Rwanda the good will of God and under God's control? Who could claim such a thing? What perverted faith blames such atrocities on God?

A parent suffers the death of a child and some say, probably as kindly as they can, "Don't worry, God is in control. It's all part of God's plan and even though you can't see it now, it is actually a good thing." That is of no comfort at all. How could that attitude instill any sense of trust or security when it fosters a belief in a God who can do literally anything, and we have to accept that it is good? God may well redeem even the grief of losing a child, but to say the death and the loss is good, and God's will, is ludicrous.

Some take the view that specific events, like the death of a child, might not be good in themselves but part of the will of God in order to bring about some larger good. Even that is a mockery of the God we see in Jesus. It presents God as a conscious abuser who causes evil events as a means towards a favored end. Unless you believe that God causes evil, the very presence of evil proves that God is not in control.

To say that God is sovereign, or Lord of all, does not have to imply that God always gets what God wants. God's *ability* to control everything does not imply that God does *in fact* control everything. Although the universe could have been created with every aspect controlled by God, the God presented by Jesus chose the path of love instead. God is love, and hence God is a risk taker. Love can always be resisted, otherwise it is not love. Love always entails risk, especially the risk of being rejected.

From the history of God's interactions with humanity as recorded in the Bible, God is well-aware of this and accepts the risk. God created everything good, only to see the perfection marred by human sin. The prophet Samuel noted that "the Lord your God was your king" (1 Samuel 12:12), and yet Israel rejects God's kingship by asking for a human king. Jesus wishes he could gather the children of Jerusalem together like a hen gathering chicks, but it didn't happen because they were not willing (Matthew 23:37). Jewish leaders in Jesus' day "rejected God's purpose for themselves" (Luke 7:30).

In all these cases and more, God did not get what God wanted. People thwart God's will. Did God want Adam and Eve to sin? No. Did God want Israel to have a king? No. Whenever Jesus talks about "whoever does the will of my Father" (e.g. Matthew 12:50), doesn't that imply there are people who do *not* do the will of the Father?

God has always taken the initiative and continues to take the initiative. God often brings good out of suffering. God sends rain and sun to bless all people, regardless of their moral status or their attitude to God (Matthew 5:45). Even on behalf of people who don't ask for it, God stands with open arms—but that does not stop people from going their own way (Isaiah 65:1–3). God could not control everything and yet be love. Love and control are incompatible.

I have already mentioned 1 Timothy 2:3–4, where Paul claims that God wants all people to be saved. That verse[141] poses a dilemma for most of today's Evangelical Christians who believe (a) that everything in the Bible is true, (b) that some people get saved and others don't and (c) that God is in control. This verse shows that those three beliefs are incompatible with each other. At least one of them must be wrong. If the verse is true but some people don't get saved, then here is a case where God is not in control because God's will for all to be saved is not fulfilled. If the verse is true and God is in control, then everyone must get saved. Or thirdly, if some people don't get saved and God is in control then the verse can't be true. You can choose any two of (a), (b) and (c) but having done so, you have to reject the third.

Different people have taken each of those options, and I guess some go further and reject all three claims. But for me, the most reasonable option is to reject (c) because there is so much Biblical evidence that God freely forsakes control.

The passage we already discussed in Philippians 2 is a primary example. The so-called "kenotic descent"—

through which Jesus emptied himself, became a servant as a man, and then gave up his life—shows how much God is willing to give up and relinquish control.

Romans 8:18–39 is another example. Paul describes creation as broken; it groans in agony (22). We too groan within that brokenness (23). He implies that God is not controlling things remotely but is sitting in the dust with us, also groaning (26). It is true that God's actions are always directed towards liberation from the bondage of decay for us and for the whole creation (20, 21, 28), but there is a lot God chooses not to do, and the decay continues. God wants good things, and sometimes we can work together with God as part of the process of bringing good things to reality, but the control over whether those good things come to pass is a complex interplay of divine and human choices and their consequences.

The good news is not that God promises some escape from the brokenness, but that God joins us in the brokenness. Not that God is in control, constraining the outcome, but that God has taken the risky step of forsaking control so we can truly be free.

This is at the core of Jesus' message: God stands in solidarity with us in the brokenness.

Notice the preface of the Philippians passage: "Your attitude should be the same as that of Jesus Christ" (Philippians 2:5). This echoes the words of Jesus himself: "As the father has sent me so I send you" (John 20:21, 17:18). We seek to reflect the character of Jesus just as he reflects the character of God. This is the mandate for the scattering church to express the attitude of *kenosis*—emptying, noncontrolling, releasing—always present in the character of God and demonstrated in the life of Jesus.

EMPOWERING AROUND THE EDGES

The consequence of this Biblical way of thinking for the scattering church is that if God is not in control, then we don't have to be either. The scattering church doesn't seek power or control but releases them both to empower others.

In the scattering church there is no centralized control or management, except that all look to God. There is no denominational structure, no internal hierarchy, and no superior from whom we must seek permission. Instead, each person seeks to live a Christ-like life wherever they are and works together with the people around them—whether they be followers of Jesus or not—to build the kingdom inaugurated by Jesus.

In this structure, power is shared from the bottom up rather than being imposed from the top down.[142]

Not all power is bad—power is simply the energy to get something done. But when power is centralized it is easily turned into abuse. The history of the church has shown time and time again that when we invest power in a central authority, we are just as prone to misuse that power as those subscribing to any other ideology. We should not therefore aim to create "Christian" power structures in the vain hope that those structures will do good from the center outwards. Instead, the scattering church avoids all power structures and encourages good around the edges.

As we grow as faithful imitators of Jesus, we exemplify a right love of ourselves, a proper respect for each other and an allegiance to God. We learn how to forgive. We act as good neighbors. We "look after the orphans and widows in their distress" (James 1:27), perhaps helping them to navigate a government bureaucracy that has reduced their welfare payments. We invite "sinners" around for dinner and gratefully accept their help when our car breaks down. We baptize in the backyard pool. We create community spaces like The Commons, even at the risk of others taking over control. We encourage young people to lead a meeting. We sit with people who are struggling and allow them to sit with us when we are struggling. We scatter seeds of hope in fields overgrown with fear. We affirm the goodness that is all around us. We help people, ourselves included, to name and disarm the things that hold us back from experiencing the fulness of life. We invite others to join us in imitating Jesus, and sometimes we even do that with words!

This is what it means to *be* the church. It is much different from "going to a church."

Because being church is more about how we live than what we do on a Sunday morning, where we live also becomes important. God could not have intervened effectively by staying in heaven. The "God with us" of the Incarnation is an important guide to mission. To scatter the Good News effectively in the world, the church needs to be incarnated in the midst of that world. To stand in solidarity with the marginalized is very difficult without living among the marginalized and becoming marginalized oneself.

I can't say I'm very good at that, and I stand in awe of groups like Servants to Asia's Urban Poor who immerse themselves in extreme poverty. There have been times when I have deliberately lived in multi-racial areas and areas of low socio-economic power, but most of my life has been in comfortable Australian suburbia. The kingdom can be, and needs to be, demonstrated there too. Our mission field is the whole world. Even in highly developed societies with a culturally Christian heritage, the message of the kingdom is a radical challenge and God's people need to be scattered there as much as anywhere else. Wherever you are, you and God are there, and so the church is there. Nevertheless, we recognize that the summons of Jesus that founded the church is more a call to "go into all the world" than to stay where we are. It is the only way yeast can work.

Empowering those on the edge rather than radiating power from the center does not mean there is no accountability or support. Just saying, "Go and do whatever you like" is not actually empowering. Followers of Jesus, wherever they are, grow into maturity through the gradual development of knowledge, habits, will, character, and experience. They need to grow the fruits of the spirit. Otherwise they have neither the wisdom to decide what to do, nor the skills to implement their decisions.

An important role of the scattering church is to foster that process of discipleship. Mentoring becomes a normal part of our lives as we learn from God, from each other, and from our interactions with God's world. When I mentioned a few paragraphs back that we might encourage young people to lead a meeting, that doesn't happen without support. The person will have seen more experienced people leading meetings; you will have helped them to reflect on those experiences and discussed what good leadership looks like in that context; someone will have planned the meeting with the young person and debriefed with them afterwards; etc. That sort of learning scaffolding is necessary in the development of faith and character just as much as it is in the development of technical and management skills. This type of discipleship avoids the controlling relationships that can occur when one person is placed in authority over another, and instead focusses on empowering each other.

THE AUTHORITY OBJECTION

A possible criticism of this call to radical decentralization is that it lacks any "covering," that is, people do not work under any authority. "Where is the accountability?" you might ask. "You'll no longer be able to guarantee right belief (orthodoxy) or right conduct (orthopraxy). How do you prevent people going off in their own direction, perhaps even forming crazy cults?"

One part of me wants to say, "But that is exactly the point!" Decentralized *does* mean not controlling through an authority structure. It *does* mean giving up the central control over what constitutes right belief. That's not a *problem* with the decentralizing, non-institutional approach: it is the very reason we'd want to do it! People *should* go off in their own direction, or more precisely, following God's direction. There is no legitimate authority apart from God, and even God tends to give up that authority rather than impose it!

But I know a more thoughtful response is necessary, and so I'll make three points: a centrally controlled church is no less likely to go astray than a decentralized one; the importance of cross-fertilization; and the importance of becoming good followers.

First, even a cursory look at the history of centralized, controlling institutions that have dominated the gathered church makes it abundantly clear that large, authority-based hierarchies are just as likely to go astray in terms of both beliefs and practice as smaller, free-thinking structures.

We saw earlier how theologically diverse the gathering church is. Huge portions of the traditional church vehemently disagree with other portions about the nature of authority, the status of the Bible, the role of women, the nature of mission, the existence of hell, etc.

There is no belief that is affirmed by all institutions that would classify themselves as "Christian" apart from the centrality of Jesus, and even that central claim is interpreted in wildly different ways. From any one particular standpoint in that landscape, most of the others have gone astray in terms of core beliefs. The size of the church is irrelevant. I know of many Protestants who deny that Catholicism is Christian. Evangelicals may say the same about Progressives. Many self-identifying Christian denominations are deeply critical of the "prosperity gospel" preached in many Pentecostal churches.

The practice of the church follows the same diverse pattern. The size of a church and the emphasis on hierarchical accountability does nothing to prevent corrupted practices. An authority structure can still give permission for unholy practices, from support for oppressive political regimes—church support for Apartheid in South Africa is a well-known example but by no means the only case—to the vast accumulation of wealth by Christian institutions and their leaders. The gathering church, with an eye on their own reputation, is also prone to covering up abusive practices, as has recently become clear in an avalanche of sexual abuse by church leaders and domestic violence encouraged by a theology that mutes the voice of women.

There is no high moral ground to take here. No church oriented towards the gathering metaphor can say, "Our system of authority and hierarchical control ensures adherence to the beliefs and practices of Jesus, and that will all be lost if we allow this radically decentralized approach."

I do not claim that the scattering church will resolve these problems. There will continue to be parts of the church that lose the plot in terms of both their beliefs and their practices. But it will be no worse than the track record of the gathering church. When that does occur, it will be in isolated pockets that soon die out rather than be perpetuated by the false legitimization of "respectable" authority structures.

Let me suggest three ways we could reduce the likelihood of drifting off the narrow path of the Gospel.

The first is a decisive willingness to follow Jesus. That should go without saying, but I think our allegiance to Jesus is often less than decisive.[143] We inevitably mix it with other motivations, both personal and collective: safety, status, respectability, political influence, etc. The church in any of its possible forms will become more aligned to the strategy of Jesus—in academic terms, we can align the *missio ecclesiae* with the *missio Dei*—when we identify and subordinate those other motives.

The second is to appreciate the value of cross-fertilization.

One thing a large, gathering church does achieve is a critical mass of people who believe roughly the same thing. A hierarchy of authority has the designed consequence that people who place themselves under the authority of the church imbibe a consistent set of beliefs from their leaders.

That may sound like a good outcome, though most will admit that it depends on the quality of teaching and the character of the leaders. On the negative side, the homogeneity that comes from generations of doctrinal in-breeding deeply entrenches one way of thinking and constantly reinforces what everyone in the church already agrees with. Even in churches where members are encouraged to ask questions, there is rarely much encouragement for those who reject the answers that are given.

Hiding under authority can easily limit the freedom to hear the new word from God. As I pointed out already, that's why we need to listen to the outsider. Hiding under authority can also dull our ability to think for ourselves or to even imagine an alternative. We become blinkered to any creative influence and unable—or unwilling—to truly hear the pain or the wisdom of those outside our co-dependent bubble.

The scattering church, on the other hand, encourages new thinking through constant exposure to varied ideas from multiple sources. The social mobility of 21st century Western culture enables a productive cross-fertilization of ideas. The scattering church takes advantage of that and becomes adept at both gaining from the exposure to new ideas and seeding kingdom ideas into the lives of others.

Through scattering we meet followers of Jesus from many different backgrounds and can compare ideas with them as a way of critically validating our own understanding. Without the grasping need to be right, we can approach belief and practice with an openness that allows us to learn from other theological traditions. Throughout that process we sift the ideas we encounter through the sieve of kingdom values. We no longer simply believe or act because some human authority has told us we should. Instead, we engage in a process of discipleship under the authority and influence of Jesus and in collaboration with other people, the goal of which is to become increasingly Christ-like in our character and values. Over time, our beliefs and practices evolve out of those embedded character and values.

Rather than encouraging cults, the scattering church actively discourages them because it gives less authority to any charismatic leader. Certainly, individuals and the people under their immediate influence may get things wrong and may mislead and abuse. But whereas in the gathered church that can affect a large group as the leaders "Lord it over" their followers, in the scattering church all are called to imitate the servanthood of Jesus (Matthew 20:24–28, Mark 10:42–45, Luke 22:24–27 [144]). Within that framework, all followers of Jesus are peers, on an equal footing before God, with equal access to God, and mutually subject to the process of correction outlined in Matthew 18.[145]

The call to servanthood leads naturally to a third suggestion that may help the church to avoid missing its way with regard to authority. We spend a lot of effort training and encouraging good leaders, but nowhere near enough effort training and encouraging good followers.

We are all leaders to our children, or as teachers in Sunday School, and most of us at one time or another lead something. We all act as role models in one form or another to the people around us. Most of us, however, aren't fundamentally leaders. Most of us are followers.

In Paul's view, leading only arises out of following. He wrote, "Follow my example, as I follow the example of Christ" (1 Corinthians 11:1). Not everyone can, or should be a leader, but all Christians should be followers. Leading in the church is only legitimate to the extent that the leader is first and foremost a faithful follower.

So how does an effective follower act? Firstly, they choose who to follow. That's an important skill. Second, effective followers actively participate rather than follow blindly. The Nuremberg Defense is not adequate. That is, it is not acceptable to say, "I was just following my superior's orders." Effective followers think for themselves and good leaders should encourage that character trait in their followers.

Good followers are critically engaged in the mission, contributing ideas and being willing to disagree. They act as examples, both inviting and showing others how to join in. They provide prayerful, practical and emotional support for their leaders. Becoming a good follower is not just an apprenticeship towards becoming a leader but can be a long-term vocation.

Given that authority ultimately comes from God and that through Jesus we have direct access to God (e.g. Ephesians 2:18), the church does not need—it never did need—a hierarchy of shepherds controlling the flock by passing down the word of God, passing down instructions, and passing down prohibitions.

PRIESTHOOD OF ALL BELIEVERS

I hope the preceding discussion has painted an alternative picture of what authority looks like in the kingdom of God. In today's world, with today's dominant approach to church, that alternative is a controversial position, just as it was in the days of Jesus and the early church. The idea of decentralizing power has been a minority view within the church since the beginning. I have not presented a detailed argument for it here but only a sketch.

To that sketch I will add one more element of the New Testament's response to the question of how authority operates: the priesthood of all believers. This itself is a contentious concept within the church as a whole, though clearly attested to by the Bible. Most churches at least pay lip-service to the notion that all members are priests, but they deny it through their structure and practice.

In Old Testament Jewish culture, the core duty of a priest was to offer sacrifices. They acted as mediators between the people and God. Other duties included taking care of the holy place in both the Tabernacle and the Temple. In the New Testament, however, these roles are made redundant by Jesus. There is no longer any need for sacrifice, nor is there a Tabernacle, Temple or altar.

In the modern church, the priest—or minister, pastor, bishop, or pope—continues to play a mediating role. Priests pray for us, absolve us of our sin, and bring God's word to us. They still control the "holy places." From a New Testament perspective, however, those core roles of a priest are either no longer relevant or are dispersed to all the people of God.

The decentralization of the priestly role is proclaimed by Peter: "You [plural] are a chosen people, a royal priesthood, a holy nation, a people belonging to God" (1 Peter 2:9). This should be read in conjunction with Exodus 19:5–6, because Peter was declaring that the church in Christ is a fulfillment of God's intention on Mt Sinai several thousand years prior. The same idea can be seen in Revelation 1:6 and 5:10, and it is implied by the description of Jesus as the new high priest, coupled with our identity as imitators of Jesus in the letter to the Hebrews.

The notion of a church scattered throughout society virtually necessitates that these verses be interpreted literally. Once you put aside a mode of operation based on gathering, there is no place for leaders who direct large groups or who control access to God. Equipping all followers of Jesus with the authority to teach, to serve, to lead, to baptize, to forgive, to pastor, etc. is essential in a scattering model.

As priests, we are no longer excluded from the "holy places" where we may encounter God. Every place is holy because every place is God-infused, and every one of us can "approach the throne of God with confidence" (Hebrews 4:16) *directly*, that is, unmediated.

Of course, this does not imply that all of us must become experts in every function. Nor does it imply that some are not specifically gifted as teachers, evangelists, carers, etc. No, the *whole* body of Christ, with *all* the gifts of God spread around from the head to the foot, is needed in the collaborative work of building the kingdom. The scattering church will encourage and recognize expertise in leadership, organizing skills, inspirational communication abilities, financial management, counselling skills and detailed theological insight. But as priests, we all have equal access to God. We are all God's representatives, or to use Paul's wonderfully kingdom-inspired phrase, God's *ambassadors* (2 Corinthians 5:20) to the people around us.

Taking the priesthood of all believers seriously leads to a delayering of church organizational structures. In modern business terms, the scattering church is a flat organizational structure, in fact hyper-flat. There is God, from whom the initiative, vision and authority emanates, and there are God's priests. We report directly to God rather than through layers of middle management. The priesthood of all believers is essentially a decentralized model that empowers people around the edges rather than controlling them hierarchically.

WHEN A CRITICAL MASS IS NEEDED

There are times when the work of the kingdom requires a critical mass of people for a particular purpose. In suggesting a radically decentralized church, I am not opposing groups of people who work together to lobby on behalf of the disempowered, to provide theological education, to foster research, to channel disaster relief and development resources, or to co-ordinate specific mission activities. All those purposes and many others are appropriate outworkings of the yeast the church scatters throughout the world. They are all important components of kingdom building, but none of them constitute the church.

An example in Australia is the Love Makes a Way organization, whose purpose is to mobilize Christian support for people seeking asylum. In the context of Australia's refusal to accept refugees arriving by boat, this is an important issue of justice where the church can and should lobby for political change.

Even in such organizations, the organizational structure and the decision making processes can all reflect the heartbeat of the scattering church: emphasizing the importance of relationships above the survival of the organization, taking a stance of embrace and inclusion, collectively discerning God's will through a recognition of our equality before God, and always expressing the character of God as we see it in Jesus.

[11]

GENEROUS AND GRACIOUS

I'VE ALREADY TOUCHED ON the role of hospitality in the scattering church. Hospitality is one outworking of a spirit of generosity that arises naturally in a church emphasizing relationship and whose default posture is open-armed inclusion. It reflects the grace of God that fills us and overflows to others.

While some of the characteristics of the scattering church are so foreign to the gathering church as to become virtually impossible within that paradigm, this is not the case with generosity and grace. Those virtues can and are expressed through the traditional, gathering church as well as through many non-faith groups. Putting aside the drive to compete, which is often forced onto us, and the fear that makes many groups fall into a mode of self-preservation, expressions of hospitality and generosity are universal attributes of human civilization. Without them, a stable group identity is hard to imagine.

Extending grace to each other is a bit more challenging than hospitality and generosity, and perhaps less common. By "grace," I mean the ability to give more than is deserved or earned, the free offering of forgiveness and mercy, the ungrudging expression of goodwill towards each other. In some cultures, the threat of "falling from grace" is a powerful mechanism of control. In cultures that equate justice with the rigid application of rules, grace can be seen as soft, even traitorous.

In the kingdom of God, however, grace is a deeply embedded virtue.[146] Jesus calls us to not judge, but to forgive and give generously (e.g. Luke 6:37–38). The last are made first. Those who work for one hour are paid the same as those who work the whole day (Matthew 20:1–16). People are forgiven seventy times seven times (Matthew 18:22). People are forgiven even before they show any sign of repentance, to the point that the law-protectors see such forgiveness as blasphemy (e.g. Matthew 9:1–8, John 8:1–11).

The kingdom of God takes it a step further than most cultures by extending hospitality, generosity and grace to all rather than just to the in-group. This attitude is already present in the Old Testament through numerous instructions to Israel to treat outsider's kindly (e.g. Leviticus 19:33–34), but re-emphasized by Jesus, who equates the way we treat strangers, the poor and the sick, and even those in prison, with the way we treat God (Matthew 25:31–46).

Jesus knows the transformative effect of hospitality so clearly that he invites himself (!) to dinner at Zacchaeus' house (Luke 19:1–10). Although a social pariah, Zacchaeus is still a "son of Abraham," that is, an heir to God's unmerited favor.

Jesus' generosity and grace are also shown in his openness to Judas. He had no qualms about sharing a meal with Judas, despite knowing that he was about to betray him (John 13:18–30). This was the Last Supper, the sacrament we still celebrate to this day in honor of that same Jesus. Yet in most churches Judas would not be allowed to participate! Why have we turned this original meal, an act of gracious hospitality in which Jesus clearly displays the first step of the Volf embrace towards Judas, into an exclusive ritual through which we emphasize to outsiders that they are not welcome in the church?

As noted before, this instruction to show love and grace to all includes our perceived enemies. In Jesus' view, that's one way we can demonstrate we are truly the children of God, because extending love to all is one of the remarkable idiosyncrasies of God (Luke 6:35, Matt 5:45).

Luke's account links love for enemies explicitly to grace, though that linkage is a bit obscured in English translations. In the New International Version we read:

> *If you love those who love you, what* <u>*credit*</u> *is that to you? Even sinners love those who love them. And if you do good to those who are good to you, what* <u>*credit*</u> *is that to you? Even sinners do that. And if you lend to those from whom you expect repayment, what* <u>*credit*</u> *is that to you? Even sinners lend to sinners, expecting to be repaid in full. But love your enemies, do good to them, and lend to them without expecting to get anything back. Then your reward will be great, and you will be children of the Most High, because he*

> is kind to the <u>ungrateful</u> and wicked. Be merciful, just as
> your Father is merciful. (Luke 6:32–36)

As German Catholic theologian Gerhard Lohfink points out,[147] the translation of "credit" is not very helpful. Other English versions use reward, thanks, praise, benefit and blessing, which perhaps are no better given that the Greek word, *charis*, has the primary meaning of loveliness, agreeableness ... even charm or beauty. The majority of times *charis* is used in the New Testament it is translated as "grace."

I have nowhere near a level of understanding of Greek to question what the majority of translators have done in Luke 6. Nevertheless, with Lohfink, I like the idea of inserting grace into these verses. It appears in four places (underlined in my quotation above)—three times in the positive, and once as the negative *acharistous*. What that reveals is something more like this:

> *If you love only within tribal or family boundaries, where is the grace in that? If you only do good to people who do good to you, where is the grace in that? If you only loan money when you're sure you'll get it back, where is the grace in that? But if you love and do good and lend to anyone—even your enemies—wow, that is a beautiful thing! That kind of charming, lovely grace is reward in itself. Those acts would show who your God really is! The God I know is kind even to those with no grace! (Matthew Clarke Revised Version)*

As the scattering church spreads the yeast of that kingdom throughout the world, joining Jesus in the goal of

giving life in all its potential fullness (John 10:10), we practice generosity and grace to ourselves, to others around us
who share the same faith, and to those around us who are
indifferent or opposed to that faith.

THE PRODIGALITY OF GOD

Tim Keller, who would probably disagree with much of my
thinking, wrote an extraordinary commentary on the so-
called parable of the prodigal son in his book, "The Prodigal God."[148] He notes that the word "prodigal" can mean
wayward in the way we normally think of the youngest son
in that parable, but the English word also means extrava-
gantly generous. Jesus' story does not actually focus on the
former meaning but on the latter.

Some versions of the Bible call this the "Story about two
sons"[149] because the eldest son seems as lost as the younger
one, and at least one uses the heading "The Story of the
Loving Father."[150] That's a better title in my mind because
it highlights the central point Jesus is making about the
nature of God. Jesus' most common term for God is "Father" and this parable demonstrates what he means by that
word.

The kingdom of God that Jesus invites us into is one
where the "king" is a father who willingly hands over the
inheritance to impetuous children and watches down the
road every day in the hope that one day they may return.
In this kingdom, the "king" casts good seed willy-nilly and
doesn't even bother to weed the garden. This "king" hangs
out with "lepers and sinners," sends rain and sunshine for
all people, including those who would consider themselves

to be enemies of God, and loves us enough to live with us and die for us. This is a profligate God, an extravagant giver who is ludicrously patient, forgiving, and gracious. This prodigal God is generous to the point of scandal and invites us into the abundance of life.

MEANWHILE, BACK AT THE COFFEE CART ...

Generosity and grace can be extremely challenging for the one who offers them. We may wonder whether we can afford to give so much away. We may feel it enables others to take advantage of us. We may struggle with the thought that those people really don't deserve what we are giving them.

On the other side of the coin, generosity and grace can also be extremely challenging for the *recipient*.

One of Annabella's favorite experiences at her coffee cart is giving away free coffees. She has a sign that says "No cash? No worries: Pay next time you come or pay it forward somewhere else and spread the kindness." You might be surprised to know how hard it is to convince someone to take a free cup of coffee!

We tried something similar on an outing with our iconvo discussion group. One summer evening, eight or ten of us caught a ferry across Sydney Harbour and then a bus to Balmoral Beach. The aim, apart from enjoying each other's company, was to observe the life of Sydney around us, to think about the difference between public life and private life and reflect on how that difference affects our faith. Teams of two or three people were each given a set of missions, like recording how many times they heard people say "thanks" or "thank you," or watching a random person for a while and then inventing a back-story for them.

Every team was given $20 and one of their missions was to give it to someone they met during the evening. For most, that turned out to be the hardest mission. I took the easy approach—when we went into a shop to buy fish and chips for our dinner, I gave the money to the cashier and said, "You guys are doing a great job tonight. I'd like you to have this extra money." That raised quizzical looks, but in the crowded café the moment quickly passed. Another team took the riskier route of walking up to a group on the beach and simply asking them to take the money. The group was immediately suspicious and refused to take it. They did, however, engage in conversation for a while. They said *they* didn't need the money and that we should find someone *really* poor and give it to them instead.

Why do most people find it difficult to accept money or help? Why is self-sufficiency and independence so valued?

One of the times I have been most blessed was when Mike, my business partner in an IT startup venture, sent me $1,000 during a time of major personal crisis for me. I was in Sydney and Mike was in Minneapolis so there wasn't much of a practical nature he could do to help or comfort me. When the $1,000 landed in my bank account I was surprised, and deeply touched by his thoughtful generosity. It wasn't that I needed the money, though it was helpful. What really encouraged me was Mike's generosity of spirit. The money was a sign of his solidarity with me, his heart-felt presence with me in spite of his physical absence. That brought a glint of grace into my darkness.

At the coffee cart, Annabella often has time to establish a relationship with the customers and has tried various approaches to explain the free coffee offer. Often it happens because Annabella only takes cash and some customers only have plastic cards. Annabella explains that she is more than happy if someone enjoys her coffee and she never gets paid for it. She encourages them to accept the gift. If they like the idea, perhaps they can pay for someone else's coffee at a different café another day just to pass the joy around.

Some people get it, and go away with not only a coffee, but with a smile and a story about this crazy lady who gives away free coffee to tell their friends. Others go off to find a money machine or dig around in their car for loose change so they can come back as soon as possible and clear the debt. Annabella explains that there is no debt, but many people cannot grasp that concept.

Sometimes customers give Annabella an extra $5 and she uses it to bless another customer later in the day. She tells that customer someone else has already paid for the coffee and she refuses to take their money. They often say, "That's a lovely idea. I'd like to do that too: please take my $5 and pay for someone else," in effect paying for their coffee anyway. But then Annabella says, "No, that's not how it works. The previous customer really wanted to bless you. If you want to bless someone another day, or at another café, that is fine. But today I want you just receive the gift."

That brings some customers to tears as they recognize the blessing for what it is: an affirmation of shared humanity.

On the other hand, it completely bamboozles other customers. Phil in particular says, "It can't work that way! How can you run a business like that?" Now Annabella makes good money from coffee sales, but she's not there for the money. She's there to build community. Phil is probably annoyed because everything in his past experience has reinforced the idea that relationships are based on transactions, and on the moral duty of keeping the accounts even. Annabella explains to him that money is less important than human flourishing. He says, "That's just not how the world works!" to which Annabella replies, "But it doesn't have to be like that." Phil shakes his head ... but he has become a regular customer and perhaps over time he is starting to understand.

Still others actually get angry at the whole concept. One day two middle-aged folks came in—first timers to the coffee cart. It turns out they were brother and sister, visiting their elderly mother for the day. They only had plastic cards and so Annabella started making the coffee for them while explaining that she can't do electronic transactions but that they can have the two coffees for free. They say no, that's no good because they don't live in the area and won't be able to return to pay her back later. Annabella reiterates what "free" means and says a bit more about the heartbeat of community and generosity we hope to foster. The brother seemed to understand, but the sister went off to find an ATM. When she returned with cash, Annabella said she wouldn't take it! The coffees are made and there is a stand-off. "Here's my money." "Yes, but these are for free." She moves from confusion to annoyance and agitation to anger. Her brother says to her, "Look, you are always doing things for other people, why not accept something from someone else?" She counters "That's not what happens in my world. No one is ever concerned about me, people don't just *give* me things!" It seemed to Annabella that this lady could not accept a gift because it would undermine her internal victim story. Nevertheless, the brother convinced her, and they left with two free coffees. We wondered, prayerfully, about what direction their conversation took in the car as they drove off to their mother's house.

That's the disruption of grace. It seems unfair. Grace *should* be outrageous and confusing, precisely because it *is* unfair. Grace is not only personally challenging, it is also risky and sociologically subversive. It subverts the culture of transaction and obligation and offers in its place a kingdom economy based on gifts.

[12]

CREATIVELY SUBVERSIVE

A NON-INSTITUTIONAL CHURCH THAT consciously forsakes control in order to build a kingdom that enables human flourishing will need to be creatively and continually subversive. Against the backdrop of a church that has been sleeping with the "principalities and power" of the world for centuries, this may come as a surprise, but the Bible, and in particular the gospel of Christ, has always been subversive.

By "subversive" I mean acting with the intention of undermining an established system.[151] This can be explained best by some examples.

THE BIBLE IS SUBVERSIVE

In Chapter 7 I discussed the New Testament metaphor about new wine and old wineskins (Matthew 9:14–17, Mark 2:18–22, Luke 5:33–39). This is a subversive metaphor in that it questions the ongoing value of the existing social and religious structures of the day. It does not directly confront those structures nor deny that they have value, but it undermines them by noting that they are not suited for what God is now doing in the work of Jesus. Matthew, Mark, and Luke all locate this metaphor in the context of Jesus' comments about religious fasting. But this is just one of many contexts in which Jesus re-directs his audience's thinking in a way that inevitably undermines their acceptance of the old system.

Jesus' suite of six, "You have heard it said ... but I tell you ..." sayings in Matthew 5 is another example of the same. While he does not directly confront the Old Testament Laws (in fact he prefaces the whole discussion with an explicit affirmation of the Law), he undermines the way those Laws have been practiced by asserting a more important set of ethical principles.

Jesus' actions often disrupt social conventions in ways that subvert the cultural presuppositions that conflict with his good news of the kingdom of God. For example, he hangs out with lepers, allows "sinners" and the "unclean" to touch him, pardons a women whom the Law says should have been stoned, speaks with women alone, allows a woman to sit at his feet as a student, questions many common economic expectations,[152] and presents a Samaritan as a hero. Through behaviors like those, Jesus implicitly questioned the value of established practices and moral norms and undermined their authority.

Numerous cases show that Jesus preferred a strategy of subversion over direct confrontation. His silence before Pilate is a perfect example. Another is his attitude to paying taxes. In Matthew 17:24–27 Jesus arranges for Peter to pay the so-called Temple Tax and yet subverts the practice by claiming that as a son of the Temple he is actually exempt from the tax. Another time, when asked about paying Roman taxes, Jesus affirmed Caesar's authority to impose taxes but placed a limit on it (Matthew 22:15–22, Mark 12:13–17, Luke 20:20–26). That attitude to Rome, coupled with frequent claims to be establishing a new kingdom, gave credence to the accusation that Jesus was opposed to Caesar (Luke 23:1–2, John 19:12).

I wrote earlier about the brief parable of yeast in Matthew 13:31–33 and Luke 13:18–21, but there is one more aspect of that parable that highlights the subversive nature of Jesus' story-telling. As Robin Meyers explains,[153] here we see Jesus using a women engaged in home duties as a symbol of the sacred activity of God. How well would that have gone down in the first-century patriarchal culture? Furthermore, in virtually every other reference to yeast in the Bible, it is a metaphor for moral corruption. For instance, Luke relates yeast to hypocrisy (12:1) and Paul compares it to malice and wickedness (1 Corinthians 5:6–8). The word would have been a red flag to Jesus' original audience, a signal that this yeast is going to disrupt everything. But Jesus turns that image upside down and teasingly affirms that the flour of the old is going to be "corrupted" by the yeast of the kingdom.

Of course, there are other cases where Jesus *directly* challenges the establishment, especially the religious establishment. Repeatedly calling the Pharisees a "brood of vipers" (Matthew 3:7, 12:34, 23:33) and the sevenfold "Woe to you, teachers of the law and Pharisees, you hypocrites!" (Matthew 23) are clear examples of Jesus taking the role of prophet to declare the word of God to corrupt leaders in power.

The subversive character of God's interaction with the world is not limited to the Gospels. The same flavor can be seen in the descriptions of early church growth in Acts (e.g. Stephen's speech before being stoned in Acts 7), in the Epistles (e.g. the metaphoric characterization of Rome as Babylon in 1 Peter 5:13), and quite dominantly in Revelation in which the collapse of the prevailing powers is replaced by a new Jerusalem.

The Old Testament is just as counter-cultural and subversive, though we often miss those aspects because we aren't familiar with the social contexts in which the old texts were written. In a world where child sacrifice was common, Moses heard God forbid the practice (Leviticus 20:1–5, Deuteronomy 18:10). When virtually all ancient literature affirmed the common human practice of blaming the victims for the calamities that befell them, the Bible repeatedly affirms the innocence of victims.[154] In a world where political regimes force their power onto the masses, the Old Testament describes numerous examples of prophets who undermined that power through word and demonstration.

THE CHURCH AT ITS BEST IS SUBVERSIVE

The early church continued this subversive strategy of Jesus. In traditional church settings I have often heard how the early church refused to pray to the Roman gods and were martyred for not affirming the divinity of Caesar. I have less often heard that in early church home groups masters, slaves, men, and women treated each other as equals; that in the first couple of centuries Christians were known for rescuing abandoned babies;[155] or that many early Christians refused to join armies.[156] All these acts are politically and culturally subversive.

There have been many times through subsequent history that the church has stood up against the dominant culture. Speaking insistently and acting prophetically in the light of unhealthy "powers and principalities," the church has brought about positive change. Of course, that has to be honestly balanced against times when the church fostered incredibly unjust and ungodly social change, times when the church has been co-opted by the ruling powers, and times when we have been reprehensibly silent.[157]

Even though the Roman Empire co-opted the church into its military machinery, and even though the Pope turned the church into an army during the Crusades of the 11th–13th centuries, and even though the church has been complicit in numerous acts of international aggression since then, there have always been pockets of Christians who maintained the reconciling, peacemaking tradition of the early followers of Jesus. Though in the minority, they have confronted and undermined the dominant political discourse by prophetically proclaiming that this is not the way of the Kingdom envisaged by Jesus. They have verbally called for a change of attitude, and on occasion engaged in planned acts of non-violent protest, but more importantly they have demonstrated a viable alternative. The Anabaptist tradition has generated many examples of this, but there are many others, including the Catholic Worker Movement, L-Arche International, the Corrymeela Community in Ireland, and the National Initiative for Reconciliation in South Africa prior to the ending of Apartheid.

The church at its best can, and does, lobby for social and political change, especially on issues of justice. Like many voices from the margins, they are typically ignored or suppressed by the established political and religious powers.

Some of this subversion may be achieved through the traditional gathering church.[158] But recovering the subversive nature of the church is very difficult when that model has been so overwhelmingly co-opted by the dominant social regime. This type of subversion is not a natural fit to the gathering church paradigm. Although some progress may be made by tacking a subversive element onto the old structure, I believe a more fundamental change—a paradigm shift—is required.

THE ROMANS 13 OBJECTION

Something needs to be said about the inevitable objection that "Paul clearly instructs us in Romans 13 to submit to legitimate earthly authorities, not subvert them." But in the end, this is a fairly shallow objection and not a lot needs to be said.

It is true that Paul writes, "Everyone must submit to the governing authorities, for there is no authority except that which God has established" (Romans 13:1) and Peter writes similarly in 1 Peter 2:13–25. I think it is clear that both writers promote an attitude of respect, co-operation, humility—a combination usually translated as "submission"—and that applies not only to the ruling authorities but to bosses, spouses, and to each other. The goal is to live as free people (1 Peter 2:16), while using that freedom in ways that respect everyone (v. 17) and work with legitimate authorities to promote the common good.

Both writers also make it abundantly clear that this posture towards earthly rulers is not a dogmatic rule. Their words *assume* that the rulers "punish those who do wrong and commend those who do right" (1 Peter 2:14, and similar in Romans 13:3–4). Legitimate authority enables justice, cares for those in need, and creates a stable society in which all people can flourish. Such rulers "hold no terror for those who do right" (Romans 13:3).

But what should we do when those assumptions are not true?

Both writers demonstrate what to do when earthly rulers do not follow the pattern of justice and misuse their authority. Peter opposes the rulers of his community and is thrown into jail in Acts 4 and again in Acts 5 and again in Acts 12.

Paul's opposition to ruling authorities resulted in him being beaten and imprisoned in Philippi (Acts 16:16–40). He caused riots in Thessalonica (Acts 17:1–9) and Ephesus (Acts 19). He was in conflict with the governor of Damascus and would have been arrested had he not slipped out a window (2 Corinthians 11:32–33). He stirred up so much trouble for the authorities in Jerusalem that they imprisoned him and later sent him to Rome for judgement (Acts 21–26).

Are we to conclude that neither Peter nor Paul followed their own rule about obeying the authorities? By no means! Their actions to confront and subvert the errors of the ruling authorities is totally consistent with their attitude of respect, co-operation, and humility. When earthly authorities are due respect and honor then we should give them respect and honor (Romans 13:7). But where an earthly ruler does not support justice or care for those in need, they do not in fact deserve respect or honor, and our proper response is like Peter's to the Sanhedrin and the Jewish High Priest: "We must obey God rather than human beings!" (Acts 5:27–29).

Furthermore, the most loyal supporter of any authority is not one who slavishly does what they are told. Loyal support sometimes requires disagreement and confrontation, like the example of the prophet Nathan with King David (2 Samuel 12). Even when we support an authority, an institution, a leader or a government, we can—and should—also challenge, disrupt and undermine any actions or policies that do not conform to properly understood principles of love and justice.

Peter and Paul both lived and preached subversively, and their instructions in Romans 13 and 1 Peter 2 in no way contradict the church's mandate to continue that subversion of human power structures.

TRANSFORMANCE ART

In the previous section I emphasized the subversive stance the scattering church takes towards the prevailing political and cultural structures. But our subversive stance also disrupts personal attitudes as well. We all display dominant, habitual, and often unconscious patterns of thinking that are called into question by the Gospel. Our personal biases, stereotypes, and unquestioned assumptions can all block the yeast of the Gospel from leavening our lives. Rather than reinforce what we already believe, as most gathering churches do, an important role of the scattering church is to question, challenge, and disrupt those habitual thought patterns.

Peter Rollins has developed a variety of subversive techniques that purposely disrupt and decenter the participants' thinking to get them to honestly confront themselves and each other, and through that be released from the idols of certainty and satisfaction. One such technique involves the curation of an immersive theatrical event, a space in which participants engage with a challenging idea through multiple senses. There is likely to be music, drama, food, and discussion. There is likely to be ambiguity, confusion, and discovery. There is likely to be more questions than answers. In some ways, the event is like a piece of performance art. The audience is always part of the performance, not merely spectators and the goal is transformation rather than entertainment. Rollins calls this "transformance art."

I have previously mentioned The Escape Goats, an informal group hosted by Annabella and myself that attempts to nourish people who have become disillusioned with church, faith, and God. Most of our events are private discussions around a meal, but we have attempted one public event in the style of Rollins' transformance art.

The venue was The Commons (see Chapter 9), and the core of the event was a dramatised reading of Ursula Le Guin's short story, *The Ones Who Walk Away from Omelas.*[159] Upon arriving, the attendees were greeted with some live violin and guitar music, food to nibble as people socialized, and relaxed evening lighting with a spotlight on a single comfortable armchair.

Dressed formally as the Master of Ceremonies, I welcomed people with an introduction that went something like this:

> *Our desire is to create spaces and relationships in which it is safe to voice doubt, uncertainty, loss, and confusion. Many of us here tonight have been hurt, betrayed, abused, and abandoned—by God just as much as by other people—and we find very few contexts to rest in the shared existential disappointment. Sometimes we need to find a desert in the oasis of bright lights and the glamour of modern life.*
>
> *On the other hand, however much we feel that life and faith are problematic, there are times like this with good food and wine and stories to share, when we glimpse something better; something more substantial and more nourishing.*
>
> *I would also like to acknowledge the traditional custodians of the land on which we meet today and pay my respects to the Elders, past and present[160].*
>
> *Tonight, we hope you are both nourished and disrupted. The disruption is core to any transformance art, so I don't apologies for that. Transformance art invites the audience to participate: to watch and listen, and to also ponder and discuss.*

> *So tonight, you will need your imagination and your hon-*
> *esty as we listen to a story written in 1973 by Ursula Le*
> *Guin. And I wish it was needless to say ... you will need re-*
> *spect for the imagination and honesty of the others around*
> *you.*
>
> *After the story, there will be an opportunity to share our*
> *responses. So please take another drink, find a seat and get*
> *comfortable. The story is about to begin.*

A young man entered and I handed him a large story-book. He sits in the armchair, opens the book and starts to read, much like an uncle reading a bedtime story to some children. The familiar bedtime reading context and the warm décor belied the disruptive ideas in Le Guin's story.

The story describes the idyllic city of Omelas, reminis-cent of a fairytale, a bright happy place at the commence-ment of their summer festival. But beneath the surface there is an ugly truth: one that everyone knows but chooses to ignore. We are assured that all the gaiety and prosperity of the city depends on this dark truth.

During the story, the reader became more animated and expressive. He crossed the room to a darkened corner where a closed door hides us from the ugly truth. He opened it to peer inside, then shut it firmly again.

After the reading, I facilitated a conversation in a World Café style through which everyone can contribute their re-actions and reflections. World Café is a wonderful ap-proach that enables a broad, evolving conversation in which everyone can participate, even when the group is large.

I seeded three rounds of discussion with suggestions designed to unpack the story's many layers without prescribing any specific questions that needed to be answered. I noted that on the surface the story is about the social ideal of utopia and what a society was willing to allow to happen in order to achieve the greatest happiness for the greatest number of people: an issue that is surely relevant to our Australian society. The story can also be read with Freud and Jung in mind, and perhaps asks what each of us personally repress in order to be happy. Thirdly, there is a decidedly religious aspect to the story. Must somebody else suffer for our salvation?

In each of those layers, Le Guin's story questions the status quo by revealing the repressed truth about the cost of maintaining that status quo, and that includes an important challenge to the shadow-side of Christianity.

There were about 30 people at the event and the discussion was as vibrant as we had hoped. Some joined us a week later to further reflect on the story and its personal impact. The event also created some new connections between the participants and opened the way for future relationships.

CREATIVE

To some, subversion may sound too negative an idea, one that only criticizes and destroys. But in giving this chapter the title "Creatively Subversive," I intended to convey something more positive.

In many ways the society in which we find ourselves is just as broken as the one Jesus occupied in the first century. To effectively bring God's light into our world, we need to be as creative, as innovative, as Jesus was. Like Jesus, we too live incarnationally, that is, we embody God's presence in the world. That includes highlighting the brokenness and demonstrating an alternative.

By "highlighting the brokenness," I do not mean that we stand in judgement of the world as though we are above all of that and are somehow superior to it. The subversion I mean comes through embracing the brokenness of life, recognizing the ways we are enmeshed in it, and yet channeling God's light to reveal the potential of everyone flourishing in the midst of that brokenness.

To achieve this, we will need to subvert the dominant view of relationships as power-based and transactional. We will need to re-assert that the basis for a person's value rests on the foundation of being God's image-bearer rather than being economically productive. We will need to show the value of community over individualism. We will need to challenge the shallowness of digitally-mediated interactions and re-establish the importance of face-to-face communication. We will need to question the neo-liberal economic vision of global progress.[161] We will need to subvert humanity's exploitative relationship to the planet earth. We will need to help people rethink justice, identity, forgiveness, human rights, responsibilities, respect, sin, blame, sacrifice, salvation, and a hundred other social constructs.

We will need to consistently ask what love looks like in every situation.

There is a lot to subvert!

Our subversion is creative in both intent and expression. Subversion acts creatively rather than critically and destructively. The aim is not simply to disrupt, but to give life and hope through that disruption. Through subverting the existing paradigms, the intent is to generate new thinking that enables all to flourish. I am sure some readers will claim that these are liberal, progressive, politically left concerns that lie outside the "proper" goal of evangelism, but against that I assert that these are all missional imperatives because they all impact how effectively Jesus' vision for a new kingdom can be realized.

Our practical approach to this subversion also needs to be expressed creatively if it is to be effective. Saying and doing the same old thing is unlikely to inspire the world to join us! The vision of the kingdom is ancient, but its implementation and its "sales pitch"—the way we formulate the invitation to join us—is dynamic. God is always doing something new, hence the way kingdom values are expressed, indeed the entire way the presence of God is incarnated, will depend on the people and the culture in which it is expressed.

The extent that the church simply mimics its surrounding culture is the extent to which it is irrelevant and useless. Subversion should use all the creativity God has given us to stand out as radically different through creating safe spaces, warm relationships, challenging discussions, and generous, caring and inclusive communities that enthuse people about the Good News of the kingdom.

CONTINUAL

This task of creative subversion will never end. The reason is not because the system we oppose is so massive and entrenched we will never be able to dismantle it. No, it is a never-ending task because every new thing that comes out of the process will itself need to be subverted!

We have seen that process throughout history: it is embedded in the dialectic nature of social and religious progress. Every advance will encounter its own internal limitations, causing the need for a new alternative in opposition to the previous position. Out of the conflict between those two positions a synthesis arises that improves on them both. But eventually this new synthesis encounters limitations that result in a new opposing idea and the need for a new synthesis, and so on.

I do not expect that the scattering church will create utopia. Whatever it creates will need to be tested, critiqued, challenged, and further improved, even if that means throwing away some of the good results so that God can pollinate something even better.

God continually produces new wine that requires new wineskins. There are plenty of examples of this continual subversion in the Bible, and in a sense this process is a distinguishing feature of the Christian story. Many ideas, common and accepted, and even given divine authority in one period of Biblical history are later subverted and replaced with a step forward in God's revelation to us.

For instance, consider the trajectory of sacrifice in the Bible. In early civilizations the processes of scapegoating and human sacrifice to appease the gods were common. The early books of the Bible struggle to differentiate the Hebrew God from these other sacrifice-demanding gods. Some passages depict a vengeful, jealous God who demands human sacrifice, but in other passages human sacrifice is forbidden. God seems to subvert the very ritual that God was understood to have instituted. God tells Abraham to kill Isaac, but an angel provides a ram instead. Later, the prophets claim that God doesn't want blood sacrifices at all! What God has really wanted all along is that we act justly, love mercy, and walk humbly (Micah 6:8). God inhabits the Tabernacle and then the Temple, but later we learn that God cannot be contained by such structures and that everyone will know God because of God's presence within them. God doesn't want blood sacrifices, but then allows Jesus to be killed as an innocent victim on behalf of others. We learn that there is a difference between Jesus' self-giving personal sacrifice and the forced sacrifice of someone killing another. Later still, we are told that there is a sacrifice that God wants from us—the willing sacrifice of our own living bodies and minds (Romans 12:1–2).

My point is that the Bible often does not present just a single position on key theological concepts, but an unfolding revelation. We have not received the full and final story from God, and I do not believe we ever will. Every step forward with God becomes a step in our past that positions us for the next step forward. That's true for us as individual followers of Jesus, and for the church as a whole. Consequently, there is no sacred, unassailable, "right" way to do things that stands beyond question. It is not that we subvert "the world" just once, replace it with a better institution and then the job is done.

Peter Rollins makes a similar point regarding identity. Rather than seeking to define a collective self-image—what he calls a tribal identity—to demarcate who's in and who's out, Rollins proposes that the central challenge of Christianity is to continually undermine *any* attempt to define tribal identities. In the Crucifixion we see the subversion and abandonment of all identity so there is no longer Jew nor Gentile, slave nor free, male nor female. This subversion needs to be applied to the personal and collective "Christian" identity as well.[162]

Following Jesus may well lead us to subvert the established notions of "church" and "Christian." Such notions, even if themselves established by the Gospel, need to be challenged by the same Gospel, especially when they become terms that separate and exclude.

One major reason why the scattering church needs to be continually subversive is that, unless it does so, it will soon become re-institutionalized. This, I think, is the biggest danger faced by the whole of the so-called "emerging church movement." The scattering church does not seek to replace one institutional form with another, but resist the urge to centralize power in any institution.

The scattering church can be re-institutionalized or re-normalized through its differentiating features being co-opted by existing institutional churches who hope they can patch the subversive ideas onto their existing fabric without any changes in their foundational gathering ideal. It can also happen when a new idea becomes established enough to gain respectability. Then through normal human socialization processes, it becomes regulated, controlled, and institutionalized.

We live subversively because we belong to the kingdom of heaven rather than to any earthly kingdom. In declaring our primary allegiance to Jesus, we inevitably place ourselves in a position that is incompatible with many of the values and priorities of whatever culture we find ourselves. That includes the "Christian" culture of English-speaking Western nations.

[13]

FREE TO IMPROVISE

WAY BACK NEAR THE BEGINNING of this book I drew attention to the metaphor of wind in Jesus' discussion with Nicodemus. In the middle of that discussion, Jesus says, "The wind blows wherever it pleases. You hear its sound, but you cannot tell where it comes from or where it is going. So it is with everyone born of the Spirit" (John 3:8).

I noted that in both Greek and Hebrew, the word for wind also means breath and spirit.

Jesus reasonably assumed Nicodemus had experienced the physical wind so via the metaphoric calculus he reminds Nicodemus that God is also dynamic and untamed. Because of this, the Spirit of God cannot be contained within the rigid script of pharisaical rules that Nicodemus brought into the discussion. Through the metaphor, he asks Nicodemus to ponder what it means to be born of the wind, to be blown by the breath of God.

Untamed freedom is so central to the message of the Gospel and to Paul's theology, that even the conservative evangelical theologian F. F. Bruce titled one of his books, *Paul: Apostle of the Free Spirit.*

"Where the Spirit of the Lord is, there is freedom" (2 Corinthians 3:17). We have been freed from dietary rules (Romans 14:14,20; 1 Corinthians 10:25–26), freed from the Law of Moses (Romans 7:6), freed from sin (Romans 6:22), freed to truly live (2 Corinthians 3:6), freed to love (Galatians 5:13–14,), freed to be free! (Galatians 5:1).

The new life is like a seed that a farmer throws up in the air on a windy day. The farmer doesn't know where the wind comes from—in fact has no control over the wind at all. The seeds are blown to God-knows-where. This is like the life of one born of the Spirit. We are not restricted to one rigid tradition that dictates the only way things can be done, but we are thrown in the air and blown by the wind/spirit/breath of God.

THEO-DRAMA

The history depicted in the Bible is a dynamic progression of interactions between humanity and God, more like a conversation than a lecture. Hans Urs von Balthasar (1905–1988) called it the "theo-drama."

Balthasar was a Swiss, Catholic theologian, a friend of Karl Barth, and a Jesuit for the middle 30 years of his life.[163] Starting in 1973, he published a massive five-volume work that "shows how many of the trends of modern theology ... point to an understanding of human and cosmic reality as a divine drama."[164] Balthasar views the interactions between God and humanity as an unfolding drama with God as the author, Jesus as the chief actor, and the Spirit as director. The creativity of those three contributors is expressed in a theatre (the world) through a performance (history) that involves all of humanity in the cast.

Balthasar views history as Christo-centric, with a script driven from above at God's initiative, and yet the unfolding drama is enacted from below.[165] That is, God initiated the drama but did not control or impose from above. Instead, God joined with us, through the incarnation, to put into action the divine script. That could only happen through the "kenotic descent" described by Paul in Philippians 2. Kenosis, that is the self-emptying of Jesus, is a central concept in Balthasar's writings as he follows Jesus' descent not only from the infinite to the finite, but from human life to the depths of hell.[166] For Balthasar, this process of self-emptying is a fundamental quality of God.[167]

That's a very different picture of the interplay between God and humanity than we often hear from the traditional church. How many people have suffered under the "umbrella of power" through which God supposedly tells senior church leaders what to do, who then tell their congregations what God supposedly requires? Rather than acting as a director-dictator, God forgoes the right to top-down control in order to participate in the evolving drama from below.

The self-giving descent of God results in an elevation of corrupted humanity. Balthasar notes that a central feature of Jesus' mission is this "wondrous exchange"[168] that occurs between God and humanity through the incarnation. This echoes the radical statement by Athanasius—the Bishop of Alexandria in the 4th century—that "He was incarnate that we might be made god,"[169] that is, so that the divine image in us might be restored.

A dramatic interpretation of history leads to an important shift in the way we might answer the question, "Who am I?" Both Athanasius in the 4th century and Balthasar in the 20th emphasized that being the Word of God is not an arbitrary role that Jesus assumed while embodied here on earth. On the contrary, we understand the intent of the incarnation by recognizing that its core, its essence, is the nature of the Word's *mission*.

This shift in thinking, from viewing Jesus' identity in terms of a *role* he played to viewing it in terms of *mission*, also applies to the rest of humanity. Our essence does not depend on some arbitrary role we might play but on our mission. The dramatic tension established in the Bible does not end with the final verse of Revelation because the story continues. "The man who is a serious co-actor with God ... contribute[s] to the unfolding of this dramatic tension."[170] That is to say, we share with Jesus not only something of the same divine image, but also the same continuing mission to redeem the world and to make the Father known.

Sorry for the technical mumbo-jumbo. The key points to note for our purposes are that...

- There is a theologically solid understanding of the Bible that views history as an unfolding drama, initiated by God, in which we are all players.

- Jesus' identity and all our human identities spring from God's mission to redeem the world.
- An essential component of the drama is the self-emptying character of God demonstrated by the life and death of Jesus.

I suppose someone may object that this dramatical perspective treats life too lightly, as though we are merely acting rather than taking things seriously. That is certainly not Balthasar's or my intention. Theo-drama in no way suggests we are "just performing" or acting out a false persona for entertainment. No, what's intended is to view drama as a useful metaphor, so that via the metaphoric calculus we can better understand the dynamic nature of mission. As with every metaphor, not everything about drama can be applied to mission. In particular, the idea of an actor filling the role of some character who is not their real self is not relevant. As Balthasar notes, it is not some role we play that defines us, but the authentic enactment of our mission. We *are* our acted character, and that character evolves over time as the missional plot unfolds.

IMPROVISATION

A fairly obvious question arises once you start thinking about life and mission as a theo-drama. That's the question of what sort of drama it is? A comedy? Tragedy? Farce?

One way of thinking about theo-drama—perhaps the normal approach for a centralized, institutional church— is that to be faithful followers of Jesus we must meticulously adhere to God's script. Any deviation is sin, rebellion, and unfaithfulness.

On the other hand, several contemporary theologians have suggested that the theo-drama is improvisational. One such writer is Kevin Vanhoozer, who agrees with Balthasar that "The Christian life is fundamentally *dramatic*, involving speech and action on behalf of Jesus' truth and life. It concerns the way of living truthfully, and its claims to truth cannot be isolated from the way of life with which it is associated."[171] That's true for each of us individually, but also for the followers of Jesus collectively: "The church is a company of players gathered together to stage scenes of the kingdom of God for the sake of a watching world."[172]

Rather than conceiving of church as a setting in which a fixed script is performed repeatedly, Vanhoozer writes that "to be faithful in its witness, the church must constantly be different. Indeed, at times it must even *improvise.*"[173]

I am fascinated by the idea of improvisation in both music and drama, though it is an area in which I have no skills whatsoever! But I am even more fascinated by how an improvisational approach could help us understand life, church, and mission. The seeds of that idea go way back to my childhood on a farm. My father was a master at working with whatever resources were available. Farmers say that if something can't be fixed with fencing wire and baling twine then it can't be fixed! That's improvisation at its finest.

We have always known—haven't we?—that there is no set script for us to follow in life. Each life is unique; none is a repeat performance of a previous life or of some ideal life scripted by God. Too many plot twists are thrust upon us for that. I was made most aware of that when I became a parent. We cannot learn how to be a parent without being one! No book or advice from other parents can prepare us for what we experience with our own children. There is no correct parenting script, we each have to make it up as we go. In parenting, and indeed in the whole of life, we have to improvise.

That does not mean that as a parent, or as a follower of Jesus, we live without boundaries or guidance. Improvisation does not mean the players can do anything at all. One only has to think of jazz improvisation to see that there are boundaries, guiding principles, and a structure within which improvisation takes place. Jazz improv requires a musical theme, a chord sequence, and a rhythm that are all agreed to by the whole band. It requires practice and coordination between the musicians.

Improv acting works in the same way. The players are constrained by a theme and a setting but collaborate creatively within those boundaries. Each performance will vary, sometimes even to the surprise of the actors, but the essence remains because it arises out of a shared vision of the drama's purpose.

Some short-form improv is staged competitively, with the theme and setting only revealed shortly before the curtain rises. Even in that context, the best improv teams can negotiate roles in real time as the play unfolds because they know each other well, have a shared understanding of performance dynamics, and have practiced together previously.

When it comes to relating this to the church and to mission, I am more interested in long-form dramatic improv where a director communicates a clear purpose to the actors and the same play is staged multiple times. For instance, someone might design a series of improv performances to raise awareness of domestic violence. The actors will understand the intended message (perhaps that psychological abuse is as damaging as physical abuse), and the possible roles (perhaps a husband, wife and a neighbor). They will en-role themselves and then act naturally according to those roles. Together with the director they may identify several phrases or events that act as anchors for the performance, then they will practice so that the flow between those key moments becomes natural.

In improv, the action progresses as the actors respond to each other, and in some cases respond to the audience's reactions. Improv theatre has a well-established set of techniques that provide structure and move the action forward. Of chief importance are the twin processes of offering and accepting.

Let's extend the domestic violence example a bit more to show how that works. Suppose that near the start of the play, a husband and wife enter their home. No-one knows where they have just come from, not even the actors. The audience doesn't even know who they are. The man says "Aaagh, I'm soaked! Why don't you ever remember to bring the umbrella?"

This is new information. As an improvised line, even the person acting as the wife did not know it previously. Technically, it is an "offer" to which the wife needs to respond.

She could of course say, "Don't be stupid, you've got the umbrella in your hand" or "What do you mean? It's not even raining." That would be termed "blocking"—a refusal to accept the offer—and would generally not be considered a good idea because it blocks the progress of the improv.

To advance the story, an offer must be accepted. The wife could say "Sorry"—and in the context of a domestic abuse story that simple response may say a whole lot about the way the two people relate to each other. She might not risk any further words, or she might say, "Well I tried to find it but you didn't leave it in the umbrella stand," which both accepts the "offer" and extends it. To that, the husband may reply loudly, "Don't you dare try to blame this on me!" and the foundation is quickly laid for an evolving relational conflict.

Isn't the interaction between God and humanity a similar series of offers, blocks and acceptances?

If the world is a stage on which we are actors, can you see how the idea of improv captures the way the theo-drama unfolds? The play's overall trajectory is set by God, but the details of how the performance progresses depend on the constant interplay between God's initiatives, our responses, and God's responses to our responses. With Jesus on stage with us, the whispers of the Spirit as director in our ears, and an ever-changing set around us, we interact creatively to carry the divine storyline through many conflicts towards an ultimate resolution.

We do not slavishly follow a static script, but build our character around our missional identity, and then, acting in character, we co-write the play with God.

Imagine a church whose basic mode of operation is formed around the idea of improv. I don't mean they run church services with an acting team doing improv plays instead of the sermon. I mean a church that sees its mission, it's engagement with the world, as an evolving play, directed by God but not dictated by God, responsive to the flow of offering and accepting with God, with other actors, and even with the audience.

Samuel Wells captures this improvisational approach to mission well:

> *The Bible is not so much a script that the church learns and performs as it is a training school that shapes the habits and practices of a community. This community learns to take the right things for granted, and on the basis of this faithfulness, it trusts itself to improvise within its tradition. Improvisation means a community formed in the right habits trusting itself to embody its traditions in new and often challenging circumstances; and this is exactly what the church is called to do.* [174]

A church like that would be agile and responsive, flexibly adapting its structure, its location, its leadership model and its rituals to the changing culture around it. Such a church would inevitably learn to listen more than to proclaim. We would listen to the whispers of the director. We would listen to each other on the stage, including to the voice of Jesus. We would listen to the audience to understand how our message is being received. We would probably come to realize that the distinction between actors on stage and the audience is misconceived and that everyone is actually part of the improv, for it is the history of the world that is on stage rather than just the church.

Such a church would also make mistakes. It would sometimes block God's offers. It would sometimes advance the storyline in ways that increase conflict rather than lead towards resolution. It would sometimes speak with multiple, conflicting voices and cause confusion rather than clarity. None of those risks differ from the mistakes the church has made repeatedly since Peter's improv offer to Jesus that he didn't really need to die—which Jesus blocked with the famous words, "Get behind me Satan!" (Matthew 16:22–23). That was only four verses after the church was summoned into being!

The difference between understanding mission as improvisational and understanding it as tightly scripted is not that either make more, or less mistakes, but that the former is not afraid of mistakes.

In many churches you believe what you are told to believe and do what you are told to do. There is one right way—God's way—and any deviation from the script is viewed as sinful. In churches like that, people risk censure if they rock the boat. People are discouraged from trying anything new, expressing their doubts, or questioning authority. People become motivated to do the right thing out of fear of the consequences if they do not. Failure is attributed to not following the script correctly, as though God's will dictates one specific path for each of us. These churches may admit that it is sometimes difficult to discover God's will, but once found there is no choice but to obey.

In the scattering church that embraces improvisation, however, people are encouraged to question and experiment. God gives us permission, in fact constantly forces us, to make our own decisions. God draws us forward with a vision of the abundant life that could be, and we can choose how to respond to that offer. There are many ways to live a God-inspired life, and the script of our lives is written as it occurs in a partnership between us and God. There will inevitably be conflicts, mistakes and failures along the way, but they are part of our dialog with God through which we learn and grow. As individuals and as a church, we seek to embody the character of Jesus so that over time, as we make our spiritual lives natural and our natural lives spiritual, we create a performance that aligns to our missional calling.

I was once asked, within a church of the first type, whether God was really in the driving seat in my life. At the time that was a helpful question that many of us pondered. Now I question the analogy and wonder what God makes of it. Is God really our chauffeur? I am more inclined to imagine Jesus in the passenger seat, turning to face me in the driver's seat and asking me excitedly, "So, where are we going today?"

OVERACCEPTING

Applying improvisation as a metaphor for the church's *modus operandi* becomes more powerful and subversive by considering the role of overaccepting.

Overaccepting is a third option for responding to an offer, apart from blocking and accepting. In improv theatre, to overaccept is to accept an offer not grudgingly but with a resounding "YES!"[175] Samuel Wells imports this idea into theo-drama by defining overaccepting as "accepting in the light of a larger story."[176] While accepting an offer may mean simply a resigned acknowledgement or reserved support, overaccepting enthusiastically embraces the offer and creatively weaves it into something greater.

In my example of an improv with a husband accusing his wife of forgetting the umbrella, my proposal of her responding with a timid "Sorry" is a begrudging acceptance. But suppose the third person in the scene, a neighbor, says, "You know, that's the third time you've blamed Sally for something this morning. I reckon there's something deeper going on—do you want to talk about it?" Such a response neither blocks nor accepts the husband's negativity. It uses the husband's comment to draw the conversation into something that could become transformative and redemptive.

The Bible is full of responses like this. Jesus turning water into wine at the wedding in Cana (John 2:1-11) is one example. In response to his mother's offer, "They have no more wine," Jesus initially blocks with "My time has not yet come." But his blocking words are reversed by the overacceptance of his actions. He does not simply accept the wine shortage but enthusiastically deals with the situation by miraculously supplying more wine, and of greater quality, than anyone could have expected. The event is marked in John's mind as the first public sign of Jesus' glory, and acts as a paradigmatic example of God's extravagant generosity.

God is a chronic overacceptor, taking every noble and evil offer thrown up by humanity, and weaving them into something good.[177] The scattering church follows that same path, always seeking to improvise in ways that creatively weave every offer into a larger story of restoration. Many examples of overaccepting could be drawn from church history, although there are equally many examples of blocking and grudging acceptance.

To choose one current and controversial issue, how might improvisation apply to our response to transsexual people? A small percentage of people have always felt uncomfortable with their birth sex, but for complex social and medical reasons there are now more options for such people to express themselves in the gender they feel most comfortable. Individuals with gender dysphoria, and the broader social possibilities of gender reassignment, throw an offer into the theo-drama. How should the church respond?

Blocking is always an option. We can say that the stance of transsexuals is wrong, sinful, counter to God's intention, and resist the social movement to permit gender reassignment.

Acceptance is also an option. We can acknowledge, even sympathize with the anguish of people with gender dysphoria, and resign ourselves to the need for society to do something about such people.

We can also try a middle road, which some Christians describe as "loving the sinner but hating the sin." This amounts to blocking the offer, since the transsexual stance is still labelled as sin, but with a resigned acceptance that the "problem" needs to be addressed with pastoral compassion.

There is not a lot of Biblical "script" to guide us on this issue. Perhaps the most relevant guidance about gender confusion comes from the treatment of eunuchs. In the face of the blocking stance of Deuteronomy 23:1, the witness of the New Testament is a radical overacceptance. In Acts 8, Philip, led by an angel (26) and the Spirit (29), welcomed a eunuch into Jesus' new community and passed on God's blessing to him through an impromptu baptism. The encounter is used within the Acts narrative to emphasize the larger story line from a Jewish-only portrayal of the Christian message towards an extension of that message to the whole world.[178] Philip overaccepts the offer of a challenging social situation in order to bless a social pariah; Luke overaccepts the event in recognition that it demonstrates the trajectory of God's plan to bless all people.

What would that pattern of overacceptance look like in the case of a transsexual in the 21st century?[179] First, we would view individual transsexuals, and the movement to validate transsexuals' social identity, as a gift rather than as a threat. In line with my comments in Chapter 9, about God speaking to us through the marginalized, we would seek to be evangelized by the good news transsexuals may bring to us. What might they teach about the way Jesus cares for the one over the 99, about the innocence of victims, about the foundations of personal identity, or about faithful integrity in adversity?

The scattering church proficient in improvisation could warmly embrace people who have bravely, and probably fearfully, changed their bodies to reflect who they truly are. Through overaccepting transsexuals, we celebrate God's power to transform.

MEANWHILE, BACK AT THE COFFEE CART ...

Annabella's coffee carts create many unusual situations in which improv is the only reasonable basis for operating.

The customers are as varied as Australian society: middle class office workers, tradies, police, transgender, gay, fire fighters, an elderly homeless indigenous man. One customer had just visited her partner in jail. Another didn't have any money but offered Annabella some marijuana in exchange for a coffee. In the flow of the day, Annabella often engages in accidental counselling with people who share significant challenges in their lives, like the lady who sat with us one Christmas in tears because it was the first Christmas since her husband had died. There are many whose names we might not know—though Annabella remembers what type of coffee they drink!—who have shared their life stories.

We also hear a rich assortment of conversations and opinions. From the weather, the latest reality TV show and the weekend football results to Australia's policy on asylum seekers, the impact of coffee waste on the environment, and whether the professionalization of the funeral industry ends up being impersonal, over-priced, and exploitative.

This is the modern life we all share and there could never be a pre-written script for responding to that wide range of people and topics. Neither the Bible nor church tradition has scripts we can re-perform in the context of a

missional coffee cart where a customer offers some marijuana as payment for a coffee!

Instead, Annabella constantly asks herself, "What
would love look like in this situation?" and improvises.

Take, for instance, Sue's difficulties with her teenage
son Ryan.[180] Sue is a regular customer who lives a few
blocks away. Ryan is finishing high school but bored, despondent, and angry. He watches computer screens too
much, lies on his bed most of the day and feels little connection with other people. Sue is a single mum at her wits'
end trying to encourage Ryan, especially fearing that he
might be starting to take drugs. She spoke with Annabella
after he started kicking holes in the walls of their home.
She was looking for a tradesperson who could do the necessary repair work.

Annabella spoke with Sue about restorative justice and
suggested that rather than just getting someone else to fix
the damage, there might be value in Ryan being part of the
repair work. Sue agreed but had no idea who would have
both the physical skills and the relational approach to make
that work. Through the conversation Sue was clearly asking Annabella to be involved—and that step of being given
permission to help is a crucial step in any relational assis-
tance.

As it happened, by the grace of God, that very day Annabella was introduced to a handyman with an interest in
restorative justice! He was an older man in the same church
community as Annabella's accountants. All Annabella did
was seed some ideas about a helpful way of approaching the
challenge from the perspective of shalom and then

introduce people to each other. But out of that improvised response, a mentoring relationship was formed between the effectively fatherless Ryan and an older man of God. The older man could not only pass on some practical skills but also help Ryan recover his dignity, removing the shame of his anger by enabling him to repair the damage he had caused. Situations like that, where people are valued and nurtured rather than punished, create opportunities for God's redemptive work as well.

A more challenging situation for us arose from the way we interacted with a business associate. The relationship started well but later unraveled, and we were left with a conflict we have not yet resolved.

It all started when David planned to open a café and wine bar, but a substantial amount of renovations were needed before that could happen. David's parents, who were providing the funds for the renovation, wanted to be sure there was a sufficient market potential, so they asked Annabella to temporarily set up her coffee cart on the site. We were happy to do so and built a good trade over several months. Since the renovations were still incomplete, we were asked to stay longer ... and longer ... and longer, until we had many regular customers, a local reputation for excellent coffee and great atmosphere, and three years had passed.

When David was finally ready to open part of his vision—not the whole café yet, but at least a take-away coffee window—he set a date four weeks in the future for us to move out. That gave us four weeks to find a new location for our business and let our customers know what was happening. Into that mix, the owner of a local shop offered us a warehouse space that had just become available behind her shop. We imagined turning that warehouse into a community center: locating one of the coffee carts there semi-permanently while encouraging multiple uses for the space, including the packaging and marketing of fabric imported from Ghana to fund a maternity clinic we had been supporting for several years. The space could be turned into a drop-in center for mums with young children, film nights, art exhibitions, etc.

The problem was the location was only 200 meters from where we were previously and David feared that all the customers would migrate to our new location, causing his café/wine bar to fail. In our minds, the two ventures were so different in their intentions we would not be in competition. Some customers would come to our new location because of the casual, almost non-commercial, atmosphere and the various community activities happening in the space. People who wanted food at lunch or wine at night would go to David's. There are enough coffee drinkers around to support both of us.

Annabella and I had differing opinions about what was the right thing to do, and hadn't finalized anything. David, however, became more and more irate, insisting that we move further away. Rather than the four weeks we had agreed to, he disconnected our power during business on a Saturday morning and required us to pack up all our equipment and be gone by the end of the day.

With the help of friends we hurriedly exited. The shop owner down the street allowed us to set up there on short notice, with the helpful attitude that we could sort out the rental details later. That location has worked well for us, providing a wonderful place to extend the community-building we enjoy.

David's coffee window opened three days later and for two months he seemed to have a good stream of customers. During that time, he continued to act aggressively towards us. We responded as calmly as possible, not directly addressing the conflict but hoping the success of his business would have its own calming effect on him.

At the moment the conflict continues, and unfortunately, we tend to avoid each other. David has closed the coffee window and continues with his renovations with the intention of opening the full café/wine bar as soon as possible.

Your response to this story may be that this is purely a business problem rather than a missional one. But mission and business are not unrelated. Our work, whether it be as a salaried employee or a business owner, is just as much a part of kingdom building as the relationships we form elsewhere, our support of international development projects, the faith discussion groups, the transformance art, our choices with how we spend money, the way we raise our children, and the ways we answer questions about why we do what we do. All of this happens because we share a common humanity that bears the image of God and because we try to follow the ethics of Jesus. The nature of employment and business, our ethical stance within those business contexts, the ways we relate to work colleagues, business partners and customers—these all reflect our missional values.

A broken relationship with David is an important missional consideration. It is not the only nor the ultimate consideration, but nevertheless we struggled with knowing
what love looked like in that situation. Having to improvise
with very little time for other options, we ended up going
with the option that David most objected to. We stayed beyond the normal activation period to support David until
he completed the renovations. That seemed like a loving
response to him at the time, but in retrospect setting a
more rigid and earlier exit date would have been more loving. That's part of the messiness of improv.

To repeat what I've said before: there is no script from
the Bible or church tradition that can simply be recited in
cases like this. Instead, we understand the summons of Jesus to work with him to build a new kingdom as a call to a
set of values that enable us to improvise as new situations
arise.

We always spoke honestly with David and tried to maintain an open channel of communication and co-operation.
We listened to his concerns without being railroaded and
made sure none of our actions could be seen as retaliation
that would escalate the conflict. We hoped for his success
and tried to create a scenario in which both businesses and
each of us personally could flourish. Although we still hope
for reconciliation at some time in the future, we are in the
dark about how to respond with overacceptance.

One thing we have learnt from this improvisation is the
importance of an exit strategy. When starting a new venture, be it a business activation or a church, we will think
more about how to navigate the ending. If we had agreed

with David about how the activation was going to end ahead of time, we both would have had clear and shared expectations that may have avoided the conflict. I think the same is true for church gatherings: many do not know how to recognize when they should finish and move on to something else because the exit strategy is never discussed. On the contrary, most gathering churches are established with the implied hope that they will forever grow and never end. In a scattering church, on the other hand, ending and moving on are essential components of the goal.

SUMMARY

We need an improv approach because the Bible and church tradition do not give a complete enough script for us to address the varied cultural contexts and questions we face.

The scattered church does not have to fear getting it wrong. We can try something and perhaps fail. We will not always get it right, but God will not smite us for that. The redemptive life of the kingdom is an evolving, open-ended story. We need not fear an overlord who will punish any variation from the script. On the contrary, God is here with us, developing the script from below in a continual conversation with the watching world.

[14]

ETHICS, VALUES, AND THE SACRED

ONE OF THE REASONS SOME MAY fear the role of improvisation in the church is that, by moving away from the idea of a static script, it seems to open the door too widely to mistakes and even heresy. Shouldn't we just stick to the rules or accept the instructions of someone in authority? I have already noted that the loss of centralized control is a benefit of the scattering church model rather than a shortcoming. But still, the problem is that if we aren't following a script or some clear set of rules, what keeps the church on the "straight and narrow"?

My threefold answer starts with the importance of following the example of Jesus. Jesus is the Word of God, and in his life among us as documented in the Gospels, we see a normative example of how to live. Prior to any abstract theorizing about the meaning of Jesus' death and resurrection we should study his life and build a model of normal Christian behavior on that foundation. Jesus' life is the cornerstone of our personal and communal ethics.

How did Jesus relate to his heavenly Father? How did Jesus care for himself? How did Jesus relate to religious authorities and their rules? How did Jesus relate to social outcasts? How did Jesus act towards those in need? What was his approach to conflict? How did he interact with the natural environment? What was his approach and teaching about money?

The New Testament writers describe a rich array of episodes in Jesus' life that answer such questions and provide a model around which to build our own character and behavior.

The second principle to help the church stay on course, after the importance of following Jesus, is that we hold fast to Jesus' vision of where we are going.

One of the primary tasks of leaders is to communicate a clear vision of the goal towards which they are leading. If the followers catch on to that vision and make it their own, they will naturally make personal decisions that head towards the shared goal. Rather than defining a pre-paved road that followers must travel, good leaders inspire their followers about where they are going and then get out of the way so everyone can work together to reach the goal.

Jesus had a clear understanding of where he was going and spent three years passing that vision on to his disciples. His first recorded sermon acts as a manifesto of that goal: he came to bring good news to the poor, freedom for prisoners, sight for the blind, and to release the oppressed

(Luke 4:18). He came so that we might all flourish (John 10:10).

Luke also notes that "Jesus resolutely set out for Jerusalem" (Luke 9:51) even though he knew that rejection and death awaited him there (Luke 9:22). In Luke's account, the arc of the Gospel narrative swings inexorably towards the doom awaiting in Jerusalem. Jesus calls those of us who wish to be followers to share the same willingness to give up our lives (Luke 9:23–27). In a sense, suffering in Jerusalem is our shared goal. Reading more deeply, however, we see that "Jerusalem" is a means towards the greater goal of reconciliation. Jesus also knew that he would rise again (Luke 9:22) and it was "for the joy set before him" that he endured the suffering (Hebrews 12:2).

Do we, personally and as a church, set out for the metaphorical Jerusalem with a joyous vision of what will happen beyond Jerusalem? Or do we get sidetracked by other visions that perhaps involve less suffering along the way?

Jesus' goal, his joy, was to fulfil the mission he articulated at the beginning of his ministry. As Paul wrote to the Colossians, all things were created by Jesus and for Jesus, and God's plan is that through Jesus all things in heaven and earth will be reconciled, that is set right, restored (Colossians 2:15–23). Jesus' goal is freedom and flourishing for all in a kingdom where everything is set right. That vision is what should direct our paths as well, because Jesus calls us to be ambassadors of this new kingdom who continue that same ministry of reconciliation (2 Corinthians 5:18–20).

Thirdly, within the context of Jesus' example and his goal of reconciliation, we also learn a set of kingdom values that guide our decisions and actions.

Some goals leave open the question of how to achieve them. Some goals encourage the idea that the end justifies the means. For instance, when we tell sports figures that "winning is everything," or the more extreme version, "winning isn't everything; it is the only thing," we sanction any means whatsoever to win. As a society, we reinforce that idea through our worship of celebrities and the huge amounts of money we pay to be entertained by them. Explicitly and implicitly we convey the belief that a person's value depends on their winning. As a result, there is huge pressure on players to bend the rules and be self-centered. Society can hardly blame professional sports players who care little for other people in their lives, swimmers who take performance-enhancing drugs, cricketers who tamper with the ball, or players who verbally and physically abuse their opponents.

If the goal of the church was to dominate the world, forcing every knee to bow before Christ, then all sorts of varied tactics could, and have been legitimized to attain that goal. We could show by example why living as a Christian is better. We could launch a global education program to rationally convince others to join us. But we could also destroy parts of the world to make the remaining people more controllable. We could threaten people with hell, establish national laws to force businesses to close on Sunday, impose prohibitions against alcohol, or launch Crusades to reclaim Jerusalem. It would not matter why people were on their knees, so long as they complied. Any form of social, psychological and physical coercion could be "divinely sanctioned" to ensure that everyone was "Christian."

On the other hand, some goals have the effect of regulating the means through which the goal may be achieved. Consider, for example, the difference between the goal of gaining a university medical degree and the goal of becoming a good doctor. The former allows the possibilities of cheating in exams, finding the university with the shortest/cheapest/easiest course requirements, and bribing a university administrator. You could study hard, practice for years and even develop your empathy with patients, but those steps are not required by the first goal. Those steps are, however, essential for the second goal. The goal of becoming a good doctor constrains how you go about achieving it in a way that the goal of gaining a university medical degree does not.

What means are available to the church if our goal is to work with Jesus towards the reconciliation of all things in heaven and on earth? Reconciliation cannot be coerced but requires an earnest concern for the welfare, for the *shalom*, of all. As we build Jesus' kingdom, our mode of operation is as important as the end goal. The way we act as we travel towards the goal is an important part of the Christian message.

As before, we look to the example of Jesus. We cannot naively imitate each action of Jesus—we don't for instance need to walk everywhere in sandals and speak Aramaic—but instead we learn as apprentices who gradually come to understand our Master's way of thinking. We soak up Jesus' values and apply them through improvisation to the circumstances we encounter each day.

No doubt the followers of Jesus will disagree as to what those core values are. We might all agree to the centrality of love and use Paul's list of love's attributes in 1 Corinthians 13 to clarify the meaning of love. Love on its own, however, is not a clear enough principle to avoid disagreements about how the principle of love should be translated into action. The path of discipleship is largely a process of understanding and practicing what love looks like. What does it mean to love God with all your heart, soul and mind? What does it mean to love one's neighbor? What does it mean to love one's self? (Matthew 22:35–40, Mark 12:28–34, Luke 10:25–37).

The answers lie in a deepening understanding of other values displayed and taught by Jesus: values such as respecting each other's autonomy, non-violence, a non-coercive approach to motivating inner personal change, self-sacrifice, servanthood, kindness, patience, generosity, a trust in the abundance of God, friendships and community, hospitality, and forgiveness. These and other values fueled the behavior of Jesus and inform our understanding of love.

As we align our decisions and action to those of Jesus, the basis of our ethical decision-making shifts from being rule-based to being values-based. We do not live without constraints as though every possible action is OK. Neither do we live so constrained by rules that we have no choice and no responsibility. Neither do we live somewhere in the middle ground with some balance of freedom and rules.

Instead, the follower of Jesus makes ethical choices on another dimension: the dimension of kingdom values based on love. We are freed from the Law so that we can more fully love.

The import of 1 Corinthians 10:23–24 is that our ethical decisions are no longer to be made on the basis of what we are permitted to do or required to do by the constraints of any law. Rather, ethical decisions are made on the basis of what is beneficial, constructive, and other-centric.

Such an approach to ethics is inherently improvisational. We mature as disciples of Jesus by learning to imitate his character and making his values our own. On that foundation—the cornerstone of Christ's own example, his goal of the reconciliation of all things, and the values he displayed and taught—we become actors in the theodrama who can live out their mission through acting authentically in character. We do not stringently follow a script or law, but take responsibility as moral agents and improvise in line with the intentions and values of the Director.

RITUAL REVISITED

I noted in Chapter 2 that traditional rituals create belonging, but they also exclude outsiders. Rituals create a symbolic link with, and a yearning for, a spiritual reality, but do so at the risk of undermining the important connection to the here and now.

In the church, rituals reflect an understanding of what it means to be holy or sacred. That's why our core rituals are called "sacraments," by which we imply that these are not just any old ritual but *sacred* rituals. For the most part, the view enacted in these rituals by the traditional church is that the sacred is wholly other, set apart from this sinful world. The sacred is pure, godly, innocent, perfect, holy, only to be found in the spiritual realm rather than here on earth.[181] That traditional view also recognizes that occasionally the sacred breaks through into the physical world. This is seen most boldly in the Incarnation, when God, the source of the sacred, bridged the divide between heaven and earth and became human. But the same dynamic can be seen in various sacred places, objects, rituals, and times—all particular instances of God's presence manifested in the physical world.

We metaphorically think of heaven above, earth below, and hell underneath. Although we no longer believe that layered picture literally, the metaphorical implications still affect our thinking. We continue to think of the three as separated realms, of heaven as spiritual and earth as merely physical, of heaven as superior and the earth as inferior. But that's a worldview based more on Plato's theory of forms, Dante's *Divine Comedy,* and Milton's *Paradise Lost* than on the Bible.

I don't think the understanding of the sacred as wholly other is affirmed by Jesus. Rather than continuing the view of a separation between the spiritual heaven above and the physical world below, I see Jesus affirming the sacredness of creation. The sacred did not "break in" when Jesus was born. The world has always been sacred for it was made by God, sustained by God, and loved by God. Everything is sacred because everything is infused with God.

As David writes in Psalm 139, there is nowhere we can go where God is not present. God is present inside and outside the church. Our mission is not to bring God into some new place, for God was already there before us. God is present in the Eucharist but also in the middle of war zones, at times of birth and death, in both our successes and our failures. God is present during every act of violence, every rape, every murder, every drug overdose, and every suicide. God is always and everywhere present.

God's presence does not imply God's approval of every event. There are many places and times when God's will is not done. If it were not so, then Jesus would not have instructed his disciples to pray "Your will be done on earth as it is in heaven" (Matthew 6:10).

Understanding the sacred in terms of God's continual and comprehensive presence with us changes the nature of ritual in the scattering church. If the church is gathered or scattered, God is present. But whereas a traditional religious approach uses rituals to orient people towards the sacred wholly other, Jesus' approach uses rituals to anchor people in the sacred here-and-now, and to celebrate God's presence.

KEVIN'S WHISKY CIRCLE

The emerging church movement has generated many new ideas about how a church gathering might be curated. The church in general is now more open to experimenting with liturgical forms.

One idea I am seeing more frequently is a pop-up church. This follows the commercial model of pop-up stores that sell something out of a vacant shop front or warehouse for a short time and then close down. Pop-up churches can be a strategy for a gathering church to activate a new location. They may rent a space for one night or for a series of meetings over a month and then decide whether there is enough interest to establish something longer term, or simply move on to another pop-up location.

I am more interested in how pop-up churches could work with a scattering mindset. A pop-up church could be a great way of scattering seeds and initiating relationships without any intention of establishing a permanent gathering. Given the mobile nature of people's lives and the transient nature of many social activities, it makes perfect sense to invite people to a once-off church event in which they can encounter God.

But for that to be effective our traditional understanding of liturgy needs to be recrafted. How can a pop-up church both demonstrate kingdom values and invite people into that kingdom? What sort of event would interest people? How do you engage them once they are there? What's the balance between entertaining, informing, and challenging? How can the décor, food, music, and program structure all combine to convey a particular message? How can the interpersonal connections facilitated by the event be nurtured afterwards?

My favorite example of that mindset is The Whisky Circle, an invention of my friend Kevin Crouse.

Imagine being invited to an evening involving a public discussion group crossed with a whisky tasting. The Whisky Circle branding features the four words Human,

Doubt, Fringe, and More. You buy your ticket online for $50 and turn up at a licensed cafe where there is a live musician and some finger food. People mingle for a while before being asked to take a seat in loosely concentric circles around a central table.

On the central table sit several bottles of whisky, which the master of ceremonies for the evening introduces and passes around. Everyone gets a chance to savor them and to comment. One of them is an Irish whiskey called *Writers Tears*, which gives the MC an excuse to introduce the guest speaker, who just happens to be an Irish author and theologian. He gets to talk for a while and others sitting around the table start a conversation with him. If you like, you can just listen from the outer circles, but the MC invites anyone who wants to join the conversation to take a seat at the table or just throw in a question from wherever they are.

There is no formal end to the evening, but after the main conversation at the table winds up many other conversations waft around the room until closing time.

On the surface, The Whisky Circle looks like a simple social gathering but it is not hard to see that there is an underlying liturgical structure in which ritual plays an important role. The décor of the meeting space, the invitations and branding, the hand-shaking and chatting when people arrive, the curated discussion, the sharing of drinks poured into small glasses from a common bottle—all these actions emphasize that something deeper is going on than simply tasting a selection of whiskies.

Kevin has put a good deal of thought into the atmosphere and flow of the evening. The slightly random but concentric seating enables people to choose their own level of engagement. The layout suggests there is a structure but one that has permeable boundaries. It provides opportunities for those who want to participate while simultaneously giving permission for others to just observe. This reflects a desire to create a safe space that promotes honesty and a respect for varied opinions. Kevin's intention is to foster an alternative way to gather within a community (in this case the community of whisky drinkers in western Sydney), a way that includes and values people regardless of their faith backgrounds, and through which an open-ended dialog can be facilitated. There is no sales pitch or attempt to convert people, only a willingness to listen.

The Whisky Circle is deliberately provocative, designed to disrupt pre-conceptions about faith and alcohol. Whisky is also called *aqua vitae*, the water of life, and of course it is a spirit! So Kevin playfully links the whisky tasting to religious themes.

The ritual around a group tasting anchors the gathering in a shared appreciation of something earthy and real. At the same time, the ritual creates a space and time in which participants may sense the deeper reality of something present but often not acknowledged. Not all will recognize or name that presence as God at first, but it is a taste of the kingdom that may become clearer to them later.

One of the important aspects of ritual is that repeating them inspires deeper reflection. After attending The Whisky Circle a few times, people start to notice the repeating elements and may realize that they are deliberate. In a reflective mood they will naturally ponder what it means, and why it was done that way? What taste does that repeating experience leave on my palate? Does it enliven me in a way that makes me want more?

It is important that the whisky tasting is a *shared* experience. It is also important that the focus is something already known and familiar. That focus, along with the setting, is a natural part of the participants' lives. People are not invited to enter a "holy" space like a traditional church building that is foreign to their normal routine, but to locate the sacred within their normal experience. It calls people to see the sacred that is already in their midst, to see and acknowledge each other, and in their shared experience endue the mundane with meaning.

Jesus' use of Baptism and Eucharist share that same flavor. He draws on people's existing familiarity with washing and shared meals but turns those mundane events into metaphors for something transcendent. Rather than thinking of these rituals as symbols of the remote, holy and wholly other, we can conceive of them as celebrations of God's presence in the sacred here and now.

The traditional institutional interpretation of these rituals separates them from the common person's daily experience by controlling when, where, and by whom they can be performed. That interpretation also separates the physical symbol from its spiritual referent and prioritizes the latter over the former, implying that the physical event is unimportant and only the "spiritual reality" is significant.

But surely Jesus wanted his followers to encounter themselves, each other, and God anew *within* the grounded event. *Within* the ritualized washing of baptism with its undertones of suicide, and *within* the brokenness of bread with all its cannibalistic undertones,[182] Jesus sought to embrace his followers in the divine presence. He was not asking them to downgrade their connection with the physical washing and eating in order to experience a higher sacred truth. Rather, he was encouraging them to upgrade their understanding of the earthly acts of washing and eating to see that they are already sacred. In this way, Jesus used ritual to celebrate God's presence. He promised the disciples that he would always be present (Matthew 28:20), and a core intention of the Eucharistic ritual was to be a continuing reminder of that presence.

The Whisky Circle is a great example of the roles liturgy, ritual, and the sacred play in a scattering church. Firstly, it emphasizes the incarnational approach to mission: rather than expecting people to step out of their culture to encounter God, The Whisky Circle presents the message of Jesus' kingdom within the existing community by using an activity culturally familiar to the participants. Secondly, although the event may be ephemeral, the structure, the discussions, and the relationships forged by the events open opportunities for personal disruption and transformation. Thirdly, the values behind the events—especially respect, inclusion, celebration, creativity, humility, service, and hospitality—demonstrate the values of Jesus' kingdom. Fourthly, the ritual of sharing a drink together anchors the event in this world, while at the same time drawing attention to the transcendent.

[15]

WHAT SUCCESS LOOKS LIKE

L ET'S TRY TO PULL ALL THE THREADS together and picture what this scattering church model might look like. In particular, how would anyone know if such a church was being effective?

Why do we rely on the physical size of a church building and the number of attendees to measure success? Even when we consciously affirm the importance of depth of discipleship, we still easily fall into a state of envy about churches with more people than ours. House churches and other small faith communities seem less significant: they are certainly less prominent and less obvious, but that does not mean they are less effective.

Part of the allure of large churches is that the number of people involved is easier to measure than the depth of discipleship. Another part of the allure is that we have bought into the dominant cultural metaphor that bigger is better.

On the other hand, if we move away from institutional survival and bums-on-seats metrics, then what is left to show we are succeeding?

The church plays a core role as part of Jesus' strategy to build an upside-down kingdom. The church is God's agent, helping to bring the kingdom of heaven to earth, a kingdom that is radically different than any other kingdom humanity has ever experienced. In the English-speaking world of the 21st century, the type of church that can achieve this mandate is not the same as the type of church we have inherited from previous generations.

I've described our cultural context as:
- Personally mobile
- Relying on digital technologies
- Affected by postmodern assumptions
- Increasingly post-institutional.

In that context, I have drawn on the rich, Biblical image of scattering to propose an approach to being church that is:
- Non-institutional
- Relational
- Embracing and inclusive
- Radically decentralized
- Generous and gracious
- Continually subversive
- Free to improvise.

While proposing a scattering church I have been highly critical of the dominant metaphor of a church as a gathering. I am not saying the gathering metaphor is the wrong way to think of church, and that scattering is the only right or Biblical approach. But I am saying that the scattering approach is consistent with the values, teaching, and practice of Jesus, and that it is a more culturally appropriate approach for our postmodern, post-institutional times.

An effective church will work like yeast and salt: small amounts spread throughout the world, seasoning everything with the values of the kingdom. The transformative effect of such a church does not depend at all on large institutions or hierarchical control. We will spread like wild mustard, a weed whose seeds are blown everywhere by the breath of God.

To be a bit cruder, the church is like manure. If you pile it up it just stinks! But if you spread it out and dig it into the soil then it becomes amazing fertilizer. If the church were more like that, scattered throughout society, then the good seed blown by God would be nourished and grow into an unstoppable kingdom. So let's become more like dogs marking each tree and electricity pole. Let's spread our "scat" far and wide! To paraphrase Jesus, "By their scat you will recognize them!"

Let us be known not by our large numbers and prominent buildings but by widespread personal examples of integrity and faith.

Let us be known not by our formidable political influence but by our grassroots relational support for the orphans, widows, prisoners, LGBTQI, refugees and other marginalized people with whom we live side-by-side.

Let us be known not by our confidence in being right, but by our love.

Let us be known not by our preaching, our glossy marketing campaigns, or the reach of our radio stations, but by our willingness to listen.

Let us be known not as an arrogant elite who impose their vision on society and coerce people to conform to that vision, but as an incarnational movement that demonstrates the reality of the Gospel through the invasive yeast of mercy.

Let us live with an unswerving allegiance to Jesus and work with him to build a kingdom in which all people can flourish.

DWELLING OUTSIDE OF OUTSIDE OF THE CAMP

One final Biblical metaphor I would like to apply to the church is the idea of being outside the camp.

In the Old Testament, "outside the camp" was where the lepers and other unclean people were banished (e.g. Numbers 12:10–15, Leviticus 13:40–46). It was where you went to the toilet (Deuteronomy 23:12–13) and where convicted law-breakers were killed (e.g. Numbers 15:32–36, Leviticus 24:10–23). To be "outside the camp" came to mean, metaphorically, to be discarded, outcast, disgraced. "Dis-graced" is an amazing word really. Someone from whom grace has been removed. Or someone towards whom grace has been denied.

In other Old Testament passages, those negative connotations of being outside the camp are balanced by positive images. For instance, certain parts of the ritual sacrifice of animals needed to be performed outside the camp (e.g. Exodus 29:14, Numbers 19:1–10, Leviticus 16:27).

More significantly, after the debacle with the Golden Calf, Moses set up a tent outside the roaming Israelites' camp, where anyone could go to inquire of the Lord (Exodus 33:7–11). God's presence was visibly portrayed by a pillar of cloud at that tent rather than inside the camp.

The writer of Hebrews merges the negative and positive aspects of this "outside the camp" metaphor and applies it to the death of Jesus. In Hebrews 13:11–13 we read:

> *The high priest carries the blood of animals into the Most Holy Place as a sin offering, but the bodies are burned outside the camp. So Jesus also suffered outside the city gate to make the people holy through his own blood. Let us, then, go to him outside the camp, bearing the disgrace he bore.*

In this passage, the city of Jerusalem is like "the camp." Via the metaphoric calculus, we recognize the author's intent—that just as disgraced people and sacrificed animals suffered outside the camp, so too Jesus suffered outside the city.

Who is normally outside the camp? The leper, the unclean, the lawbreaker, and in our day the refugee, the drug dealer, the transgender person. And Jesus. That is where God appears and where we should be too.

The reason to dwell "outside the camp" is not derived from some exclusive theology of a chosen remnant, as though we have the hidden truth and have to tell everyone else they are wrong. It is to embrace the full scope of human life, with all its color and joy and trauma, rather than hiding out in "Christian" ghetto camps. Only when we are outside of the camp can we leaven the whole world.

Many parts of the church seek to metaphorically set up their tent outside the secular city. That is, they see their goal as being to draw people out from the dominant culture and into their new gathering. But I don't think this idea of a new gathering of believers outside the city is what the Biblical metaphor means. The call to dwell "outside the camp" is not a call to set up a new camp. To the extent that parts of the church have set up a new camp outside the city, the invitation of Jesus is to come *outside of* outside of the camp. For it is on the very outer edge, where the lepers and unclean live, that Jesus' presence is made visible.

If you are inside the gathered church, I hope this book has shown that there is nothing to fear about those actively working with God outside of the institutional structures. The slow demise of Christendom does not signal the end of Jesus' influence in the world. On the contrary, the Bible supports the idea that the work of God is scattered like seeds, blown by the wind of the Spirit, outside the camp. You are welcome to come out with us and enjoy the fresh air!

If you are already outside, you are in good company! You may be branded a leper and theologically unclean, but this is where God is made visible. I hope the conceptual framework I have given in this book encourages you to not feel guilty about where the wind of God has blown you. I hope the practical ideas and stories inspire your path so you can be co-creators with Jesus of the forever new and subversive kingdom of God.

Notes

[1] Recipes on the website
www.turningteardropsintojoy.com/books.

[2] Tickle, *The Great Emergence*.

[3] Lakoff and Johnson, *Metaphors We Live By*.

[4] All Bible quotations are taken from the New International Version.

[5] For some long bedtime reading, you might like the 59-page compendium by Montefiore, "A Tentative Catalogue of Biblical Metaphors."

[6] A linguistic example is the history of the word "convoluted." To be convoluted originally referred to a physical object that had convolutions—twisted, tortuous, winding structures—such as the human brain or a ram's horn. Later on, the word was metaphorically applied to unnecessarily complicated thought processes, explanations, and bureaucratic processes. Whoever first described the process of selecting a bishop as "convoluted" was applying an apt metaphor. But now the metaphoric usage is so common that we take it as the literal meaning and rarely hear the original meaning.

[7] St Augustine, "De Moribus Ecclesiae," chap. 30:62. See also Shealy, "The Church as Bride and Mother: Two Neglected Theological Metaphors" and Gomez, "Mother Church as Metaphor in Key Early Patristic Writers and Vatican II."

[8] See for instance The Economist, "Jesus, CEO."

[9] Explicitly in Chapter 3, but really this is an important aspect of their whole work.

[10] Lakoff and Johnson, *Metaphors We Live By*, 5.

[11] Author unknown, but perhaps written in the 1980's and probably associated with the Emmanuel Covenant Community.

[12] I have taken some of these ideas from Hal Lindsay's article that was first published in the home-church magazine "Voices in the Wilderness" in the 1980's and more recently republished in Miller, "Brothers, Sisters." The full text can also be found at http://www.home-church.org/voicesdocs/chrc-fam.html

[13] Merriam Webster, "Definition of CHURCH"; Oxford Dictionaries, "Church | Definition of Church in English by Oxford Dictionaries."

[14] Partridge, *Origins*; Collins Online Dictionary, "Ecclesia."

[15] The exceptions are mostly because the verse refers to an assembly of people other than the Christian church: Acts 7:38 and Hebrews 2:12 relate to Israel; Acts 19:32 and 41 relate to a crowd in Ephesus. 1 Corinthians 14 is the exception to the exceptions! Although the exact same word ἐκκλησίαις occurs in both verse 33 and 34, the NIV translators have chosen to use "congregation" the first time and "churches" the second time.

[16] An often quoted example of this (though probably apocryphal according to Hutchins, "'The Whisky Was Invisible', or Persistent Myths of MT") is an episode in the early days of automated language translating by computer. The story goes that some time before 1962 a computer system was asked to translate Matthew 26:41, "The spirit is willing, but the flesh is weak," from English into Russian. When the same system was prompted to translate the resulting Russian back into English,

the computer typed out "The vodka is strong but the steak is lousy!"

[17] Encyclopaedia Britannica, "Solon: Greek Statesman and Poet."

[18] Hirsch and Frost, *Rejesus*, 32 and http://www.vergenetwork .org/2011/01/01/alan-hirsch-what-is-a-missional-community-printable.

[19] "Catechism of the Catholic Church, Paragraph 5: THE COMMUNION OF SAINTS."

[20] Bible Hub, "Strong's Greek: 1290. Διασπορά (Diaspora)."

[21] In a list of 17 factors influencing the early spread of Christianity as part of his massive two-volume work *Early Christian Mission*, Eckhard Schnabel places Roman political stability at the head of the list. Safe travel and the use of Greek as a common language enabled the faith to spread even in the midst of persecution. Further down the list he mentions several other factors that resonate with the core thesis of this book and which are just as relevant to our modern context: the centrality of love, charity and social inclusion. (*Schnabel, Early Christian Mission*, 1556.)

[22] Excerpts of Blumhardt's letters to his son-in-law can be found in Blumhardt, *Everyone Belongs to God.*

[23] The ideas in this paragraph and the next are taken from an interview with the contemporary historian of missions Andrew Walls. (Walls, "The Expansion of Christianity.")

[24] Cartoon drawn by Hannah Sunderland and used with her permission. Based on an idea from the Twitter account of Saji George (@S_A_J_I).

[25] http://web.archive.org/web/20131117215719/http://www .christenacleveland.com/2012/10/die-heretic-the-absurdity-of-divisions-in-the-church.

26   See   https://www.theguardian.com/stage/2005/sep/29 /comedy.religion, or a live version at https://www.youtube.com /watch?v=l3fAcxcxoZ8. I reproduce the joke here with permission from Emo Philips.

27 A third I could have included would be *The Scattering: Imagining a Church that Connects Faith and Life* by Dwight L. DuBois. Like the two books I do discuss, DuBois gives primary place to the gathered church but emphasizes the urgency of empowering church members to see that most of their mission lies outside the church walls. He rightly notes that we suffer from a kind of autoimmune disease that "establishes institutional survival as its real agenda at the expense of connecting the following of Jesus with serving everyday neighbors." (Dubois, *The Scattering*, page X.)

28 Hammett, *The Gathered and Scattered Church*, xvi–xviii.

29 Hammett, ix.

30 Hammett, ix.

31 Hammett, ix.

32 Hammett, x.

33 Hammett, 13.

34 Hammett, 15.

35 Hammett, 17.

36 Hammett, 18.

37 Hammett, ix.

38 Halter and Smay, *AND*, 13.

39 Halter and Smay, 18.

40 Halter and Smay, 25.

41 Halter and Smay, 17.

42 Halter and Smay, 64.

43 Halter and Smay, 104.

44 Halter and Smay, 96.

[45] I say "impossible" because the history of the church, and disagreements within the current church, shows that there is not one clearly defined "Christian" morality. We could never disentangle what we take to be God's instructions about right living from the spaghetti of cultural norms. We need more humility than that. Even if that were possible, imposing rules on what people believe and how they act—whether through guilt, peer pressure or legislation—does not create followers of Jesus, nor does it equate to the kingdom of God that Jesus preached about. And even if imposing "Christian" morality on a group of people were an effective means of creating followers of Jesus, it remains impossible to create a "Christian country" because of a fundamental category error—a country is not the sort of thing that can be "Christian." People follow Jesus; a country cannot.

[46] Jim Palmer, in *Inner Anarchy: Dethroning God and Jesus to Save Ourselves and the World*, quoted at https://www .facebook.com/Nobody.JimPalmer/posts/10155644218125592.

[47] For a more detailed understanding of Anabaptism, see Estep, *The Anabaptist Story*, Becker, *Anabaptist Essentials* or www.anabaptistnetwork.com.

[48] See The Anabaptist Mennonite Network at https://amnetwork.uk.

[49] Although Yoder's writings have been influential in the development of my own faith, I have become very reluctant to quote him because of the disgraceful way he manipulated people for his own pleasure. Some of his actions are inconsistent with his writings and that duplicity calls into question the basis of his ethical framework. If a key proponent of a theology that values right relationships cannot live out that value, then perhaps the theology is wrong. Nevertheless, I still find his understanding of church and how the church should engage with the world to be

compelling. So I still draw on some of his analysis in the belief that the insights can stand even though the author has fallen.

[50] Yoder, "Let the Church Be the Church," 175.

[51] Gish, *Living in Christian Community*, 324.

[52] See Yoder, *The Politics of Jesus* for a clear description on the Anabaptist view on that topic. Another insightful analysis, from an Anglican point of view, is Prior, *Jesus and Power*.

[53] Bonhoeffer, *Letters and papers from prison*, 140.

[54] Market Access Consulting and Research, "Christian Media Project Qualitative Research," 23.

[55] From McCrindle research, reported in Eternity News, "Church Seen as Irrelevant to Australians' Lives."

[56] Simon is the Executive Director of the Centre for Public Christianity in Sydney. I heard him use this phrase during a seminar in 2018.

[57] Brown, "Michael Gove Is Right – Christianity Has Become a Laughing Stock."

[58] Based on an annual survey by Gallup. For the question "Please tell me how much confidence you, yourself, have in ... the church or organized religion", 43% of respondents in 1973 answered "A great deal" compared to only 20% in 2018. On the other end of the scale, the percentage of people who responded "Very little" more than tripled from 7% to 24% (Gallup Inc, "Religion.")

[59] McCrindle, "A Demographic Snapshot of Christianity and Church Attenders in Australia."

[60] McCrindle, "Church Attendance in Australia."

[61] Gallup Inc, "Religion", with the percentage of people who never attend a church or synagogue doubling in that period, from 14% to 28%.

[62] Barna, *Revolution*, 38.

[63] Packard and Hope, *Church Refugees*, quoted in Vaughn, "Are You Fed Up With Church?"

[64] Packard and Hope, *Church Refugees*, Kindle loc. 231.

[65] Derived from several statistics in McCrindle, "Faith and Belief in Australia: A National Study on Religion, Spirituality and Worldview Trends." 45% of the population identify with Christianity but only 7% are "extremely involved" and a further 15% attend at least monthly, leaving 23% who attend less than monthly.

[66] Thurston and ter Kuile, "How We Gather," 6.

[67] In this context I will deliberately hold off expressing any judgement on the validity of these postmodern ideas. My point is not to agree nor disagree with them, but to note how deeply they affect the attitudes of people living in the Western world of the early 21st century. There are some on the conservative side who think we should fight against these influences and maintain the value of pre-postmodern beliefs. There are others who are already writing about moving not back but beyond postmodernism. But the factors I have mentioned remain core to the culture in which we live at the moment and necessitate a rethinking of how the church can effectively engage in a world where postmodernism is the dominant perspective.

[68] McCrindle, "Faith and Belief in Australia: A National Study on Religion, Spirituality and Worldview Trends," 26.

[69] The Guinness Book of Records lists the University of Karueein as the "oldest existing, and continually operating educational institution in the world", founded in 859 CE (Guinness World Records, "Oldest Higher-Learning Institution, Oldest University")

[70] http://www.anglicancommunion.org

[71] Bouma, *Australian Soul*, 33–37.

[72] Touraine, *The Post-Industrial Society* is the later English translation.

[73] The Open Source and free software movements are also significant examples. I am writing this book on a laptop running Microsoft Windows and Microsoft Word, but I could move away from those commercial products produced by one of the world's largest institutions. If I chose to, I could use non-proprietary (and free!) software such as Linux and LibreOffice. Many thousands of software developers around the world explicitly reject the institutional mindset and embrace a decentralized model of collaboration that produces world-class software that is often available for free.

[74] Online Direct Democracy at www.onlinedirectdemocracy.org

[75] "Royal Commission into Institutional Responses to Child Sexual Abuse" at www.childabuseroyalcommission.gov.au

[76] Both McCrindle and the Australian National Church Life Survey

[77] Bible Hub, "Strong's Greek: 4687. Σπείρω (Speiró)."

[78] Bible Hub, "Strong's Greek: 4650. Σκορπίζω (Skorpizó)."

[79] Bible Hub, "Strong's Greek: 1287. Διασκορπίζω (Diaskorpizó)."

[80] I know it's a total side-track, but my father was a farmer and my first university degree was in maths, so I just have to add a comparison to modern crop yields. From what I can gather from agricultural research on the Internet, a modern wheat farmer would expect a 70% establishment rate, compared to the 25% in Jesus' parable. A modern wheat plant yields about 110 grains on average—whereas Jesus seems to assume that in his time the *best* possible outcome would be 100. So overall, a modern farmer would expect a multiplication rate of about 77 compared to Jesus' 16.

The ROI in today's approach, however, is not so far ahead of Jesus' model as the yield might suggest. Jesus' sower scatters the seed and then does nothing but watch. A modern farmer has to pay for machinery, fuel, fertilizer, irrigation, pesticides and herbicides. Those costs contribute to the higher yields, but reduce the financial ROI considerably.

[81] The online Celebrity Atheist List includes an entry for him at www.celebatheists.com/wiki/Bill_Hayden, and he was awarded the title of Australian Humanist of the Year in 1996 because "As Governor General he publicly declared himself an atheist and spoke, without fear despite criticism, in favour of voluntary euthanasia and other causes supported by Humanists." (www.hsnsw.asn.au/ahoy.html)

[82] Bowling, "Former Atheist and Political Leader Bill Hayden Baptised at Age 85 at St Mary's Church, Ipswich."

[83] Kärkkäinen, *Introduction to Ecclesiology*, 21.

[84] Barna, *Revolution*, 39. The change of attitude from "doing church" to "being church" is also one of four shifts that form the basis of Dave DeVries' Missional Transformation process (https://www.missionalchallenge.com/mt-4-from-doing-church-to-being-church).

[85] Snyder, *The Community of the King*, 13.

[86] N. T. Wright goes so far as to say that this is what the Gospels are all about—that through the life of Jesus, we come to learn that God is king. For a summary of that view, see Wright, "The Cross and the Kingdom"; for the full story, see Wright, *How God Became King*.

[87] There has been extensive discussion about this alignment from many theological perspectives. A web search for "*missio ecclesiae* and *missio Dei*" will lead to many resources.

[88] Kreminski, *Urban Spirituality*, 31, see also Helland and Hjalmarson, *Missional Spirituality* and Hirsch and Frost, *Rejesus*. To some extent I question this use of the term "missional" because every organisation, religious or not, is missional in that it has a goal. To be missional is simply to be purposive. The key issue is not whether an organisation or activity is missional, but what specific mission is being advocated. Nevertheless, "mission" is used within Christian contexts in such a pervasive way, with a specifically sacred sheen, that I will go along with that usage.

[89] See Gish, *Living in Christian Community* and Yoder, "A People in the World." I note in passing that Stanley Hauerwas endorses the same view (Hauerwas, *With the Grain of the Universe*, 219; Hauerwas, "Beyond the Boundaries: The Church as Mission").

[90] Gish, *Living in Christian Community*, 25; Yoder, "A People in the World," 74. I must also note here that many Anabaptists who take this view on mission see a different relationship between church and kingdom than what I have presented. Rather than thinking of the church as God's agent for establishing the kingdom, some Anabaptists virtually equate the church with the kingdom of God (Finger, "Kingdom of God.") Scot McKnight, for instance, is a leading contemporary theologian with Anabaptist leanings, for whom the church and the kingdom are effectively the same thing. In McKnight's ecclesiology there can be no kingdom work outside of the church McKnight, *Kingdom Conspiracy*, 206..

[91] Winter, "The Two Structures of God's Redemptive Mission" but see a full reprint at http://www.undertheiceberg.com/wp-content/uploads/2006/04/Sodality-Winter%20on%20Two%20Structures1.pdf.

[92] I wonder actually, whether the modality/sodality distinction is as easy to derive from the New Testament as Winter seems to think. This is not my area of expertise but there is certainly no *explicit* separation in the New Testament between these two modes of operation. Perhaps the implicit separation that Winter sees is a retrospective reading of church history into the text.

[93] The usual translation in that verse is "dwelt among us" but the Greek σκηνόω (skénoó) literally means to pitch or live in a tent Bible Hub, "Strong's Greek: 4637. Σκηνόω (Skénoó)."

[94] I wouldn't over-emphasize this distinction between God desiring the tabernacle but David desiring a temple. The temple plays an important role itself in New Testament theology. Jesus is seen as the true temple (John 2:18–22) just as much as the true tabernacle. The church and Jesus together are also compared to a new temple in which God lives (Ephesians 2:19–22). Nevertheless, the point is important: God wanted a mobile tabernacle but David wanted a static temple, and the symbolism of the two are quite different.

[95] Snyder, *The Problem of Wine Skins*, 67.

[96] Snyder, 73.

[97] Bonhoeffer, *Letters and papers from prison*, 88.

[98] Bonhoeffer, 89.

[99] Bonhoeffer, 90.

[100] Bonhoeffer, 101.

[101] Bonhoeffer, 102.

[102] As with several themes in this book, I cannot allocate space to a full description or argument for anarchism. If the idea intrigues or disturbs you, I suggest reading Andrews, *Christi-Anarchy*. for a contemporary description that includes extensive examples of how the idea can work in practice. For a more theoretical

account, try Ellul, *Anarchy and Christianity*, first published in French in 1988.

[103] Bonhoeffer, *Life Together*, 21.

[104] Bonhoeffer, *Letters and papers from prison*, 139.

[105] A reference to the classic book on discipleship by R. E. Coleman *The Master Plan of Evangelism*.

[106] Hughes et al., *Building Stronger Communities*, 32.

[107] See the downloadable report from the web site (Thurston and ter Kuile, "How We Gather.")

[108] What some call "communities of locality", e.g. Hughes et al., *Building Stronger Communities*, 16.

[109] The idea actually goes back to the very beginnings of the church. I highly recommend Robert Banks' book *Paul's Idea of Community*.

[110] Bonhoeffer, *Life Together*, 21.

[111] Bonhoeffer, 31.

[112] Bonhoeffer, 23.

[113] Bonhoeffer, 38.

[114] As Robert and Julia Banks note, "Home churches are better experienced than explained." Nevertheless, if you have not experienced that style of church and do not know where to start, I thoroughly recommend their book *The Church Comes Home.* as a starting point.

[115] Jackson and Jackson, *Living Together in a World Falling Apart*.

[116] The most influential of which was Gish, *Living in Christian Community*.

[117] PhD research by Jim McKnight estimated that 2,500–4,000 people lived in about 180 such communities in the mid-1980s (McKnight, *Australian Christian Communes*, 37.)

[118] See also the parallel passage in Luke 11:14-26.

[119] Bonhoeffer, *Life Together*, 36.

[120] See Volf, *Exclusion and Embrace*, 140–47 for the full story.

[121] Volf, 143.

[122] Volf, 146.

[123] Volf, 147.

[124] powell and Menendian, "The Problem of Othering."

[125] Girard, *The Scapegoat*; Girard, *I See Satan Fall like Lightning*.

[126] Australian Bureau of Statistics, "3412.0 - Migration, Australia, 2016-17."

[127] Phillips, "Boat Arrivals and Boat 'Turnbacks' in Australia since 1976."

[128] 93.5% acceptance rate for boat-arrivals in 2010–11 and 91% in 2011–12, compared to 62.2% and 67.7% respectively for all asylum seekers (Reilly, "FactCheck"). This article does not show the acceptance rate for the non-boat category, but by mathematical necessity it has to be even lower than the "All arrivals" category.

[129] e.g. in Volf, "Living with the Other."

[130] Volf, "Soft Difference: Theological Reflections on the Relation Between Church and Culture in 1 Peter," 24.

[131] Much more has been said about this by authors such as Rene Girard, Gil Bailie, Michael Hardin and James Alison. If that territory is unfamiliar to you, I particularly recommend Hardin, *The Jesus Driven Life* and Bailie, *Violence Unveiled*.

[132] Rohr, "The Myth of Redemptive Violence."

[133] I take the phrase "everyone belongs to God" from a book by 19th century Lutheran pastor Christoph Blumhardt: a series of letters he wrote to his son-in-law who was a missionary in China. Those letters show how respectful, permeable boundaries can

translate into cross-cultural mission work. (Blumhardt, *Everyone Belongs to God.*)

Another aspect of everyone belonging to God can be found in the three parables in Luke 15 that I have discussed elsewhere: the lost sheep, the lost coin and the lost son. Rob Bell makes an interesting observation about those three stories (Bell, "Jesus H. Christ | Part 7 - You Are Already at the Party"): in all cases, there is never any suggestion the thing that is lost does not always belong to the respective owners. The sheep belongs to the shepherd and is loved and treasured by the shepherd throughout. The coin belongs to the woman and is loved and treasured by her throughout. The two sons are always sons, loved and treasured by their father throughout. Via the metaphoric calculus, Jesus intends for us to recognize that in the kingdom of heaven, we always belong to God. Our personal state of lostness never means that we are rejected by God. As though the woman who represents God, having lost a coin, would say "Oh well, its not my coin any more. I never really wanted it anyway." No! The God of this kingdom searches for us all, watches down the road for us all, and rejoices when we are found. But during our lostness we are still loved, treasured and belong to God.

[134] Bennett, "Riddle of the Week #18: An Engineer, a Physicist, and a Mathematician Build a Fence." is one rendition of the puzzle.

[135] See also Kopas, "Outsiders in the Gospels: Marginality as a Source of Knowledge."

[136] e.g. Gittins, *Bread for the Journey*, chap. 4.

[137] Rollins, *The Idolatry of God*, chap. 7.

[138] The Commons no longer exists in the form I describe here. Although their website has disappeared, you can look up historical information and photos from the Internet Archive's

Wayback Machine. This quote is taken from 4 Feb 2017: http://web.archive.org/web/20170219001920/http://www .thecommons.org.au/about/mission-and-values/.

[139] See for instance https://www.huffpost.com/entry/on-the-edge-of-the-inside_b_829253 and https://cac.org/the-edge-of-the-inside-2019-07-09.

[140] Used with the permission of David Hayward, https://nakedpastor.com.

[141] 2 Peter 3:9 echoes the same thought. So Paul and Peter agree on that principle.

[142] An idea that on the surface sounds like a form of scattering church is Steve Murrell's proposal of a wiki church. Murrell founded the Victory church in the Philippines in 1984 with a structure modelled on Wikipedia. "Imagine if every believer, not just paid leaders, were engaged in ministry. That's a Wiki Church." (Murrell, *WikiChurch*, 5) It's a great aim, though I do not think it bears much relation to the Wikipedia model beyond the common feature that both encourage the involvement of many people. Wikipedia is an example of modern anarchy at work. It builds consensus by encouraging people to contribute knowledge from a neutral point of view. In seeking to be encyclopedic, Wikipedia discourages opinion and original research.

The prefix "wiki" does not actually refer to the way Wikipedia engages with its contributors. It is derived from the Hawaiian word for "quick," and co-opted by Wikipedia because of the type of technology used to create web pages that anyone can quickly edit.

Murrell's idea of a wiki church certainly does not mean a quick church, nor a "user-editable" church in which everyone can throw in competing ideas to form consensus from the bottom-up. Nor is a wiki church an attempt to foster a neutral point of view about theology. Although Murrell's approach to church building is successful from a numbers perspective—Victory apparently grew to 52,000 members by 2011—it still follows a gathering model in which top-down discipleship creates an institutional hierarchy.

Other mega-church leaders have recognized the challenges inherent to that context: especially how do you avoid focusing on the leader's gifts rather than activating and empowering everyone's gifts? Francis Chan, who at one time lead a church of 5,000 people, left because of that frustration and started a new model of connected house churches called *We Are Church* (Lynn, "Francis Chan Goes Into Detail With Facebook Employees on Why He Left His Megachurch"). From my outsider's perspective, that is more of a step towards the scattering church than Murrell's wiki church approach.

[143] Recovering this allegiance to Christ in the church is the key theme of a recent book by Kenneth D. Butcher, *The Church - What on Earth Is It?* but I think it is only the first step. People across the religious spectrum recognize the authority of Jesus and give their allegiance to him. I do not doubt that many people whose beliefs and practices are opposed to mine are nevertheless just as committed to the way of Jesus as I am. When they and I are both willing to follow the same Lord, there is still a lot of hard work to be done to understand each other and to hear what the Spirit has to say about our purpose and mode of operation.

[144] I like the way Luke remembers this saying of Jesus, especially his sarcastic reference to leaders who impose their will on their subjects while all the time claiming to be "benefactors." Ever seen that in the church?

[145] Just in case I am misunderstood as quoting this passage to support a kind of closed group where only the "faithful"—i.e. those who agree with us—are accepted and the "sinner" is excluded, let me point out that when Jesus says "If he refuses to listen even to the church, treat him as you would a pagan or a tax collector", we should consider Jesus' own approach to pagans and tax collectors. They were precisely the people he liked to hang out with!

[146] If that's unfamiliar territory for you, I recommend Yancey, *What's so Amazing about Grace?*

[147] Lohfink, *Jesus of Nazareth*, 196.

[148] Keller, *The Prodigal God.*

[149] Easy-to-Read Version and the Contemporary English Version.

[150] International Standard Version, but see also The Passion and the New English Translation.

[151] "Subversion" can also mean overthrowing, but that's not the connotation I am drawing on. Overthrowing suggests an act of power whereby one aggressively attacks and overwhelms the other. It should be clear from the tenor of everything else I have written in this book that I am not advocating any form of violent or militaristic coup. Rather than overthrowing, the subversion I describe here is more about digging under the roots of an ill-conceived system until it eventually caves in on itself.

[152] I'm thinking here about passages like Matthew 18:23–35, Matthew 20:1–16, Luke 16, Luke 21:1–4 ... the list can go on and on because Jesus said a huge amount about money and how the attitude to money in the kingdom stood in stark contrast to the attitudes of his day.

[153] Meyers, *The Underground Church*, chap. 7.

154 This is a major theme in the writings of Rene Girard. I recommend Bailie, *Violence Unveiled* as an entry to Girard's claim that the impetus for our modern concern for victims springs from the Bible.

155 I've heard, but not been able to check, that reliable documentation of that practice is described in the *Encyclopedia of Ancient Christianity* in its entry on "Child."

156 See for instance Origen, writing in about 248 CE, "We no longer take up sword against nation, nor do we learn war anymore, having become children of peace, for the sake of Jesus, who is our leader" (*Against Celsus 5:33*, in Roberts, Donaldson, and Coxe, *Ante-Nicene Fathers*, vol. IV). See Ryan, "The Rejection of Military Service by the Early Christians" for a more thorough analysis.

157 See the first few chapters of Andrews, *Christi-Anarchy* if you have any doubt about the injustices committed by the historical church.

158 That is certainly the hope that Robin Meyers expresses in *The Underground Church*. and Michael Frost in *Keep Christianity Weird*.

159 There are PDF versions online and if you have not already read it, I thoroughly recommend doing so. It is less than 3,000 words, so it won't take long and I guarantee it is worthwhile.

160 For readers outside Australia: this "acknowledgement of country" is a common inclusion in events lead by politically conscious groups. It acknowledges the long presence of indigenous people in this land, while not quite admitting that we are invaders occupying their land. We emphasized the acknowledgement of country in this transformance art event especially because it is a subversive statement that links the "ugly truth" in Le Guin's story to the reality of Australian

history. I'm not sure if anyone recognized the connection that evening, but we throw lots of seeds around like that, knowing that not all will germinate.

[161] Good examples of doing this are Walsh, *Subversive Christianity* and Volf, *Flourishing*.

[162] Rollins, *The Idolatry of God*. Rollins accepts we cannot divest ourselves of all identity, but we can hold our identity, or identities, lightly. When we enter a shared space to encounter each other, and to encounter ourselves through those others, we can temporarily leave our identity at the door.

[163] Cross and Livingstone, "Balthasar, Hans Urs Von"; Henrici, "Hans Urs von Balthasar: A Sketch of His Life," 7–22.

[164] Quoted from the Hans Urs von Balthasar internet archive at http://readingvonbalthasar.blogspot.com.au/p/theo-drama_15.html.

[165] See for example Balthasar, *Theo-Drama*, 1992, 15.

[166] MacKinnon, "Some Reflections on Hans Urs von Balthasar's Christology with Special Reference to Theodramatik II/2 and III," 165; Treitler, "True Foundations of Authentic Theology," 171–73.

[167] Quash, "The Theo-Drama," 151; Balthasar, *Mysterium Paschale*, vii.

[168] Balthasar, *Theo-Drama*, 1992, 237.

[169] Athanasius, *On the Incarnation*, sec. 54.

[170] Balthasar, *Theo-Drama*, 1988, 645.

[171] Vanhoozer, *The Drama of Doctrine*, 15.

[172] Vanhoozer, 32.

[173] Vanhoozer, 128.

[174] Wells, *Improvisation*, 12.

[175] Johnstone, *Impro*, 101–3.

[176] Wells, *Improvisation*, 109. Wells' use of the term "overaccepting," though it is becoming more common in theo-dramatic discourse, does not exactly match the term's usage in improv theatre. I think the idea of overaccepting as a third way of responding to an offer is Wells' own invention, albeit an insightful one.

[177] For detailed analyses of God's overacceptance, see Wells, chap. 9; Cowdell, *René Girard and the Nonviolent God*, chap. 7. The ultimate example is of course the Incarnation, which starts with an overaccepting of human life and ends with an overaccepting of death (Wells, *Improvisation*, 113). "Jesus doesn't block the cross by refusing it. He doesn't simply accept it and go to his death. Instead, God overaccepts the cross in the resurrection." (Faith and Leadership, "Samuel Wells.")

[178] Clarke, "Philip and the Ethiopian Eunuch."

[179] Some may claim there is a significant difference between eunuchs and transsexuals: that transgendering is a personal choice whereas being forcibly castrated is not. But the difference is not so clear cut. The gender dysphoria that causes people to choose to undertake gender reassignment is almost certainly never a self-selected state. No-one would choose the social and physical trauma of being transsexual if it could be avoided. Conversely, Jesus noted that some people choose for themselves to be eunuchs (Matthew 19:12).

[180] This situation actually happened twice, with two totally unconnected teenage boys. My retelling combines some details from both instances.

[181] This is a perhaps more of a depiction of common thought rather than a formal doctrinal position. Nevertheless, it underlies Émile Durkheim's well-regarded definition (from 1915) of religion as "a unified system of beliefs and practices relative to

sacred things, that is to say, things set apart and surrounded by prohibitions—beliefs and practices that unite its adherents in a single moral community called a church, all those who adhere to them" (Durkheim, *The Elementary Forms of the Religious Life*, 47). Although Durkheim uses a broad definition of "sacred" that encompasses human communal activity, he maintains an opposition between the sacred and the profane, and argues that the church uses belief, ritual and other practices to promote the sacred and protect it from the profane.

The wholly otherness of the sacred is also key to the view of religion espoused by historian Mircea Eliade, even though he writes perceptively about the importance of hierophanies, that is, the frequent times when the wholly other sacred breaks through into the physical world. (Eliade, *The Sacred and the Profane*.)

[182] These may be shocking ideas I suppose. But Romans 6:4 and Colossians 2:12 require us to interpret baptism as a willing self-offering to die under the water. Jesus' own words in John 6:51–58 explicitly address the appearance of cannibalism. The third century historians Tertullian (*Apology* 7), Origen (*Against Celsus*, 6.27) and Minucius Felix (*Octavius* 9) all cite accusations against Christians of infanticide and cannibalism.

Bibliography

Andrews, Dave. *Christi-Anarchy: Discovering a Radical Spirituality of Compassion*. Eugene, Or.: Wipf & Stock, 2012.

Athanasius. *On the Incarnation*. Translated by John Behr. Popular Patristics Series, no. 44a. Yonkers, N.Y: St Vladimir's Seminary Press, 2011.

Australian Bureau of Statistics. "3412.0 - Migration, Australia, 2016-17." Australian Bureau of Statistics, July 27, 2018. http://www.abs.gov.au/AUSSTATS/abs@.nsf/DetailsPage/3412.02016-17?OpenDocument.

Bailie, Gil. *Violence Unveiled: Humanity at the Crossroads*. New York: Crossroad Pub., 1997.

Balthasar, Hans Urs von. *Mysterium Paschale: The Mystery of Easter*. San Francisco: Ignatius Press, 2000.

———. *Theo-Drama: Theological Dramatic Theory (Vol. 1 - Prolegomena)*. San Francisco: Ignatius Press, 1988.

———. *Theo-Drama: Theological Dramatic Theory (Vol. 3 - The Dramatis Personae: The Person of Christ)*. Translated by Graham Harrison. San Francisco: Ignatius Press, 1992.

Banks, Robert J. *Paul's Idea of Community: The Early House Churches in Their Cultural Setting*. Revised edition. Grand Rapids, Mich: Baker Academic, 1994.

Banks, Robert J, and Julia Banks. *The Home Church: Regrouping the People of God for Community and*

Mission. Sutherland, N.S.W.; Tring: Albatross Books ; Lion, 1986.

Barna, George. *Revolution*. Wheaton, Ill: Tyndale House Publishers, 2005.

Becker, Palmer. *Anabaptist Essentials: Ten Signs of a Unique Christian Faith*. Harrisonburg, Virginia: Herald Press, 2017.

Bell, Rob. "Jesus H. Christ | Part 7 - You Are Already at the Party." The RobCast, October 28, 2018. https://robbell.podbean.com/e/jesus-h-christ-part-7-you-are-already-at-the-party/.

Bennett, Jay. "Riddle of the Week #18: An Engineer, a Physicist, and a Mathematician Build a Fence." Popular Mechanics, March 3, 2017. https://www.popularmechanics.com/science/math/a25508/riddle-of-the-week-18/.

Bible Hub. "Strong's Greek: 1287. Διασκορπίζω (Diaskorpizó)." Bible Hub. Accessed September 13, 2018. https://biblehub.com/greek/1287.htm.

———. "Strong's Greek: 1290. Διασπορά (Diaspora)." Bible Hub. Accessed September 13, 2018. https://biblehub.com/greek/1290.htm.

———. "Strong's Greek: 4637. Σκηνόω (Skénoó)." Bible Hub. Accessed October 26, 2018. https://biblehub.com/greek/4637.htm.

———. "Strong's Greek: 4650. Σκορπίζω (Skorpizó)." Bible Hub. Accessed September 13, 2018. https://biblehub.com/greek/4650.htm.

———. "Strong's Greek: 4687. Σπείρω (Speiró)." Bible Hub. Accessed September 13, 2018. https://biblehub.com/str/greek/4687.htm.

Blumhardt, Christoph Friedrich. *Everyone Belongs to God: Discovering the Hidden Christ.* Walden, New York: Plough Publishing House, 2015.

Bonhoeffer, Dietrich. *Letters and papers from prison.* Edited by Eberhard Bethge. London: SCM Press, 1985.

———. *Life Together.* New York: Harper & Row, 1954.

Bouma, Gary D. *Australian Soul: Religion and Spirituality in the Twenty-First Century.* Cambridge, UK ; New York: Cambridge University Press, 2006.

Bowling, Mark. "Former Atheist and Political Leader Bill Hayden Baptised at Age 85 at St Mary's Church, Ipswich." The Catholic Leader, September 18, 2018. http://catholicleader.com.au/uncategorized/former-atheist-and-political-leader-bill-hayden-baptised-at-age-85-at-st-marys-church-ipswich.

Brown, Andrew. "Michael Gove Is Right – Christianity Has Become a Laughing Stock." *The Guardian*, April 2, 2015, sec. Opinion. https://www.theguardian.com/commentisfree/2015/apr/02/michael-gove-christianity-detached-british-culture.

Bruce, F. F. *Paul: Apostle of the Free Spirit.* Rev. ed. Exeter: The Paternoster Press, 1977.

Butcher, Kenneth D. *The Church - What on Earth Is It? The Church Identity Crisis and Reinstating the Headship of Christ.* Condor, A.C.T.: Kenneth D. Butcher, 2013. http://www.whatisthebiblicalchurch.com/.

Catechism of the Catholic Church. "Catechism of the Catholic Church, Paragraph 5: THE COMMUNION OF SAINTS." Accessed February 14, 2019. http://www.vatican.va/archive/ENG0015/__P2B.HTM.

Clarke, Matthew C. "Philip and the Ethiopian Eunuch (Acts 8:26-40)," October 2014.

http://matthew.clarke.name/christian/commentary-on-specific-bible-verses/philip-and-the-ethiopian-eunuch.

Coleman, Robert Emerson. *The Master Plan of Evangelism.* New Jersey: Fleming H. Revell Company Old Tappan, 1978.

Collins Online Dictionary. "Ecclesia." Collins Online Dictionary. Accessed January 6, 2018. https://www.collinsdictionary.com/.

Cowdell, Scott. *René Girard and the Nonviolent God.* Notre Dame: University of Notre Dame Press, 2018.

Cross, F.L., and E.A. Livingstone, eds. "Balthasar, Hans Urs Von." In *The Oxford Dictionary of the Christian Church,* 3 rev. ed., 2009. http://www.oxfordreference.com.ezproxy.csu.edu.au/view/10.1093/acref/9780192802903.001.0001/acref-9780192802903-e-626?rskey=1Jh8HN&result=1.

Donaldson, Julia. *Room on the Broom.* Picture Puffins. New York, NY: Puffin Books, 2003.

Dubois, Dwight L. *The Scattering: Imagining a Church That Connects Faith and Life,* 2015.

Durkheim, Émile. *The Elementary Forms of the Religious Life.* Translated by Joseph Ward Swain. Mineola, N.Y: Dover Publications, Inc, 2008.

Eliade, Mircea. *The Sacred and the Profane: The Nature of Religion.* Translated by Willard R. Trask. A Harvest Book. San Diego: Harcourt, 1987.

Ellul, Jacques. *Anarchy and Christianity.* Translated by Geoffrey W. Bromiley. Eugene, OR: Wipf & Stock, 2011.

Encyclopaedia Britannica. "Solon: Greek Statesman and Poet." Encyclopaedia Britannica. Accessed January 14, 2018. https://www.britannica.com/biography/Solon.

Estep, William Roscoe. *The Anabaptist Story.* Grand Rapids: Eerdmans, 1975.

Eternity News. "Church Seen as Irrelevant to Australians'
Lives: New Survey," February 3, 2015.
https://www.eternitynews.com.au/archive/church-seen-
irrelevant-australians-lives-new-survey/.

Faith and Leadership. "Samuel Wells: Improvising
Leadership." Faith and Leadership, March 26, 2012.
https://faithandleadership.com/multimedia/samuel-wells-
improvising-leadership.

Finger, Thomas N. "Kingdom of God." Global Anabaptist
Mennonite Encyclopedia Online, 1990.
https://gameo.org/index.php?title=Kingdom_of_god&oldi
d=162926.

Frost, Michael. *Keep Christianity Weird: Embracing the
Discipline of Being Different*, 2018.

Gallup Inc. "Religion." Gallup.com, 2019.
https://news.gallup.com/poll/1690/Religion.aspx.

Girard, René. *I See Satan Fall like Lightning*. Maryknoll, N.Y. :
Ottawa : Leominster, Herefordshire: Orbis Books ;
Novalis ; Gracewing, 2001.

———. *The Scapegoat*. Johns Hopkins paperbacks ed.
Baltimore: Johns Hopkins University Press, 1989.

Gish, Arthur G. *Living in Christian Community: A Personal
Manifesto*. Sutherland, Australia: Albatross Books, 1979.

Gittins, Anthony J. *Bread for the Journey: The Mission of
Transformation and the Transformation of Mission*. Wipf
and Stock, 1993.

Gomez, Cristina Nava Lledo. "Mother Church as Metaphor in
Key Early Patristic Writers and Vatican II." Charles Sturt
University, School of Theology, St Mark's National
Theological Centre, 2015.
https://researchoutput.csu.edu.au/ws/portalfiles/portal/93
14831.

Guinness World Records. "Oldest Higher-Learning Institution, Oldest University." Guinness World Records. Accessed October 12, 2018. http://www.guinnessworldrecords.com/world-records/oldest-university/.

Halter, Hugh, and Matt Smay. *AND: The Gathered and Scattered Church*. Exponential Series. Grand Rapids, Mich: Zondervan, 2010.

Hammett, Edward H. *The Gathered and Scattered Church: Equipping Believers for the 21st Century*. 2nd ed. Macon, Ga: Smyth & Helwys Pub, 2005.

Hardin, Michael. *The Jesus Driven Life : Reconnecting Humanity with Jesus*. Lancaster, PA: JDL Press, 2010.

Hauerwas, Stanley. "Beyond the Boundaries: The Church as Mission." In *Walk Humbly with the Lord: Church and Mission Engaging Plurality*, edited by Viggo Mortensen and Andreas Østerlund Nielsen, 53–69. Wm. B. Eerdmans Publishing, 2010.

———. *With the Grain of the Universe: The Church's Witness and Natural Theology : Being the Gifford Lectures Delivered at the University of St. Andrews in 2001*. London: SCM Press, 2002.

Helland, Roger, and Len Hjalmarson. *Missional Spirituality: Embodying God's Love from the inside Out*. Downers Grove, Ill: IVP Books, 2011.

Henrici, Peter. "Hans Urs von Balthasar: A Sketch of His Life." In *Hans Urs von Balthasar: His Life and Work*, edited by David L. Schindler, 7–44. Communio Books. San Francisco: Ignatius Press, 1991.

Hirsch, Alan, and Michael Frost. *Rejesus: A Wild Messiah for a Missional Church*. Grand Rapids, Mich.: Baker Books, 2008.

Hughes, Philip, Alan Black, Peter Kaldor, John Bellamy, and
    Keith Castle. *Building Stronger Communities*. Sydney:
    University of New South Wales Press, 2007.

Hutchins, John. "'The Whisky Was Invisible', or Persistent
    Myths of MT," June 1995.
    http://www.hutchinsweb.me.uk/MTNI-11-1995.pdf.

Jackson, Dave, and Neta Jackson. *Living Together in a World
    Falling Apart*. New Leaf Library. Carol Stream, Ill:
    Creation House, 1974.

Johnstone, Keith. *Impro: Improvisation and the Theatre*.
    London: Eyre Methuen, 1981.

Kärkkäinen, Veli-Matti. *Introduction to Ecclesiology:
    Ecumenical, Historical & Global Perspectives*. Downers
    Grove, Ill: InterVarsity Press, 2002.

Keller, Timothy J. *The Prodigal God : Recovering the Heart of
    the Christian Faith*. New York: Riverhead Books, 2011.

Kopas, Jane. "Outsiders in the Gospels: Marginality as a Source
    of Knowledge." *The Way* 33, no. 2 (April 1993): 117–26.

Kreminski, Karina. *Urban Spirituality: Embodying God's
    Mission in the Neighborhood*, 2018.

Lakoff, George, and Mark Johnson. *Metaphors We Live By*.
    Chicago: University of Chicago Press, 1980.

Lohfink, Gerhard. *Jesus of Nazareth: What He Wanted, Who
    He Was*. Translated by Linda M Maloney, 2012.
    http://www.myilibrary.com?id=750523.

Lynn, Sheryl. "Francis Chan Goes Into Detail With Facebook
    Employees on Why He Left His Megachurch." Christian
    Post, June 29, 2017.
    https://www.christianpost.com/news/francis-chan-goes-
    into-detail-with-facebook-employees-on-why-he-left-his-
    megachurch-190136/.

MacKinnon, Donald. "Some Reflections on Hans Urs von
    Balthasar's Christology with Special Reference to

Theodramatik II/2 and III." In *The Analogy of Beauty: The Theology of Hans Urs von Balthasar*, edited by John Kenneth Riches, 164–79. Edinburgh: T. & T. Clark, 1986.

Market Access Consulting and Research. "Christian Media Project Qualitative Research," September 2003. http://www.martinjohnsoncommunications.com.au/_literature_127781/JAAL_Research_paper.

McCrindle. "A Demographic Snapshot of Christianity and Church Attenders in Australia," April 18, 2014. https://mccrindle.com.au/wp-content/uploads/A-Demographic-snapshot-of-Christianity-and-church-attenders-in-Australia_McCrindle.pdf.

————. "Church Attendance in Australia." McCrindle, March 27, 2013. https://mccrindle.com.au/insights/blogarchive/church-attendance-in-australia-infographic/.

McCrindle, Mark. "Faith and Belief in Australia: A National Study on Religion, Spirituality and Worldview Trends." McCrindle, May 2017. https://faithandbelief.org.au/.

McKnight, Jim. *Australian Christian Communes*. Cobbity: Trojan Head Press, 1990.

McKnight, Scot. *Kingdom Conspiracy: Returning to the Radical Mission of the Local Church*. Grand Rapid, Michigan: Brazos Press, 2014.

Merriam Webster. "Definition of CHURCH." Accessed September 13, 2018. https://www.merriam-webster.com/dictionary/church.

Meyers, Robin R. *The Underground Church: Reclaiming the Subversive Way of Jesus*. London: SPCK, 2012.

Miller, Hal. "Brothers, Sisters." In *Called to Community: The Life Jesus Wants for His People*, edited by Charles E. Moore, 22–26. Walden, New York: Plough Publishing House, 2016.

Montefiore, C.G. "A Tentative Catalogue of Biblical
  Metaphors." *The Jewish Quarterly Review* 3, no. 4 (July
  1891): 623–81.

Murrell, Steve. *WikiChurch*. Lake Mary, Fla: Charisma House,
  2011.

Oxford Dictionaries. "Church | Definition of Church in English
  by Oxford Dictionaries." Oxford Dictionaries. Accessed
  September 13, 2018.
  https://en.oxforddictionaries.com/definition/church.

Packard, Josh, and Ashleigh Hope. *Church Refugees:
  Sociologists Reveal Why People Are DONE with Church
  but Not Their Faith*. Loveland, Colorado: Group
  Publishing, 2015.

Partridge, Eric. *Origins: An Etymological Dictionary of
  Modern English*. 4. ed., Repr. London: Routledge, 1991.

Phillips, Janet. "Boat Arrivals and Boat 'Turnbacks' in
  Australia since 1976: A Quick Guide to the Statistics."
  Parliament of Australia, January 17, 2017.
  https://www.aph.gov.au/About_Parliament/Parliamentary
  _Departments/Parliamentary_Library/pubs/rp/rp1617/Qu
  ick_Guides/BoatTurnbacks.

powell, john a., and Stephen Menendian. "The Problem of
  Othering: Towards Inclusiveness and Belonging."
  Othering and Belonging, no. 1 (Summer 2016).
  http://www.otheringandbelonging.org/the-problem-of-
  othering/.

Prior, David. *Jesus and Power*. The Jesus Library. Hodder and
  Stoughton, 1987.

Quash, Ben. "The Theo-Drama." In *The Cambridge
  Companion to Hans Urs von Balthasar*, edited by Edward
  T. Oakes and David Moss, 143–57. Cambridge
  Companions to Religion. Cambridge, U.K. ; New York:
  Cambridge University Press, 2004.

Reilly, Alex. "FactCheck: Are Australia's Refugee Acceptance Rates High Compared with Other Nations?" The Conversation, August 20, 2013. http://theconversation.com/factcheck-are-australias-refugee-acceptance-rates-high-compared-with-other-nations-17151.

Roberts, Alexander, James Donaldson, and A. Cleveland Coxe Menzies, Allan, eds. *Ante-Nicene Fathers: The Writings of the Fathers down to A.D. 325*. Peabody, Mass.: Hendrickson Publishers, 1994.

Rohr, Richard. "The Myth of Redemptive Violence." Center for Action and Contemplation, May 1, 2017. https://cac.org/myth-redemptive-violence-2017-05-01/.

Rollins, Peter. *The Idolatry of God: Breaking Our Addiction to Certainty and Satisfaction*. 1st Howard Books trade paperback ed. New York: Howard Books, 2013.

Ryan, Edward A. "The Rejection of Military Service by the Early Christians." *Theological Studies* 13, no. 1 (March 1952): 1–32.

Schnabel, Eckhard J. *Early Christian Mission*. Downers Grove, Ill.: Leicester, England: InterVarsity Press; Apollos, 2004.

Shealy, Wayne. "The Church as Bride and Mother: Two Neglected Theological Metaphors." Family Ministry Today: The Centre for Christian Family Ministry at the Southern Baptist Theological Seminary, 2012. http://www.sbts.edu/family/2012/10/01/the-church-as-bride-and-mother-two-neglected-theological-metaphors/.

Snyder, Howard A. *The Community of the King*. Downers Grove, Ill: Inter-Varsity Press, 1977.

———. *The Problem of Wine Skins: Church Structure in a Technological Age*. Downers Grove, Ill: Inter-Varsity Press, 1975.

St Augustine. "De Moribus Ecclesiae." In *A Select Library Of The Nicene And Post-Nicene Fathers Of The Christian Church*, edited by Philip Schaff, Vol. 4. T&T Clark, n.d. http://www.ccel.org/ccel/schaff/npnf104.i.html.

The Economist. "Jesus, CEO." The Economist, December 20, 2005. https://www.economist.com/node/5323597.

Thurston, Angie, and Casper ter Kuile. "How We Gather." How We Gather, 2018. https://www.howwegather.org/.

Tickle, Phyllis. *The Great Emergence: How Christianity Is Changing and Why*. Grand Rapids, Mich: Baker Books, 2008.

Touraine, Alain. *The Post-Industrial Society*. [1st American ed.] edition. New York: Random House, 1971.

Treitler, Wolfgang. "True Foundations of Authentic Theology." In *Hans Urs von Balthasar: His Life and Work*, edited by David L. Schindler, 169–82. Communio Books. San Francisco: Ignatius Press, 1991.

Vanhoozer, Kevin J. *The Drama of Doctrine: A Canonical-Linguistic Approach to Christian Theology*. 1st ed. Louisville: Westminster John Knox Press, 2005.

Vaughn, Patrick. "Are You Fed Up With Church? 30 Million Say, 'Yes!'" *Huffington Post* (blog), August 13, 2015. https://www.huffingtonpost.com/patrick-vaughn/are-you-fed-up-with-churc_b_7941012.html.

Volf, Miroslav. *Exclusion and Embrace: A Theological Exploration of Identity, Otherness, and Reconciliation*. Nashville: Abingdon Press, 1996.

———. *Flourishing: Why We Need Religion in a Globalized World*. New Haven, CT: Yale University Press, 2016.

———. "Living with the Other." Ministry Magazine, March 2007. https://www.ministrymagazine.org/archive/2007/03/living-with-the-other.html.

————. "Soft Difference: Theological Reflections on the Relation Between Church and Culture in 1 Peter." *Ex Auditu* 10 (1994): 15–30.

Walls, Andrew. "The Expansion of Christianity." Religion Online, 2000. https://www.religion-online.org/article/the-expansion-of-christianity-an-interview-with-andrew-walls/.

Walsh, Brian J. *Subversive Christianity: Imaging God in a Dangerous Time.* Eugene, Oregon: Wipf & Stock, 2014.

Wells, Samuel. *Improvisation: The Drama of Christian Ethics.* Michigan: 9781540960115, 2018.

Winter, Ralph D. "The Two Structures of God's Redemptive Mission." *Missiology: An International Review* 2, no. 1 (January 1974): 121–39. https://doi.org/10.1177/009182967400200109.

Wright, N. T. *How God Became King: The Forgotten Story of the Gospels*, 2016.

————. "The Cross and the Kingdom: How God Became King." Text. ABC Religion & Ethics, May 28, 2014. https://www.abc.net.au/religion/the-cross-and-the-kingdom-how-god-became-king/10099242.

Yancey, Philip. *What's so Amazing about Grace?* Grand Rapids, MI: Zondervan, 1997.

Yoder, John Howard. "A People in the World." In *The Royal Priesthood: Essays Ecclesiological and Ecumenical*, edited by Michael G. Cartwright, 65–101. Grand Rapids, Mich: Eerdmans Pub. Co, 1994.

————. "Let the Church Be the Church." In *The Royal Priesthood: Essays Ecclesiological and Ecumenical*, edited by Michael G. Cartwright, 168–80. Grand Rapids, Mich: Eerdmans Pub. Co, 1994.

————. *The Politics of Jesus.* 2nd ed. Grand Rapids, Mich. : Carlisle, UK: Eerdmans ; Paternoster Press, 1994.

Printed in Great Britain
by Amazon